Case Study
Research
Fourth Edition

APPLIED SOCIAL RESEARCH
METHODS SERIES

Series Editors
LEONARD BICKMAN, Peabody College, Vanderbilt University, Nashville
DEBRA J. ROG, Westat

Case Study Research

Design and Methods

Fourth Edition

Robert K. Yin

APPLIED SOCIAL RESEARCH METHODS SERIES

Volume 5

Los Angeles • London • New Delhi • Singapore • Washington DC

For information:

SAGE Inc.
2455 Teller Road
Thousand Oaks, California 91320
E-mail: order@sagepub.com

SAGE India Pvt. Ltd.
B 1/I 1 Mohan Cooperative
　Industrial Area
Mathura Road, New Delhi 110 044
India

SAGE Ltd.
1 Oliver's Yard
55 City Road
London EC1Y 1SP
United Kingdom

SAGE Asia-Pacific Pte Ltd
33 Pekin Street #02-01
Far East Square
Singapore 048763

Printed in the United States of America

Library of Congress Cataloging-in-Publication Data

Yin, Robert K.
Case study research : design and methods/Robert K. Yin.—4th ed.
　　p. cm.—(Applied social research methods v. 5)
Includes bibliographical references and index.
ISBN 978-1-4129-6099-1 (pbk.)
1. Case method. 2. Social sciences—Research—Methodology. I. Title.

H62.Y56 2009
300.72′2—dc22

2008019313

This book is printed on acid-free paper.

09　10　11　12　10　9　8　7　6　5　4　3　2

Acquisitions Editor:	Vicki Knight
Associate Editor:	Sean Connelly
Editorial Assistant:	Lauren Habib
Production Editor:	Catherine M. Chilton
Copy Editor:	Gillian Dickens
Typesetter:	C&M Digitals (P) Ltd
Proofreader:	Annette R. Van Deusen
Indexer:	Sylvia Coates
Cover Designer:	Candice Harman
Marketing Manager:	Stephanie Adams

Contents

Foreword

It is a privilege to provide the foreword for this fine book. It epitomizes a research method for attempting valid inferences from events outside the laboratory while at the same time retaining the goals of knowledge shared with laboratory science.

More and more I have come to the conclusion that the core of the scientific method is not experimentation per se but rather the strategy connoted by the phrase "plausible rival hypotheses." This strategy may start its puzzle solving with evidence, or it may start with hypothesis. Rather than presenting this hypothesis or evidence in the context-independent manner of positivistic confirmation (or even of postpositivistic corroboration), it is presented instead in extended networks of implications that (although never complete) are nonetheless crucial to its scientific evaluation.

This strategy includes making explicit other implications of the hypotheses for other available data and reporting how these fit. It also includes seeking out rival explanations of the focal evidence and examining their plausibility. The plausibility of these rivals is usually reduced by ramification extinction, that is, by looking at their other implications on other data sets and seeing how well these fit. How far these two potentially endless tasks are carried depends on the scientific community of the time and what implications and plausible rival hypotheses have been made explicit. It is on such bases that successful scientific communities achieve effective consensus and cumulative achievements, without ever reaching foundational proof. Yet, these characteristics of the successful sciences were grossly neglected by the logical positivists and are underpracticed by the social sciences, quantitative or qualitative.

Such checking by other implications and the ramification-extinction of rival hypotheses also characterizes validity-seeking research in the humanities, including the hermeneutics of Schleiermacher, Dilthey, Hirst, Habermas, and current scholarship on the interpretation of ancient texts. Similarly, the strategy is as available for a historian's conjectures about a specific event as for a scientist's assertion of a causal law. It is tragic that major movements in the social sciences are using the term *hermeneutics* to connote giving up on the goal of validity and abandoning disputation as to who has got it right. Thus, in addition to the quantitative and quasi-experimental case study approach that Yin teaches, our social science methodological armamentarium also needs a humanistic validity-seeking case study methodology that, although making no use of quantification or tests of significance, would still work on the same questions and share the same goals of knowledge.

As versions of this plausible rival hypotheses strategy, there are two paradigms of the experimental method that social scientists may emulate. By training, we are apt to think first of the randomized-assignment-to-treatments model coming to us from agricultural experimentation stations, psychological laboratories, randomized trials of medical and pharmaceutical research, and the statistician's mathematical models. Randomization purports to control an infinite number of rival hypotheses *without specifying what any of them are.* Randomized assignment never completely controls these rivals but renders them implausible to a degree estimated by the statistical model.

The other and older paradigm comes from physical science laboratories and is epitomized by experimental isolation and laboratory control. Here are the insulated and lead-shielded walls; the controls for pressure, temperature, and moisture; the achievement of vacuums; and so on. This older tradition controls for a relatively few but explicitly specified rival hypotheses. These are never controlled perfectly, but well enough to render them implausible. Which rival hypotheses are controlled for is a function of the disputations current in the scientific community at the time. Later, in retrospect, it may be seen that other controls were needed.

The case study approach as presented here, and quasi-experimentation more generally, is more similar to the experimental isolation paradigm than to the randomized-assignment-to-treatments model in that each rival hypothesis must be specified and specifically controlled for. The degree of certainty or consensus that the scientific community is able to achieve will usually be less in out-of-doors social science, due to the lesser degree of plausibility-reduction of rival hypotheses that is likely to be achieved. The inability to replicate at will (and with variations designed to rule out specific rivals) is part of the problem. We should use those singular-event case studies (which can never be replicated) to their fullest, but we should also be alert for opportunities to do intentionally replicated case studies.

Given Robert Yin's background (Ph.D. in experimental psychology, with a dozen publications in that field), his insistence that the case study method be done in conformity with science's goals and methods is perhaps not surprising. But such training and career choice are usually accompanied by an intolerance of the ambiguities of nonlaboratory settings. I like to believe that this shift was facilitated by his laboratory research on that most hard-to-specify stimulus, the human face, and that this experience provided awareness of the crucial role of pattern and context in achieving knowledge.

This valuable background has not kept him from thoroughly immersing himself in the classic social science case studies and becoming in the process a leader of nonlaboratory social science methodology. I know of no comparable text. It meets a longstanding need. I am confident that it will become a standard text in social science research methods courses.

—Donald T. Campbell
Bethlehem, Pennsylvania

Preface

Congratulations! You are reading the best edition of *Case Study Research* to date. This fourth edition contains more material, is more readable, and has more practical value than previous editions. The book was first published 25 years ago, and this fourth edition is actually the book's fifth published version, because there was a revised edition (1989) in addition to the three earlier editions (1984, 1994, and 2003).

The book's enduring objective is to guide you and other investigators and students to do case study research rigorously. The book claims to be distinctive in several ways. First, it presents the breadth of the case study method, but also at a detailed level. Other texts do not offer this same combination. Thus, the earlier versions of this book have been used as a complete portal to the world of case study research. Among its most distinctive features, the book provides

- a workable technical definition of the case study method and its differentiation from other social science research methods (Chapter 1),
- an extensive discussion of case study design (Chapter 2), and
- a continually expanding presentation of case study analytic techniques (Chapter 5).

These features are important because case study design and analysis tend to create the greatest challenges for people doing case studies.[1] Sandwiched between Chapters 2 and 5, the book also has two extensive and important chapters pertaining to preparing for and then collecting case study evidence.

Second, the book refers to numerous case studies, in different academic and applied fields. These references will increase your access to existing and (often) exemplary case studies. Most of the citations are contemporary, making the works easy to retrieve. However, to avoid losing connectivity with "roots," the citations also include older works that might be out of print but still deserving of being recognized. The specific references are found in BOXES sprinkled throughout the chapters. Each BOX contains one or more concrete examples of published case studies, to illustrate points made in the text. In this fourth edition, the BOXES now cover more than 50 different case studies, about a quarter of them newly cited in comparison to the earlier editions of this book.

Third, the new material in the BOXES complements other new technical material located throughout the book. The new information demonstrates how the case study as a research method appears to be advancing, despite vigorous attention to (and disproportionate funding support for) other methods, such as experimental designs.

In fact, Chapter 1 discusses the complementarity between case studies and experiments, including an important new reference to the centrality of case studies in clinical psychology (Veerman & van Yperen, 2007). Chapter 1 also contains a more elaborate discussion of the limitations of randomized field trials when the unit of analysis is a collective rather than an individual. Similarly, this new edition points out several features that parallel Paul Rosenbaum's (2002) important work in *non*experimental research designs. The parallel features include the desirability of having elaborate theories as starting points; the use of "case control" or "retrospective" designs; the importance of collecting and presenting data to support or reject rival explanations, as if to represent theories of their own; the value of the nonequivalent, dependent variables design as a form of pattern matching; and replication strategies as an essential approach to multiple-case analysis.

This edition also gives greater attention to two critical topics now addressed more fully in Chapter 2. The first is the definition of the "case" being studied (a concrete entity, event, occurrence, action, but not an abstract topic such as a concept, argument, hypothesis, or theory). The second is more guidance on the substance (not just the form) of a case study's initial questions and a suggested three-stage approach that may help readers to define their initial questions.

Similarly, the new edition devotes more attention to the mixing of quantitative and qualitative data as part of the same case study. The possibilities and variations in mixed methods designs gain explicit attention at the end of Chapter 2, and Chapter 6 has modest guidance on composing case studies in relation to mixed methods research. New examples of quantitative analyses, including the use of hierarchical linear models and structural equation models as applied to certain facets of a case study, appear in Chapter 5. These examples reinforce this book's original and continuing position regarding the case study method as one that can embrace both quantitative and qualitative data.[2]

Finally, new material in Chapter 3 discusses human subjects protection, the role of institutional review boards (IRBs), and the interplay between obtaining IRB approval and the final development of the case study protocol and conduct of a pilot case.

Aside from these technical enhancements, this fourth edition contains several features aimed at making the book more useful and practical. First, each chapter starts with a "tip." The tip poses key questions and answers for the core material in the entire chapter. The tips therefore enable readers to know quickly how hard they will want to focus on any given chapter. An easily understood tip might suggest that the chapter only needs brief perusal. Conversely, a tip that appears confusing or obscure might suggest the need for a close reading.

Second, the practical exercises for each chapter have been upgraded. Previous editions also had five such exercises for each chapter, but the fourth edition revises some of them and then locates them throughout each chapter, rather than at the end of the chapter as in the past. Each exercise therefore appears next to the chapter section that is most pertinent to the exercise. The upgrading and relocation of the exercises should increase their practical value.

Third, the end of each chapter, besides having one or more endnotes, now has a new cross-referencing table. The table indicates where readers may seek more extensive excerpts or fuller renditions of the case studies referenced in the chapter's BOXES and text. Although readers always can refer to the original case study publication, the table indicates whether excerpts also appear in either of two anthologies that deliberately collected these materials (Yin, 2003, 2004). The anthologies only contain excerpts, but they nevertheless serve to broaden the exposure to the case studies for readers who may not be ready (or willing) to work with the original literature.

Finally, the chapter titles and subtitles have been revised to be more friendly. They should still communicate the basic coverage of each chapter but also suggest what readers will gain by studying the chapter. Likewise, this preface is entirely new and attempts to point out the new edition's important features. As with previous editions, the chapter titles are followed with a brief abstract that summarizes the chapter's contents.

One possible motivation for all these changes, expanding technical topics and making the book more practical, may derive from an observation that I (and many others) have long had (but cannot explain): the remarkable ability of young people to conduct computer and video game operations easily and with little apparent instructional guidance. The young learn fast. However, they also may come equipped with more skills and intuitions than previous generations.

This observation has, curiously, influenced the revisions in the fourth edition. As being suggested by this preface, I have not hesitated to add some more difficult concepts in doing case study research. As a result of these changes, readers should be forewarned that I think this edition is "harder" (hopefully not more arcane) than earlier editions. However, successful adoption of this edition's techniques and guidance also means that case study research will be better than in the past. The ultimate goal, as always, is to improve our social science methods and practices over those of previous generations. Only in this manner can every generation make its own mark, much less establish its own competitive niche.

Given this context, two places where the book has not changed very much deserve attention. Reviewers of the third edition suggested reducing the material in Chapter 6, because many of the compositional issues seem to be related to the writing of research more generally, not limited to the writing of case studies. However, my experience has been that the writing of case studies is more critical to their communication than the writing of other types of research. Furthermore, those who have done exemplary case studies appear also to have a flair for writing (and may have been attracted to the case study method in the first place because they wanted to have the opportunity to do some good writing). Thus, Chapter 6 serves as a reminder about the importance of writing and the investigator's skills, when doing case study research.

Second, Donald Campbell's insightful foreword remains unchanged. His succinct text, written nearly 30 years ago, still stands as a masterpiece about social science methods. Within the context of today's research debates, Campbell's work continues, remarkably, to speak with freshness and direct relevance. His foreword also positions well the role of case study research as portrayed in this book. I am deeply honored by the inclusion of this foreword and have attempted to provide but a modest repayment in a subsequent publication (Yin, 2000).

Over the years, the initiation and continued evolution of this book have benefited from the advice and support of many people. I will resist creating a cumulative list acknowledging all of these people from, in some cases, many years ago. However, Prof. Leonard Bickman and Dr. Debra Rog invited me to submit the first manuscript of this book as part of their (then) new series on Applied Social Research Methods. Under their editorship, the series has become a bellwether among all of Sage's publications. I will be forever grateful to them for providing the opportunity as well as the initial feedback and encouragement in completing the manuscript. Similarly, in relation to the book's still-early editions, colleagues such as Larry Susskind at the Department of Urban Studies and Planning (Massachusetts Institute of Technology), Nanette Levinson at the Department of Computer Sciences (The American University), and Eric Maaloe (the Aarhus School of Business in Denmark) all provided opportunities to teach and learn about the case study method in different settings.

Flashing forward to this fourth edition, and as part of its preparation, Sage Publications invited seven persons to share in writing their experience in using the third edition. I did not expect Sage to divulge their identities, and they remained anonymous until well after I had integrated the comments, reworked the manuscript, and started the production process with Sage's editors. At that point, Sage chose to make the identities known. Though surprised, I nevertheless can now thank these reviewers by name. I hope they will see that their comments have influenced the edition's enhancements and updating, although I could not respond to all of the suggestions. The reviewers' diverse array of teaching experiences also appears to reflect the breadth of courses and disciplines that have found the book to be relevant:

- qualitative research methods to Ph.D. nursing students (Martha Ann Carey, Azusa Pacific University);
- doctoral course in IT research methodologies, for degree in management (Alan McCord, Lawrence Technological University);

- foundation and capstone seminars for master's in public administration (Nolan J. Argyle, Valdosta State University);
- political science (Jeffrey L. Bernstein, Eastern Michigan University);
- case study research for doctoral students in educational administration (Vincent A. Anfara Jr., University of Tennessee);
- first-year doctoral seminar in education (Pam Bishop, University of Calgary); and
- qualitative research for graduate-level course in public policy (William S. Lynn, Tufts University).

Research methods editors at Sage Publications also have, over the years, been extremely helpful in identifying ways of making the book more useful and usable for readers. For this most recent edition, I have had the pleasure of working first with Lisa Cuevas Shaw and then with Vicki Knight and Catherine Chilton. Lisa set us on a straight and productive course, and Vicki and Catherine then made sure that the final manuscript would be converted into a distinctive book, even as a fourth edition. As you can guess, we all have worked hard to make the book have its own identity, beyond being a mere retread of earlier work. Nonetheless, as with the earlier versions, I alone bear the responsibility for this fourth edition.

At the same time, I conclude this preface by repeating a portion from the preface to the third edition. In it, I suggested that anyone's ideas about case studies—and about social science methods more generally—must have deeper roots. Mine go back to the two disciplines in which I was trained: history as an undergraduate and brain and cognitive sciences as a graduate. History and historiography first raised my consciousness regarding the importance (and challenge) of methodology in the social sciences. The unique brand of basic research in brain and cognitive science that I learned at MIT then taught me that empirical research advances only when it is accompanied by theory and logical inquiry, and not when treated as a mechanistic data collection endeavor. This lesson turns out to be a basic theme of the case study method. I have therefore dedicated this book to the person at MIT who taught me this best and under whom I completed a dissertation on face recognition, though he might only barely recognize the resemblances between past and present, were he alive today.

NOTES

1. Readers familiar with earlier versions of this book will find that a discussion of pattern matching that formerly appeared as part of a design discussion in Chapter 2 is now found in its more appropriate place under pattern matching in Chapter 5.

2.   Esteemed quantitative researchers may even agree with this. One of them has been the lead author of an article using "case study" in its title (Cook & Foray, 2007). Readers should not take this as an example of how to do case study research, however. The article mainly contains the authors' rendition of a set of events (which apparently could not be told with quantitative methods) but does not present much evidence to support that rendition. (The rendition may be important, but whether it should be accepted as an example of case study research remains an open question.)

REFERENCES

Cook, T. D., & Foray, D. (2007). Building the capacity to experiment in schools: A case study of the Institute of Educational Sciences in the US Department of Education. *Economics of Innovation and New Technology, 16*(5), 385–402.

Rosenbaum, P. R. (2002). *Observational studies* (2nd ed.). New York: Springer.

Veerman, J. W., & van Yperen, T. A. (2007). Degrees of freedom and degrees of certainty: A developmental model for the establishment of evidence-based youth care. *Evaluation and Program Planning, 30*, 212–221.

Yin, R. K. (2000). Rival explanations as an alternative to "reforms as experiments." In L. Bickman (Ed.), *Validity & social experimentation: Donald Campbell's legacy* (pp. 239–266). Thousand Oaks, CA: Sage.

Yin, R. K. (2003). *Applications of case study research* (2nd ed.). Thousand Oaks, CA: Sage.

Yin, R. K. (Ed.). (2004). *The case study anthology.* Thousand Oaks, CA: Sage.

This book is dedicated to Hans-Lukas Teuber,
who made research a lifelong goal for
all who studied with him.

**Doing Case Study Research:
A linear but iterative process**

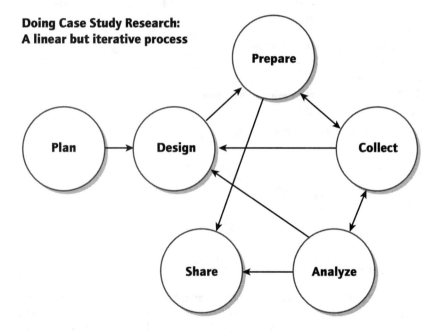

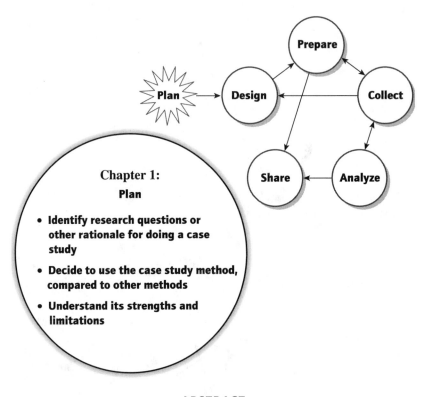

Chapter 1:
Plan

- **Identify research questions or other rationale for doing a case study**
- **Decide to use the case study method, compared to other methods**
- **Understand its strengths and limitations**

ABSTRACT

The case study is but one of several ways of doing social science research. Other ways include but are not limited to experiments, surveys, histories, and economic and epidemiologic research.

Each method has peculiar advantages and disadvantages, depending upon three conditions: the type of research question, the control an investigator has over actual behavioral events, and the focus on contemporary as opposed to historical phenomena. In general, case studies are the preferred method when (a) "how" or "why" questions are being posed, (b) the investigator has little control over events, and (c) the focus is on a contemporary phenomenon within a real-life context. This situation distinguishes case study research from other types of social science research. Nevertheless, the methods all overlap in many ways, not marked by sharp boundaries.

In case studies, the richness of the phenomenon and the extensiveness of the real-life context require case study investigators to cope with a technically distinctive situation: There will be many more variables of interest than data points. In response, an essential tactic is to use multiple sources of evidence, with data needing to converge in a triangulating fashion. This challenge is but one of the ways that makes case study research "hard," although it has classically been considered a "soft" form of research.

1

Introduction

How to Know Whether and When to Use Case Studies as a Research Method

THE CASE STUDY AS A RESEARCH METHOD

Using case studies for research purposes remains one of the most challenging of all social science endeavors. The purpose of this book is to help you—an experienced or budding social scientist—to deal with the challenge. Your goal is to design good case studies and to collect, present, and analyze data fairly. A further goal is to bring the case study to closure by writing a compelling report or book.

Do not underestimate the depth of your challenge. Although you may be ready to focus on designing and doing case study research, others may espouse and advocate other research methods. Similarly, prevailing federal or other research funds may favor other methods, but not the case study. As a result, you may need to have ready responses to some inevitable questions.

First and foremost, you should explain and show how you are devoting yourself to following a rigorous methodological path. The path begins with a thorough literature review and the careful and thoughtful posing of research questions or objectives. Equally important will be a dedication to formal and explicit procedures when doing your research. Along these lines, this book offers much guidance. It shows how case study research includes procedures central to all types of research methods, such as protecting against threats to validity, maintaining a "chain of evidence," and investigating and testing "rival explanations." The successful experiences of scholars and students, for over 25 years, may attest to the potential payoffs from using this book.

Second, you should understand and openly acknowledge the strengths and limitations of case study research. Such research, like any other, complements the strengths and limitations of other types of research. In the face of those who might only see the need for a single research method, this book believes that, just as different scientific methods prevail in the natural sciences, different social science research methods fill different needs and situations for investigating social science topics. For instance, in the natural sciences, astronomy is a science but does not

Tip: *How do I know if I should use the case study method?*

There's no formula, but your choice depends in large part on your research question(s). The more that your questions seek to explain some present circumstance (e.g., "how" or "why" some social phenomenon works), the more that the case study method will be relevant. The method also is relevant the more that your questions require an extensive and "in-depth" description of some social phenomenon.

What are some other reasons you might cite for using or not using the case study method?

rely on the experimental method. Similarly, much neurophysiological and neuroanatomical research does not rely on statistical methods. For social science, later portions of this chapter present more about the potential "niches" of different research methods.

As a research method, the case study is used in many situations, to contribute to our knowledge of individual, group, organizational, social, political, and related phenomena. Not surprisingly, the case study has been a common research method in psychology, sociology, political science, anthropology, social work, business, education, nursing, and community planning. Case studies are even found in economics, in which the structure of a given industry or the economy of a city or a region may be investigated. In all of these situations, the distinctive need for case studies arises out of the desire to understand complex social phenomena. In brief, the case study method allows investigators to retain the holistic and meaningful characteristics of real-life events—such as individual life cycles, small group behavior, organizational and managerial processes, neighborhood change, school performance, international relations, and the maturation of industries.

This book covers the distinctive characteristics of the case study as a research method. The book will help you to deal with some of the more difficult questions still frequently neglected by available research texts. So often, for instance, the author has been confronted by a student or colleague who has asked (a) how to define the "case" being studied, (b) how to determine the relevant data to be collected, or (c) what to do with the data, once collected. This book answers these questions and more, by covering all of the phases of design, data collection, analysis, and reporting.

At the same time, the book does not cover all uses of case studies. For example, it is not intended to help those who might use case studies as a teaching tool, popularized in the fields of law, business, medicine, or public policy (see Garvin, 2003; Llewellyn, 1948; Stein, 1952; Towl, 1969; Windsor & Greanias, 1983) but now prevalent in virtually every academic field, including the natural sciences. For teaching purposes, a case study need not contain a complete or accurate rendition of actual events. Rather, the purpose of the "teaching case" is to establish a framework for discussion and debate among students. The criteria for developing good cases for teaching—usually of the single- and not multiple-case variety—are different from those for doing research (e.g., Caulley & Dowdy, 1987). Teaching case studies need not be concerned with the rigorous and fair presentation of empirical data; research case studies need to do exactly that.

Similarly, this book is not intended to cover those situations in which cases are used as a form of record keeping. Medical records, social work files, and other case records are used to facilitate some practice, such as medicine, law, or social work. Again, the criteria for developing good cases for practice differ from those for doing case study research.

In contrast, the rationale for this book is that case studies are commonly used as a research method in the social science disciplines—*psychology* (e.g., D. T. Campbell, 1975; Hersen & Barlow, 1976), *sociology* (e.g., Hamel, 1992; Platt, 1992; Ragin & Becker, 1992), *political science* (e.g., George & Bennett, 2004; Gerring, 2004), and *anthropology*—and for doing research in different professional fields, such as *social work* (e.g., Gilgun, 1994), *business and marketing* (e.g., Benbasat, Goldstein, & Mead, 1987; Bonoma, 1985; Ghauri & Grønhaug, 2002; Gibbert & Ruigrok, 2007; Graebner & Eisenhardt, 2004; Voelpel, Leibold, Tekie, & von Krogh, 2005), *public administration* (e.g., Agranoff & Radin, 1991; Perry & Kraemer, 1986), *public health* (e.g., Pluye, Potvin, Denis, Pelletier, & Mannoni, 2005; Richard et al., 2004), *education* (e.g., Yin, 2006a; Yin & Davis, 2006), *accounting* (e.g., Bruns, 1989), and *evaluation* (e.g., U.S. Government Accountability Office, 1990).

You as a social scientist would like to know how to design and conduct single- or multiple-case studies to investigate a research issue. You may only be doing a case study or may be using it as part of a larger mixed methods study (see Chapter 2). Whichever, this book covers the entire range of issues in designing and doing case studies, including how to start a case study, collect case study evidence, analyze case study data, and compose a case study report.

COMPARING CASE STUDIES WITH OTHER RESEARCH METHODS IN THE SOCIAL SCIENCES

When and why would you want to do case studies on some topic? Should you consider doing an experiment instead? A survey? A history? An analysis of archival records, such as modeling economic trends or student performance in schools?[1]

These and other choices represent different research methods. Each is a different way of collecting and analyzing empirical evidence, following its own logic. And each method has its own advantages and disadvantages. To get the most out of using the case study method, you need to appreciate these differences.

A common misconception is that the various research methods should be arrayed hierarchically. Many social scientists still deeply believe that case studies are only appropriate for the exploratory phase of an investigation, that surveys and histories are appropriate for the descriptive phase, and that experiments are the only way of doing explanatory or causal inquiries. This hierarchical view reinforces the idea that case studies are only a preliminary research method and cannot be used to describe or test propositions.

This hierarchical view, however, may be questioned. Experiments with an exploratory motive have certainly always existed. In addition, the development of causal explanations has long been a serious concern of historians, reflected by the subfield known as historiography. Likewise, case studies are far from being only an exploratory strategy. Some of the best and most famous case studies have been explanatory case studies (e.g., see BOX 1 for a vignette on Allison and Zelikow's *Essence of Decision: Explaining the Cuban Missile Crisis*, 1999). Similarly, famous descriptive case studies are found in major disciplines such as

---

BOX 1
A Best-Selling, Explanatory, Single-Case Study

For over 30 years, Graham Allison's (1971) original study of a single case, the 1962 Cuban missile crisis, has been a political science best seller. In this crisis, a U.S.–Soviet Union confrontation could have produced nuclear holocaust and doomed the entire world. The book posits three competing but also complementary theories to explain the crisis—that the U.S. and Soviets performed as (a) rationale actors, (b) complex bureaucracies, or (c) politically motivated groups of persons. Allison compares the ability of each theory to explain the actual course of events in the crisis: why the Soviet Union placed offensive (and not merely defensive) missiles in Cuba in the first place, why the United States responded to the missile deployment with a blockade (and not an air strike or invasion—the missiles already were in Cuba!), and why the Soviet Union eventually withdrew the missiles.

The case study shows the explanatory and not just descriptive or exploratory functions of single-case studies. Furthermore, the lessons from the case study are intended to be generalizable to foreign affairs more broadly and also to a whole variety of complex governmental actions. In this way, the book, even more thoughtfully presented in its second edition (Allison & Zelikow, 1999), forcefully demonstrates how a single case study can be the basis for significant explanations and generalizations.

sociology and political science (e.g., see BOX 2 for two vignettes). Additional examples of explanatory case studies are presented in their entirety in a companion book cited throughout this text (Yin, 2003, chaps. 4–7). Examples of descriptive case studies are similarly found there (Yin, 2003, chaps. 2 and 3).

Distinguishing among the various research methods and their advantages and disadvantages may require going beyond the hierarchical stereotype. The more appropriate view may be an inclusive and pluralistic one: Every research method can be used for all three purposes—exploratory, descriptive, and

---

BOX 2
Two Famous Descriptive Case Studies

2A. A Neighborhood Scene

Street Corner Society (1943/1955), by William F. Whyte, has for decades been recommended reading in community sociology. The book is a classic example of a descriptive case study. It traces the sequence of interpersonal events over time, describes a subculture that had rarely been the topic of previous study, and discovers key phenomena—such as the career advancement of lower income youths and their ability (or inability) to break neighborhood ties.

The study has been highly regarded despite its being a single-case study, covering one neighborhood (under the pseudonym of "Cornerville") and a time period now nearly 100 years old. The value of the book is, paradoxically, its generalizability even to contemporary issues of individual performance, group structure, and the social structure of neighborhoods. Later investigators have repeatedly found remnants of Cornerville in their work, even though they have studied different neighborhoods and different time periods (also see BOX 20, Chapter 4, p. 111).

2B. A National Crisis

Neustadt and Fineberg's excellent analysis of a mass immunization campaign was issued originally as a government report in 1978, *The Swine Flu Affair: Decision-Making on a Slippery Disease*. The case study describes the immunization of 40 million Americans when the United States was faced with a threat of epidemic proportions from a new and potentially lethal influenza strain.

Although the case study became known as an exemplary example of a thorough and high-quality case study, the original form of the case study was difficult to obtain, having been published by the U.S. Government Printing Office, which, according to the authors, "has many virtues,...but...filling orders which do not have exact change and precise stock numbers is not one of them" (Neustadt & Fineberg, 1983, p. xxiv). As a result, a revised version of the original case study—adding new material to the original case—was later published as *The Epidemic That Never Was* (1983).

explanatory. There may be exploratory case studies, descriptive case studies, or explanatory case studies. Similarly, there may be exploratory experiments, descriptive experiments, and explanatory experiments. What distinguishes the different methods is not a hierarchy but three important conditions discussed below. As an important caution, however, the clarification does not imply that the boundaries between the methods—or the occasions when each is to be used—are always sharp. Even though each method has its distinctive characteristics, there are large overlaps among them. The goal is to avoid gross misfits—that is, when you are planning to use one type of method but another is really more advantageous.

When to Use Each Method

The three conditions consist of (a) the type of research question posed, (b) the extent of control an investigator has over actual behavioral events, and (c) the degree of focus on contemporary as opposed to historical events. Figure 1.1 displays these three conditions and shows how each is related to the five major research methods being discussed: experiments, surveys, archival analyses, histories, and case studies. The importance of each condition, in distinguishing among the five methods, is as follows.

METHOD	(1) Form of Research Question	(2) Requires Control of Behavioral Events?	(3) Focuses on Contemporary Events?
Experiment	how, why?	yes	yes
Survey	who, what, where, how many, how much?	no	yes
Archival Analysis	who, what, where, how many, how much?	no	yes/no
History	how, why?	no	no
Case Study	how, why?	no	yes

Figure 1.1   Relevant Situations for Different Research Methods

SOURCE: COSMOS Corporation.

Types of research questions (Figure 1.1, column 1). The first condition covers your research question(s) (Hedrick, Bickman, & Rog, 1993). A basic categorization scheme for the types of questions is the familiar series: "who," "what," "where," "how," and "why" questions.

If research questions focus mainly on "what" questions, either of two possibilities arises. First, some types of "what" questions are exploratory, such as "What can be learned from a study of a startup business?" This type of question is a justifiable rationale for conducting an exploratory study, the goal being to develop pertinent hypotheses and propositions for further inquiry. However, as an exploratory study, any of the five research methods can be used—for example, an exploratory survey (testing, for instance, the ability to survey startups in the first place), an exploratory experiment (testing, for instance, the potential benefits of different kinds of incentives), or an exploratory case study (testing, for instance, the importance of differentiating "first-time" startups from startups by entrepreneurs who had previously started other firms).

The second type of "what" question is actually a form of a "how many" or "how much" line of inquiry—for example, "What have been the ways that communities have assimilated new immigrants?" Identifying such ways is more likely to favor survey or archival methods than others. For example, a survey can be readily designed to enumerate the "what," whereas a case study would not be an advantageous method in this situation.

Similarly, like this second type of "what" question, "who" and "where" questions (or their derivatives—"how many" and "how much") are likely to favor survey methods or the analysis of archival data, as in economic studies. These methods are advantageous when the research goal is to describe the incidence or prevalence of a phenomenon or when it is to be *predictive* about certain outcomes. The investigation of prevalent political attitudes (in which a survey or a poll might be the favored method) or of the spread of a disease like AIDS (in which an epidemiologic analysis of health statistics might be the favored method) would be typical examples.

In contrast, "how" and "why" questions are more *explanatory* and likely to lead to the use of case studies, histories, and experiments as the preferred research methods. This is because such questions deal with operational links needing to be traced over time, rather than mere frequencies or incidence. Thus, if you wanted to know how a community successfully overcame the negative impact of the closing of its largest employer—a military base (see Bradshaw, 1999, also presented in BOX 26, Chapter 5, p. 138)—you would be less likely to rely on a survey or an examination of archival records and might be better off doing a history or a case study. Similarly, if you wanted to know how research investigators may possibly (but unknowingly) bias their research, you could design and conduct a series of experiments (see Rosenthal, 1966).

Let us take two more examples. If you were studying "who" had suffered as a result of terrorist acts and "how much" damage had been done, you might survey residents, examine government records (an archival analysis), or conduct a "windshield survey" of the affected area. In contrast, if you wanted to know "why" the act had occurred, you would have to draw upon a wider array of documentary information, in addition to conducting interviews; if you focused on the "why" question in more than one terrorist act, you would probably be doing a multiple-case study.

Similarly, if you wanted to know "what" the outcomes of a new governmental program had been, you could answer this question by doing a survey or by examining economic data, depending upon the type of program involved. Questions—such as "How many clients did the program serve?" "What kinds of benefits were received?" "How often were different benefits produced?"—all could be answered without doing a case study. But if you needed to know "how" or "why" the program had worked (or not), you would lean toward either a case study or a field experiment.

To summarize, the first and most important condition for differentiating among the various research methods is to classify the type of research question being asked. In general, "what" questions may either be exploratory (in which case, any of the methods could be used) or about prevalence (in which surveys or the analysis of archival records would be favored). "How" and "why" questions are likely to favor the use of case studies, experiments, or histories.

EXERCISE 1.1   Defining a Case Study Question

Develop a "how" or "why" question that would be the rationale for a case study that you might conduct. Instead of doing a case study, now imagine that you only could do a history, a survey, or an experiment (but not a case study) in order to answer this question. What would be the distinctive advantage of doing a case study, compared to these other methods, in order to answer this question?

Defining the research questions is probably the most important step to be taken in a research study, so you should be patient and allow sufficient time for this task. The key is to understand that your research questions have both *substance*—for example, What is my study about?—and *form*—for example, am I asking a "who," "what," "where," "why," or "how" question? Others have focused on some of the substantively important issues (see J. P. Campbell, Daft, & Hulin, 1982); the point of the preceding discussion is that the form of the question can provide an important clue regarding the appropriate research method to be used. Remember, too, the large areas of overlap among the methods, so that, for some questions, a choice among methods might actually exist. Be aware, finally, that you (or your academic department) may be predisposed to favor a particular method regardless of the study question. If so, be sure to create the form of the study question best matching the method you were predisposed to favor in the first place.

EXERCISE 1.2   Identifying the Research Questions Covered
When Other Research Methods Are Used

Locate a research study based solely on the use of survey, historical, or experimental (but not case study) methods. Identify the research question(s) addressed by the study. Does the type of question differ from those that might have appeared as part of a case study on the same topic, and if so, how?

Extent of control over behavioral events (Figure 1.1, column 2) and degree of focus on contemporary as opposed to historical events (Figure 1.1, column 3). Assuming that "how" and "why" questions are to be the focus of study, a further distinction among history, case study, and experiment is the extent of the investigator's control over and access to actual behavioral events. Histories are the preferred method when there is virtually no access or control. The distinctive contribution of the historical method is in dealing with the "dead" past—that is, when no relevant persons are alive to report, even retrospectively, what occurred and when an investigator must rely on primary documents, secondary documents, and cultural and physical artifacts as the main sources of evidence. Histories can, of course, be done about contemporary events; in this situation, the method begins to overlap with that of the case study.

The case study is preferred in examining contemporary events, but when the relevant behaviors cannot be manipulated. The case study relies on many of the same techniques as a history, but it adds two sources of evidence not usually included in the historian's repertoire: direct observation of the events being studied and interviews of the persons involved in the events. Again, although case studies and histories can overlap, the case study's unique strength is its ability to deal with a full variety of evidence—documents, artifacts, interviews, and observations—beyond what might be available in a conventional historical study. Moreover, in some situations, such as participant-observation (see Chapter 4), informal manipulation can occur.

Finally, experiments are done when an investigator can manipulate behavior directly, precisely, and systematically. This can occur in a laboratory setting, in which an experiment may focus on one or two isolated variables (and presumes that the laboratory environment can "control" for all the remaining variables beyond the scope of interest), or it can be done in a field setting, where the term *field* or *social experiment* has emerged to cover research where investigators "treat" whole groups of people in different ways, such as providing them with different kinds of vouchers to purchase services (Boruch & Foley, 2000). Again, the methods overlap. The full range of experimental science also includes those situations in which the experimenter cannot manipulate behavior but in which the logic of experimental design still may be applied. These situations have been commonly regarded as "quasi-experimental" situations (e.g., D. T. Campbell & Stanley, 1966; Cook & Campbell, 1979) or "observational" studies (e.g., P. R. Rosenbaum, 2002). The quasi-experimental approach even can be used in a historical setting, where, for instance, an investigator may be interested in studying race riots or lynchings (see Spilerman, 1971) and use a quasi-experimental design because no control over the behavioral event was possible. In this case, the experimental method begins to overlap with histories.

In the field of evaluation research, Boruch and Foley (2000) have made a compelling argument for the practicality of one type of field experiment—randomized field trials. The authors maintain that the field trials design, emulating the design of laboratory experiments, can be and has been used even when evaluating complex community initiatives. However, you should be cautioned about the possible limitations of this design.

In particular, the design may work well when, within a community, individual consumers or users of services are the unit of analysis. Such a situation would exist if a community intervention consisted, say, of a health promotion campaign and the outcome of interest was the incidence of certain illnesses among the community's residents. The random assignment might designate a few communities to have the campaign, compared to a few that did not, and the outcomes would compare the condition of the residents in both sets of communities.

In many community studies, however, the outcomes of interest and therefore the appropriate unit of analysis are at the community or collective level and not at the individual level. For instance, efforts to upgrade neighborhoods may be concerned with improving a neighborhood's economic base (e.g., the number of jobs per residential population). Now, although the candidate communities still can be randomly assigned, the degrees of freedom in any later statistical analysis are limited by the number of communities rather than the number of residents. Most field experiments will not be able to support the participation of a sufficiently large number of communities to overcome the severity of the subsequent statistical constraints.

The limitations when communities or collective entities are the unit of analysis are extremely important because many public policy objectives focus on the collective rather than individual level. For instance, the thrust of federal education policy in the early 2000s focused on *school* performance. Schools were held accountable for year-to-year performance even though the composition of the students enrolled at the schools changed each year. Creating and implementing a field trial based on a large number of schools, as opposed to a large number of students, would present an imposing challenge and the need for extensive research resources. In fact, Boruch (2007) found that a good number of the randomized field trials inadvertently used the incorrect unit of analysis (individuals rather than collectives), thereby making the findings from the trials less usable.

Field experiments with a large number of collective entities (e.g., neighborhoods, schools, or organizations) also raise a number of practical challenges:

♦ any randomly selected control sites may adopt important components of the intervention of interest before the end of the field experiment and no longer qualify as "no-treatment" sites;

♦ the funded intervention may call for the experimental communities to reorganize their entire manner of providing certain services—that is, a "systems" change—thereby creating site-to-site variability in the unit of assignment (the experimental design assumes that the unit of assignment is the same at every site, both intervention and control);

♦ the same systems change aspect of the intervention also may mean that the organizations or entities administering the intervention may not necessarily remain stable over the course of time (the design requires such stability until the random field trials have been completed); and

♦ the experimental or control sites may be unable to continue using the same instruments and measures (the design, which will ultimately "group" the data to compare intervention sites as a group with comparison sites as a second group, requires common instruments and measures across sites).

The existence of any of these conditions will likely lead to the need to find alternatives to randomized field trials.

Summary. You should be able to identify some situations in which all research methods might be relevant (such as exploratory research) and other situations in which two methods might be considered equally attractive. You also can use multiple methods in any given study (for example, a survey within a case study or a case study within a survey). To this extent, the various methods are not mutually exclusive. But you should also be able to identify some situations in which a specific method has a distinct advantage. For the *case study*, this is when

♦ A "how" or "why" question is being asked about
  ○ a contemporary set of events,
  ○ over which the investigator has little or no control.

To determine the questions that are most significant for a topic, as well as to gain some precision in formulating these questions requires much preparation. One way is to review the literature on the topic (Cooper, 1984). Note that such a literature review is therefore a means to an end, and not—as many people have been taught to think—an end in itself. Novices may think that the purpose of a literature review is to determine the *answers* about what is known on a topic; in contrast, experienced investigators review previous research to develop sharper and more insightful *questions* about the topic.

Traditional Prejudices against the Case Study Method

Although the case study is a distinctive form of empirical inquiry, many research investigators nevertheless disdain the strategy. In other words, as a research endeavor, case studies have been viewed as a less desirable form of inquiry than either experiments or surveys. Why is this?

Perhaps the greatest concern has been over the lack of rigor of case study research. Too many times, the case study investigator has been sloppy, has not followed systematic procedures, or has allowed equivocal evidence or biased views to influence the direction of the findings and conclusions. Such lack of rigor is less likely to be present when using the other methods—possibly because of the existence of numerous methodological texts providing investigators with specific procedures to be followed. In contrast, only a small (though increasing) number of texts besides the present one cover the case study method in similar fashion.

The possibility also exists that people have confused case study teaching with case study research. In teaching, case study materials may be deliberately altered to demonstrate a particular point more effectively (e.g., Garvin, 2003). In research, any such step would be strictly forbidden. Every case study investigator must work hard to report all evidence fairly, and this book will help her or him to do so. What is often forgotten is that bias also can enter into the conduct of experiments (see Rosenthal, 1966) and the use of other research methods, such as designing questionnaires for surveys (Sudman & Bradburn, 1982) or conducting historical research (Gottschalk, 1968). The problems are not different, but in case study research, they may have been more frequently encountered and less frequently overcome.

**EXERCISE 1.3   Examining Case Studies Used for Teaching
                 Purposes**

Obtain a copy of a case study designed for teaching purposes (e.g., a case in a textbook used in a business school course). Identify the specific ways in which this type of "teaching" case is different from research case studies.

Does the teaching case cite primary documents, contain evidence, or display data? Does the teaching case have a conclusion? What appears to be the main objective of the teaching case?

A second common concern about case studies is that they provide little basis for scientific generalization. "How can you generalize from a single case?" is a frequently heard question. The answer is not simple (Kennedy, 1976). However, consider for the moment that the same question had been asked about an experiment: "How can you generalize from a single experiment?" In fact, scientific facts are rarely based on single experiments; they are usually based on a multiple set of experiments that have replicated the same phenomenon under different conditions. The same approach can be used with multiple-case studies but requires a different concept of the appropriate research designs, discussed in detail in Chapter 2. The short answer is that case studies, like experiments, are generalizable to theoretical propositions and not to populations or universes. In this sense, the case study, like the experiment, does not represent a "sample," and in doing a case study, your goal will be to expand and generalize theories (analytic generalization) and not to enumerate frequencies (statistical generalization). Or, as three notable social scientists describe in their *single* case study done years ago, the goal is to do a "generalizing" and not a "particularizing" analysis (Lipset, Trow, & Coleman, 1956, pp. 419–420).[2]

A third frequent complaint about case studies is that they take too long, and they result in massive, unreadable documents. This complaint may be appropriate, given the way case studies have been done in the past (e.g., Feagin, Orum, & Sjoberg, 1991), but this is not necessarily the way case studies—yours included—must be done in the future. Chapter 6 discusses alternative ways of writing the case study—including ones in which the traditional, lengthy narrative can be avoided altogether. Nor need case studies take a long time. This incorrectly confuses the case study method with a specific method of data collection, such as ethnography (e.g., Fetterman, 1989) or participant-observation (e.g., Jorgensen, 1989). Ethnographies usually require long periods of time in the "field" and emphasize detailed, observational evidence. Participant-observation may not require the same length of time but still assumes a hefty investment of field efforts. In contrast, case studies are a form of inquiry that does *not* depend solely on ethnographic or participant-observer data. You could even do a valid and high-quality case study without leaving the telephone or Internet, depending upon the topic being studied.

A fourth possible objection to case studies has seemingly emerged with the renewed emphasis, especially in education and related research, on randomized field trials or "true experiments." Such studies aim to establish *causal* relationships—that is, whether a particular "treatment" has been effi-cacious in producing a particular "effect" (e.g., Jadad, 1998). In the eyes of many, the emphasis has led to a downgrading of case study research because case studies (and other types of nonexperimental methods) cannot directly address this issue.

Overlooked has been the possibility that case studies can offer important evidence to complement experiments. Some noted methodologists suggest, for instance, that experiments, though establishing the efficacy of a treatment (or intervention), are limited in their ability to explain "how" or "why" the treatment necessarily worked, whereas case studies could investigate such issues (e.g., Shavelson & Townes, 2002, pp. 99–106).[3] Case studies may therefore be valued "as adjuncts to experiments rather than as alternatives to them" (Cook & Payne, 2002). In clinical psychology, a "large series of single case studies," confirming predicted behavioral changes after the initiation of treatment, even may provide additional evidence of efficaciousness (e.g., Veerman & van Yperen, 2007).

Despite the fact that these four common concerns can be allayed, as above, one major lesson is that good case studies are still difficult to do. The problem is that we have little way of screening for an investigator's ability to do good case studies. People know when they cannot play music; they also know when they cannot do mathematics beyond a certain level, and they can be tested for other skills, such as the bar examination in law. Somehow, the skills for doing good case studies have not yet been formally defined. As a result, "most people feel that they can prepare a case study, and nearly all of us believe we can understand one. Since neither view is well founded, the case study receives a good deal of approbation it does not deserve" (Hoaglin, Light, McPeek, Mosteller, & Stoto, 1982, p. 134). This quotation is from a book by five promi-nent *statisticians.* Surprisingly, from another field, even they recognize the challenge of doing good case studies.

DIFFERENT KINDS OF CASE STUDIES, BUT A COMMON DEFINITION

Our discussion has progressed without a formal definition of case studies. Moreover, commonly asked questions about case studies still have been unan-swered. For example, is it still a case study when more than one case is included in the same study? Do case studies preclude the use of quantitative evidence? Can case studies be used to do evaluations? Let us now attempt to define the case study strategy and answer these questions.

Definition of the Case Study as a Research Method

The most frequently encountered definitions of case studies have merely repeated the types of topics to which case studies have been applied. For example, in the words of one observer,

> The essence of a case study, the central tendency among all types of case study, is that it tries to illuminate a *decision* or set of decisions: why they were taken, how they were implemented, and with what result. (Schramm, 1971, emphasis added)

This definition thus cites cases of "decisions" as the major focus of case studies. Other common cases include "individuals," "organizations," "processes," "programs," "neighborhoods," "institutions," and even "events." However, citing a case topic[4] is surely insufficient to establish the needed definition of case studies as a research *method*.

Alternatively, many of the earlier social science textbooks failed to consider the case study a formal research method at all (the major exception is the book by five statisticians from Harvard University—Hoaglin et al., 1982). As discussed previously, one common flaw was to consider the case study as the exploratory stage of some other type of research method, and the case study itself was only mentioned in a line or two of text.

Another definitional flaw has been to confuse case studies with ethnographies or with participant-observation, so that a textbook's presumed discussion of case studies was in reality a description either of the ethnographic method or of participant-observation as a data collection technique. Many earlier methodological texts (e.g., see L. Kidder & Judd, 1986; Nachmias & Nachmias, 1992), in fact, only covered "fieldwork" as a data collection technique and omitted any further discussion of case studies.

In a historical overview of the case study in American methodological thought, Jennifer Platt (1992) explains the reasons for these treatments. She traces the practice of doing case studies back to the conduct of life histories, the work of the Chicago school of sociology, and casework in social work. She then shows how "participant-observation" emerged as a data collection technique, leaving the further definition of any distinctive case study method in suspension. Finally, she explains how the first edition of this book (1984) definitively dissociated the case study strategy from the limited perspective of only doing participant-observation (or any type of fieldwork). The case study strategy, in her words, begins with "a logic of design . . . a strategy to be preferred when circumstances and research problems are appropriate rather than an ideological commitment to be followed whatever the circumstances" (Platt, 1992, p. 46).

And just what is this logic of design? The critical features had been worked out prior to the first edition of this book (Yin, 1981a, 1981b) but now may be restated as part of a twofold, technical definition of case studies. The first part begins with the scope of a case study:

1. A case study is an empirical inquiry that
   o investigates a contemporary phenomenon in depth and within its real-life context, especially when
   o the boundaries between phenomenon and context are not clearly evident.

In other words, you would use the case study method because you wanted to understand a real-life phenomenon in depth, but such understanding encompassed important contextual conditions—because they were highly pertinent to your phenomenon of study (e.g., Yin & Davis, 2007). This first part of the logic of design therefore helps to continue to distinguish case studies from the other research methods that have been discussed.

An experiment, for instance, deliberately divorces a phenomenon from its context, attending to only a few variables (typically, the context is "controlled" by the laboratory environment). A history, by comparison, does deal with the entangled situation between phenomenon and context but usually with *non-*contemporary events. Finally, surveys can try to deal with phenomenon and context, but their ability to investigate the context is extremely limited. The survey designer, for instance, constantly struggles to limit the number of variables to be analyzed (and hence the number of questions that can be asked) to fall safely within the number of respondents who can be surveyed.

Second, because phenomenon and context are not always distinguishable in real-life situations, other technical characteristics, including data collection and data analysis strategies, now become the second part of our technical definition of case studies:

2. The case study inquiry
   o copes with the technically distinctive situation in which there will be many more variables of interest than data points, and as one result
   o relies on multiple sources of evidence, with data needing to converge in a triangulating fashion, and as another result
   o benefits from the prior development of theoretical propositions to guide data collection and analysis.

In essence, the twofold definition shows how case study research comprises an all-encompassing method—covering the logic of design, data collection techniques, and specific approaches to data analysis. In this sense, the case study is not limited to being a data collection tactic alone or even a design feature alone (Stoecker, 1991). How the method is practiced is the topic of this entire book.

EXERCISE 1.4   Finding and Analyzing an Existing Case Study
                from the Literature

Retrieve an example of case study research from the literature. The case study can be on any topic, but it must have used some empirical method and presented some empirical (qualitative or quantitative) data. Why is this a case study? What, if anything, is distinctive about the findings that could not be learned by using some other social science method focusing on the same topic?

Certain other features of the case study method are not critical for defining the method, but they may be considered variations within case study research and also provide answers to common questions.

Variations within Case Studies as a Research Method

Yes, case study research includes both single- and multiple-case studies. Though some fields, such as political science and public administration, have tried to distinguish between these two approaches (and have used such terms as the *comparative case method* as a distinctive form of multiple-case studies; see Agranoff & Radin, 1991; Dion, 1998; Lijphart, 1975), single- and multiple-case studies are in reality but two variants of case study designs (see Chapter 2 for more).

And yes, case studies can include, and even be limited to, quantitative evidence. In fact, any contrast between quantitative and qualitative evidence does not distinguish the various research methods. Note that, as analogous examples, some experiments (such as studies of perceptions) and some survey questions (such as those seeking categorical rather than numerical responses) rely on qualitative and not quantitative evidence. Likewise, historical research can include enormous amounts of quantitative evidence.

As a related but important note, the case study method is not just a form of "qualitative research," even though it may be recognized among the array of qualitative research choices (e.g., Creswell, 2007). Some case study research goes beyond being a type of qualitative research, by using a mix of quantitative and qualitative evidence. In addition, case studies need not always include the direct and detailed observational evidence marked by other forms of "qualitative research."

And yes, case studies have a distinctive place in evaluation research (see Cronbach & Associates, 1980; Patton, 2002; U.S. Government Accountability Office, 1990). There are at least four different applications. The most important is to *explain* the presumed causal links in real-life interventions that are too complex for the survey or experimental strategies. A second application is to *describe* an intervention and the real-life context in which it occurred. Third, case studies can *illustrate* certain topics within an evaluation, again in a descriptive mode. Fourth, the case study strategy may be used to *enlighten* those situations in which the intervention being evaluated has no clear, single set of outcomes. Whatever the application, one constant theme is that program sponsors—rather than research investigators alone—may have the prominent role in defining the evaluation questions and desired data categories (U.S. Government Accountability Office, 1990).

And finally, yes, case studies can be conducted and written with many different motives. These motives vary from the simple presentation of individual cases to the desire to arrive at broad generalizations based on case study evidence but without presenting any of the individual case studies separately (see BOX 3).

BOX 3
Multiple-Case Studies: Case Studies Containing Multiple "Cases"

Case studies can cover multiple cases and then draw a single set of "cross-case" conclusions. The two examples below both focused on a topic of continuing public interest: identifying successful programs to improve U.S. social conditions.

3A. A Cross-Case Analysis following the Presentation of Separate, Single Cases

Jonathan Crane (1998) edited a book that had nine social programs as separate cases. Each case had a different author and was presented in its own chapter. The programs had in common strong evidence of their effectiveness, but they varied widely in their focus—from education to nutrition to drug prevention to preschool programs to drug treatment for delinquent youths. The editor then presents a cross-program analysis in a final chapter, attempting to draw generalizable conclusions that could apply to many other programs.

3B. A Book Whose Entire Text Is Devoted to the Multiple-Case ("Cross-Case") Analysis

Lisbeth Schorr's (1997) book is about major strategies for improving social conditions, illustrated by four policy topics: welfare reform, strengthening the child protection system, education reform, and transforming neighborhoods. The book continually refers to specific cases of successful programs, but these programs do not appear as separate, individual chapters. Also citing data from the literature, the author develops numerous generalizations based on the case studies, including the need for successful programs to be "results oriented." Similarly, she identifies six other attributes of highly effective programs (also see BOX 41A and 41B, Chapter 6, p. 173).

> **EXERCISE 1.5   Defining Different Types of Case Studies Used for Research Purposes**
>
> Define the three types of case studies used for research (but not teaching) purposes: (a) explanatory or causal case studies, (b) descriptive case studies, and (c) exploratory case studies. Compare the situations in which these different types of case studies would be most applicable. Now name a case study that you would like to conduct. Would it be explanatory, descriptive, or exploratory? Why?

SUMMARY

This chapter has introduced the importance of the case study as a research method. Like other research methods, it is a way of investigating an empirical topic by following a set of prespecified procedures. Articulating these procedures will dominate the remainder of this book.

The chapter has provided an operational definition of the case study and has identified some of the variations in case studies. The chapter also has attempted to distinguish the case study from alternative research methods in social science, indicating the situations in which doing a case study may be preferred, for instance, to doing a survey. Some situations may have no clearly preferred method, as the strengths and weaknesses of the various methods may overlap. The basic goal, however, is to consider all the methods in an inclusive and pluralistic fashion—as part of your repertoire from which you may draw according to a given situation to do social science research.

Finally, the chapter has discussed some of the major criticisms of case study research, also suggesting possible responses to these criticisms. However, we must all work hard to overcome the problems of doing case study research, including the recognition that some of us were not meant, by skill or disposition, to do such research in the first place. Case study research is remarkably hard, even though case studies have traditionally been considered to be "soft" research, possibly because investigators have not followed systematic procedures. This book tries to make your research study easier by offering an array of such procedures.

NOTES

1. The discussion only pertains to the use of these methods in the social sciences, making no claims for commenting on the use of experiments, for instance, in physics, biology, or other fields.

2. There nevertheless may be exceptional circumstances when a single case is so unique or important that a case study investigator has no desire to generalize to any other cases. See Stake's (2005) "intrinsic" case studies and Lawrence-Lightfoot and Davis's (1997) "portraits."

3. Scholars also point to the possibility that the classic experiments tend to test simple causal relationships—that is, when a single treatment such as a new drug is hypothesized to produce an effect. However, for many social and behavioral topics, the relevant causes may be complex and involve multiple interactions, and investigating these may well be beyond the capability of a single experiment (George & Bennett, 2004, p. 12).

4. Robert Stake (2005, p. 443) similarly considers the "case," and not any method of inquiry, to be the defining criterion for case study. Furthermore, Stake (1995, pp. 1–2) says that the preferred case must be a well-bounded, specific, complex, and functioning "thing" (e.g., a person or a program) and not a generality (such as the relationship among schools or an education policy).

REFERENCE TO EXPANDED CASE STUDY
MATERIALS FOR CHAPTER 1

For selected case studies cited in the text of this chapter, two anthologies contain either a more extensive excerpt or the full case study. The table below crosswalks the reference in this book to the location of the excerpt or full rendition.

CHAPTER 1 Chapter Topic and Page Numbers	Topics of Illustrative Case Studies	Reference to Lengthier Material
The Case Study as a Research Method	None	
Comparing Case Studies with Other Research Methods:		
BOX 1, p. 1-7	International relations	CSA-2
BOX 2A, p. 1-7	Neighborhoods	None
BOX 2B, p. 1-7	Health care	CSA-1
p. 1-7 text	University innovation	ACSR-4
p. 1-7 text	Drug abuse prevention	ACSR-5
p. 1-7 text	Business and industry	ACSR-6
p. 1-7 text	Crime prevention	ACSR-7

CHAPTER 1 Chapter Topic and Page Numbers	Topics of Illustrative Case Studies	Reference to Lengthier Material
p. 1-7 text	Neighborhoods	ACSR-2
p. 1-7 text	Computers in schools	ACSR-3
Different Kinds of Case Studies, but a Common Definition:		
BOX 3A, p. 1-27	Social services	None
BOX 3B, p. 1-27	Social services	None

NOTE: CSA = *Case Study Anthology* (Yin, 2004). ACSR = *Applications of Case Study Research* (Yin, 2003). The number denotes the chapter number in the book.

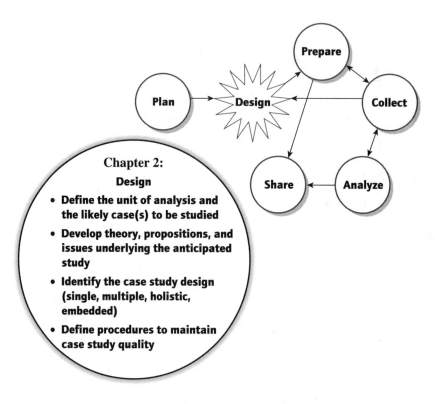

ABSTRACT

A research design is the logic that links the data to be collected (and the conclusions to be drawn) to the initial questions of study. Every empirical study has an implicit, if not explicit, research design. Articulating "theory" about what is being studied and what is to be learned helps to operationalize case study designs and make them more explicit.

Case study designs need to maximize their quality through four critical conditions related to design quality: (a) construct validity, (b) internal validity, (c) external validity, and (d) reliability. How investigators can deal with these aspects of quality control in doing case studies is discussed in Chapter 2 but also is a major theme throughout the remainder of the book.

Among the actual case study designs, four major types are relevant, following a 2×2 matrix. The first pair consists of single-case and multiple-case designs. The second pair, which can occur in combination with either of the first pair, is based on the unit or units of analysis to be covered—and distinguishes between holistic and embedded designs. Among these designs, most multiple-case designs are likely to be stronger than single-case designs. Trying to use even a "two-case" design is therefore a worthy objective, compared to doing a single-case study. Case studies also can be part of a larger mixed methods study.

2

Designing Case Studies

Identifying Your Case(s) and Establishing the Logic of Your Case Study

GENERAL APPROACH TO DESIGNING CASE STUDIES

In identifying the method for your research project, Chapter 1 has shown when you might choose to use the case study method, as opposed to other methods. The next task is to design your case study. For this purpose, as in designing any other type of research investigation, you need a plan or *research design.*

The development of this research design is a difficult part of doing case studies. Unlike other research methods, a comprehensive "catalog" of research designs for case studies has yet to be developed. There are no textbooks, like those in the biological and psychological sciences, covering such design considerations as the assignment of subjects to different "groups," the selection of different stimuli or experimental conditions, or the identification of various response measures (see Cochran & Cox, 1957; Fisher, 1935, cited in Cochran & Cox, 1957; Sidowski, 1966). In a laboratory experiment, each of these choices reflects an important logical connection to the issues being studied. Similarly, there are not even textbooks like the well-known volumes by Campbell and Stanley (1966) or by Cook and Campbell (1979) that summarize the various research designs for quasi-experimental situations. Nor have there emerged any common designs—for example, "panel" studies—such as those recognized in doing survey research (see L. Kidder & Judd, 1986, chap. 6).

One pitfall to be avoided, however, is to consider case study designs to be a subset or variant of the research designs used for other methods, such as experiments. For the longest time, scholars incorrectly thought that the case study was but one type of quasi-experimental design (the "one-shot post-test-only" design). This misperception has finally been corrected, with the following statement appearing in a revision on quasi-experimental designs (Cook & Campbell, 1979): "Certainly the case study as normally practiced should not be demeaned by identification with the one-group post-test-only design" (p. 96). In other

---

Tip: *How should I select the case(s) for my case study?*

You need sufficient access to the potential data, whether to interview people, review documents or records, or make observations in the "field." Given such access to more than a single candidate case, you should choose the case(s) that will most likely illuminate your research questions. Absent such access, you should consider changing your research questions, hopefully leading to new candidates to which you do have access.

Do you think access should be so important?

---

words, the one-shot, post-test-only design as a quasi-experimental design still may be considered flawed, but the case study has now been recognized as something different. In fact, the case study is a separate research method that has its own research designs.

Unfortunately, case study research designs have not been codified. The following chapter therefore expands on the new methodological ground broken by earlier editions of this book and describes a basic set of research designs for doing single- and multiple-case studies. Although these designs will need to be continually modified and improved in the future, in their present form they will nevertheless help you to design more rigorous and methodologically sound case studies.

Definition of Research Designs

Every type of empirical research has an implicit, if not explicit, research design. In the most elementary sense, the design is the logical sequence that connects the empirical data to a study's initial research questions and, ultimately, to its conclusions. Colloquially, a research design is *a logical plan for getting from here to there,* where *here* may be defined as the initial set of questions to be answered, and *there* is some set of conclusions (answers) about these questions. Between "here" and "there" may be found a number of major steps, including the collection and analysis of relevant data. As a summary definition, another textbook has described a research design as a plan that

> guides the investigator in the process of collecting, analyzing, and interpreting observations. It is a *logical model of proof* that allows the researcher to draw inferences concerning causal relations among the variables under investigation. (Nachmias & Nachmias, 1992, pp. 77-78, emphasis added)

Another way of thinking about a research design is as a "blueprint" for your research, dealing with at least four problems: what questions to study, what data are relevant, what data to collect, and how to analyze the results (Philliber, Schwab, & Samsloss, 1980).

Note that a research design is much more than a work plan. The main purpose of the design is to help to avoid the situation in which the evidence does not address the initial research questions. In this sense, a research design deals with a *logical* problem and not a *logistical* problem. As a simple example, suppose you want to study a single organization. Your research questions, however, have to do with the organization's relationships with other organizations—their competitive or collaborative nature, for example. Such questions can be answered only if you collect information directly from the other organizations and not merely from the one you started with. If you complete your study by examining only one organization, you cannot draw unbiased conclusions about interorganizational partnerships. This is a flaw in your research design, not in your work plan. The outcome could have been avoided if you had developed an appropriate research design in the first place.

Components of Research Designs

For case studies, five components of a research design are especially important:

1. a study's questions;
2. its propositions, if any;
3. its unit(s) of analysis;
4. the logic linking the data to the propositions; and
5. the criteria for interpreting the findings.

Study questions. This first component has already been described in Chapter 1, which suggested that the *form* of the question—in terms of "who," "what," "where," "how," and "why"—provides an important clue regarding the most relevant research method to be used. The case study method is most likely to be appropriate for "how" and "why" questions, so your initial task is to clarify precisely the nature of your study questions in this regard.

More troublesome may be coming up with the substance of the questions. Many students take an initial stab, only to be discouraged when they find the same question(s) already well covered by previous research. Other less desirable questions focus on too trivial or minor parts of an issue. A helpful hint is to move in three stages. In the first, try to use the literature to narrow your interest to a key topic or two, not worrying about any specific research questions. In the second, examine closely—even dissect—a few key studies on your topic of interest. Identify the questions in those few studies and whether they conclude with new questions or loose ends for future research. These may then stimulate your own thinking and imagination, and you may find yourself articulating some potential questions of your own. In the third stage, examine another set of studies on the same topic. They may provide support for your potential questions or even suggest ways of sharpening them.

> **EXERCISE 2.1   Defining the Boundaries of a Case Study**
>
> Select a topic for a case study you would like to do. Identify some research questions to be answered or propositions to be examined by your case study. How does the naming of these questions or propositions clarify the boundaries of your case study with regard to the time period covered by the case study; the relevant social group, organization, or geographic area; the type of evidence to be collected; and the priorities for data collection and analysis?

Study propositions. As for the second component, each proposition directs attention to something that should be examined within the scope of study. For instance, assume that your research, on the topic of interorganizational partnerships, began with the following question: How and why do organizations collaborate with one another to provide joint services (for example, a manufacturer and a retail outlet collaborating to sell certain computer products)? These "how" and "why" questions, capturing what you are really interested in answering, led you to the case study as the appropriate method in the first place. Nevertheless, these "how" and "why" questions do not point to what you should study.

Only if you are forced to state some propositions will you move in the right direction. For instance, you might think that organizations collaborate because they derive mutual benefits. This proposition, besides reflecting an important theoretical issue (that other incentives for collaboration do not exist or are unimportant), also begins to tell you where to look for relevant evidence (to define and ascertain the extent of specific benefits to each organization).

At the same time, some studies may have a legitimate reason for not having any propositions. This is the condition—which exists in experiments, surveys, and the other research methods alike—in which a topic is the subject of "exploration." Every exploration, however, should still have some purpose. Instead of propositions, the design for an exploratory study should state this purpose, as well as the criteria by which an exploration will be judged successful. Consider the analogy in BOX 4 for exploratory case studies. Can you imagine how you would ask for support from Queen Isabella to do your exploratory study?

BOX 4
"Exploration" as an Analogy for an Exploratory Case Study

When Christopher Columbus went to Queen Isabella to ask for support for his "exploration" of the New World, he had to have some reasons for asking for three ships (Why not one? Why not five?), and he had some rationale for going westward (Why not south? Why not south and then east?). He also had some (mistaken) criteria for recognizing the Indies when he actually encountered it. In short, his exploration began with some rationale and direction, even if his initial assumptions might later have been proved wrong (Wilford, 1992). This same degree of rationale and direction should underlie even an exploratory case study.

Unit of analysis. This third component is related to the fundamental problem of defining what the "case" is—a problem that has plagued many investigators at the outset of case studies (e.g., Ragin & Becker, 1992). For instance, in the classic case study, a "case" may be an individual. Jennifer Platt (1992) has noted how the early case studies in the Chicago school of sociology were life histories of such persons as juvenile delinquents or derelict men. You also can imagine case studies of clinical patients, of exemplary students, or of certain types of leaders. In each situation, an individual person is the case being studied, and the individual is the primary unit of analysis. Information about the relevant individual would be collected, and several such individuals or "cases" might be included in a multiple-case study.

You would still need study questions and study propositions to help identify the relevant information to be collected about this individual or individuals. Without such questions and propositions, you might be tempted to cover "everything" about the individual(s), which is impossible to do. For example, the propositions in studying these individuals might involve the influence of early childhood or the role of peer relationships. Such seemingly general topics nevertheless represent a vast narrowing of the relevant data. The more a case study contains specific questions and propositions, the more it will stay within feasible limits.

Of course, the "case" also can be some event or entity other than a single individual. Case studies have been done about decisions, programs, the implementation process, and organizational change. Feagin et al. (1991) contains some classic examples of these single cases in sociology and political science. Beware of these types of cases—none is easily defined in terms of the beginning or end points of the "case." For example, a case study of a specific program may reveal (a) variations in program definition, depending upon the perspective of different actors, and (b) program components that preexisted the formal designation of the program. Any case study of such a program would therefore have to confront these conditions in delineating the unit of analysis.

As a general guide, your tentative definition of the unit of analysis (which is the same as the definition of the "case") is related to the way you have defined your initial research questions. Suppose, for example, you want to study the role of the United States in the global economy. Years ago, Peter Drucker (1986) wrote a provocative essay (not a case study) about fundamental changes in the world economy, including the importance of "capital movements" independent of the flow of goods and services. Using Drucker's work or some similar theoretical framework, the unit of analysis (or "case") for your case study might be a country's economy, an industry in the world marketplace, an economic policy, or the trade or capital flow between countries. Each unit of analysis and its related questions and propositions would call for a slightly different research design and data collection strategy.

Selection of the appropriate unit of analysis will start to occur when you accurately specify your primary research questions. If your questions do not lead to the favoring of one unit of analysis over another, your questions are probably either too vague or too numerous—and you may have trouble doing a case study. However, when you do eventually arrive at a definition of the unit of analysis, do not consider closure permanent. Your choice of the unit of analysis, as with other facets of your research design, can be revisited as a result of discoveries during your data collection (see discussion and cautions about flexibility throughout this book and at the end of this chapter).

Sometimes, the unit of analysis may have been defined one way, even though the phenomenon being studied actually follows a different definition. Most frequently, investigators have confused case studies of neighborhoods with case studies of small groups (as another example, confusing a new technology with the workings of an engineering team in an organization; see BOX 5A). How a geographic *area* such as a neighborhood copes with racial transition, upgrading, and other phenomena can be quite different from how a small *group* copes with these same phenomena. For instance, *Street Corner Society* (Whyte, 1943/1955; see BOX 2A in Chapter 1 of this book) and *Tally's Corner* (Liebow, 1967; see BOX 9, this chapter) often have been mistaken for being case studies of neighborhoods when in fact they are case studies of small groups (note that in neither book is the neighborhood geography described, even though the small groups lived in a small area with clear neighborhood implications). BOX 5B, however, presents a good example of how units of analyses can be defined in a more discriminating manner—in the field of world trade.

BOX 5
Defining the Unit of Analysis

5A. What Is the Unit of Analysis?

The Soul of a New Machine (1981) was a Pulitzer Prize–winning book by Tracy Kidder. The book, also a best seller, is about the development of a new minicomputer, produced by Data General Corporation, intended to compete with one produced by a direct competitor, Digital Equipment Corporation (also see BOX 28, Chapter 5, p. 142).

This easy-to-read book describes how Data General's engineering team invented and developed the new computer. The book begins with the initial conceptualization of the computer and ends when the engineering team relinquishes control of the machine to Data General's marketing staff.

The book is an excellent example of a case study. However, the book also illustrates a fundamental problem in doing case studies—that of defining the unit of analysis. Is the "case" being studied the minicomputer, or is it about the dynamics of a small group—the engineering team? The answer is critical for understanding how the case study might relate to any broader body of knowledge—that is, whether to generalize to a technology topic or to a group dynamics topic. Because the book is not an academic study, it does not need to, nor does it, provide an answer.

5B. A Clearer Choice among Units of Analysis

Ira Magaziner and Mark Patinkin's (1989) book, *The Silent War: Inside the Global Business Battles Shaping America's Future*, presents nine individual case studies (also see BOX 35, Chapter 5, p. 161). Each case helps the reader to understand a real-life situation of international economic competition.

Two of the cases appear similar but in fact have different main units of analysis. One case, about the Korean firm Samsung, is a case study of the critical policies that make the firm competitive. Understanding Korean economic development is part of the context, and the case study also contains an embedded unit—Samsung's development of the microwave oven as an illustrative product. The other case, about the development of an Apple computer factory in Singapore, is in fact a case study of Singapore's critical policies that make the country competitive. The Apple computer factory experience—an embedded unit of analysis—is actually an illustrative example of how the national policies affected foreign investments.

These two cases show how the definition of the main and embedded units of analyses, as well as the definition of the contextual events surrounding these units, depends on the level of inquiry. The main unit of analysis is likely to be at the level being addressed by the main study questions.

Most investigators will encounter this type of confusion in defining the unit of analysis or "case." To reduce the confusion, one recommended practice is to discuss the potential case with a colleague. Try to explain to that person what questions you are trying to answer and why you have chosen a specific case or group of cases as a way of answering those questions. This may help you to avoid incorrectly identifying the unit of analysis.

Once the general definition of the case has been established, other clarifications in the unit of analysis become important. If the unit of analysis is a small group, for instance, the persons to be included within the group (the immediate topic of the case study) must be distinguished from those who are outside it (the context for the case study). Similarly, if the case is about local services in a specific geographic area, you need to decide which services to cover. Also desirable, for almost any topic that might be chosen, are specific time boundaries to define the beginning and end of the case (e.g., whether to include the entire or only some part of the life cycle of the entity that is to be the case). Answering all of these types of questions will help to determine the scope of your data collection and, in particular, how you will distinguish data about the subject of your case study (the "phenomenon") from data external to the case (the "context").

These latter cautions regarding the need for spatial, temporal, and other concrete boundaries underlie a key but subtle aspect in defining your case. The desired case should be some real-life phenomenon, not an abstraction such as a topic, an argument, or even a hypothesis. These abstractions, absent the identification of specific examples or cases, would rightfully serve as the subjects of research studies using other kinds of methods but not case studies. To justify using the case study method, you need to go one step further: You need to define a specific, real-life "case" to represent the abstraction. (For examples of more concrete and less concrete case study topics, see Figure 2.1.)

Take the concept of "neighboring." Alone, it could be the subject of research studies using methods other than the case study method. The other methods might include a survey of the relationships among neighbors, a history of the evolution of the sense of neighboring and the setting of boundaries, or an experiment in which young children do tasks next to each other to determine the distracting effects, if any, of their neighbors. These examples show how the abstract concept of "neighboring" does not alone produce the grounds for a case study. However, the concept could readily become a case study topic if it were accompanied by your selecting a specific neighborhood ("case") to be studied and posing study questions and propositions about the neighborhood in relation to the concept of "neighboring."

One final point pertains to the role of the available research literature and needs to be made about defining the case and the unit of analysis. Most researchers will want to compare their findings with previous research. For

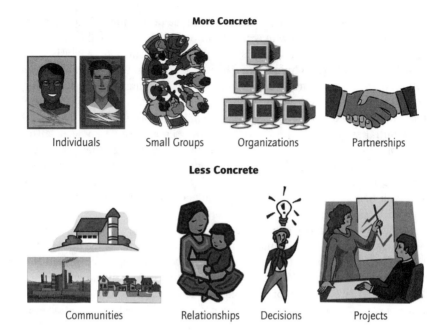

Figure 2.1   Illustrative Case Study Topics

this reason, the key definitions used in your study should not be idiosyncratic. Rather, each case study and unit of analysis either should be similar to those previously studied by others or should innovate in clear, operationally defined ways. In this manner, the previous literature also can become a guide for defining the case and unit of analysis.

EXERCISE 2.2   Defining the Unit of Analysis (and the "Case") for a Case Study

Examine Figure 2.1. Discuss each subject, which illustrates a different unit of analysis. Find a published case study on at least one of these subjects, indicating the actual "case" that was being studied. Understanding that each subject illustrates a different unit of analysis and involves the selection of different cases to be studied, do you think that the more concrete units might be easier to define than the less concrete ones? Why?

Linking data to propositions and criteria for interpreting the findings. The fourth and fifth components have been increasingly better developed in doing case studies. These components foreshadow the data analysis steps in case study research. Because the analytic techniques and choices are covered in detail in Chapter 5, your main concern during the design phase is to be aware of the main choices and how they might suit your case study. In this way, your research design can create a more solid foundation for the later analysis.

All of the analytic techniques in Chapter 5 represent ways of *linking data to propositions:* pattern matching, explanation building, time-series analysis, logic models, and cross-case synthesis. The actual analyses will require that you combine or calculate your case study data as a direct reflection of your initial study propositions. For instance, knowing that some or all of your propositions cover a temporal sequence would mean that you might eventually use some type of time-series analysis. Noting this strong likelihood during the design phase would call your attention to the need to be sure you had sufficient procedures to collect time markers as part of your data collection plans.

If you have had limited experience in conducting empirical studies, you will not easily identify the likely analytic technique(s) or anticipate the needed data to use the techniques to their full advantage. More experienced researchers will note how often they have either (a) collected too much data that were not later used in any analysis or (b) collected too little data that prevented the proper use of a desired analytic technique. Sometimes, the latter situation even may force researchers to return to their data collection phase (if they can), to supplement the original data. The more you can avoid any of these situations, the better off you will be.

Criteria for interpreting a study's findings. Statistical analyses offer some explicit criteria for such interpretations. For instance, by convention, social science considers a p level of less than .05 to demonstrate that observed differences were "statistically significant." However, much case study analysis will not rely on the use of statistics and therefore calls attention to other ways of thinking about such criteria.

A major and important alternative strategy is to identify and address rival explanations for your findings. Again, Chapter 5 discusses this strategy and how it works more fully. At the design stage of your work, the challenge is to anticipate and enumerate the important rivals, so you will include information about them as part of your data collection. If you only think of rival explanations after data collection has been completed, you will be starting to justify and design a *future* study, but you will not be helping to complete your *current* case study. For this reason, specifying important rival explanations is a part of a case study's research design work.

Summary. A research design should include five components. Although the current state of the art does not provide detailed guidance on the last two, the complete research design should indicate what data are to be collected—as indicated by a study's questions, its propositions, and its units of analysis. The design also should tell you what is to be done after the data have been collected—as indicated by the logic linking the data to the propositions and the criteria for interpreting the findings.

The Role of Theory in Design Work

Covering these preceding five components of research designs will effectively force you to begin constructing a preliminary theory related to your topic of study. This role of theory development, prior to the conduct of any data collection, is one point of difference between case studies and related methods such as ethnography (Lincoln & Guba, 1985; Van Maanen, 1988) and "grounded theory" (Corbin & Strauss, 2007). Typically, these related methods deliberately avoid specifying any theoretical propositions at the outset of an inquiry. As a result, students confusing these methods with case studies wrongly think that, by having selected the case study method, they can proceed quickly into the data collection phase of their work, and they may have been encouraged to make their "field contacts" as quickly as possible. No guidance could be more misleading. Among other considerations, the relevant field contacts depend upon an understanding—or theory—of what is being studied.

Theory development. For case studies, theory development as part of the design phase is essential, whether the ensuing case study's purpose is to develop or to test theory. Using a case study on the implementation of a new management information system (MIS) as an example (Markus, 1983), the simplest ingredient of a theory is a statement such as the following:

> The case study will show why implementation only succeeded when the organization was able to re-structure itself, and not just overlay the new MIS on the old organizational structure. (Markus, 1983)

The statement presents the nutshell of a theory of MIS implementation—that is, that organizational restructuring is needed to make MIS implementation work.

Using the same case, an additional ingredient might be the following statement:

> The case study will also show why the simple replacement of key persons was not sufficient for successful implementation. (Markus, 1983)

This second statement presents the nutshell of a *rival* theory—that is, that MIS implementation fails because of the resistance to change on the part of individual people and that the replacement of such people is the main requirement for implementation to succeed.

You can see that as these two initial ingredients are elaborated, the stated ideas will increasingly cover the questions, propositions, units of analysis, logic connecting data to propositions, and criteria for interpreting the findings—that is, the five components of the needed research design. In this sense, the complete research design embodies a "theory" of what is being studied.

This theory should by no means be considered with the formality of grand theory in social science, nor are you being asked to be a masterful theoretician. Rather, the simple goal is to have a sufficient blueprint for your study, and this requires theoretical propositions, usefully noted by Sutton and Staw (1995) as "a [hypothetical] story about why acts, events, structure, and thoughts occur" (p. 378). Then, the complete research design will provide surprisingly strong guidance in determining what data to collect and the strategies for analyzing the data. For this reason, theory development prior to the collection of any case study data is an essential step in doing case studies. As noted for nonexperimental studies more generally, a more elaborate theory desirably points to a more complex pattern of expected results (P. R. Rosenbaum, 2002, pp. 5–6 and 277–279). The benefit is a stronger design and a heightened ability to interpret your eventual data.

However, theory development takes time and can be difficult (Eisenhardt, 1989). For some topics, existing works may provide a rich theoretical framework for designing a specific case study. If you are interested in international economic development, for instance, Peter Drucker's (1986) "The Changed World Economy" is an exceptional source of theories and hypotheses. Drucker claims that the world economy has changed significantly from the past. He points to the "uncoupling" between the primary products (raw materials) economy and the industrial economy, a similar uncoupling between low labor costs and manufacturing production, and the uncoupling between financial markets and the real economy of goods and services. To test these propositions might require different studies, some focusing on the different uncouplings, others focusing on specific industries, and yet others explaining the plight of specific countries. Each different study would likely call for a different unit of analysis. Drucker's theoretical framework would provide guidance for designing these studies and even for collecting relevant data.

In other situations, the appropriate theory may be a descriptive theory (see BOX 2A in Chapter 1 for another example), and your concern should focus on such issues as (a) the purpose of the descriptive effort, (b) the full but realistic range of topics that might be considered a "complete" description of what is to be studied, and (c) the likely topic(s) that will be the essence of the description. Good answers to these questions, including the rationales underlying the answers, will help you go a long way toward developing the needed theoretical base—and research design—for your study.

For yet other topics, the existing knowledge base may be poor, and the available literature will provide no conceptual framework or hypotheses of note. Such a knowledge base does not lend itself to the development of good theoretical statements, and any new empirical study is likely to assume the characteristic of an "exploratory" study. Nevertheless, as noted earlier with the illustrative case in BOX 4, even an exploratory case study should be preceded by statements about what is to be explored, the purpose of the exploration, and the criteria by which the exploration will be judged successful.

Overall, you may want to gain a richer understanding of how theory is used in case studies by reviewing specific case studies that have been successfully completed. For instance, Yin (2003, chap. 1) shows how theory was used in exploratory, descriptive, and explanatory situations by discussing five actual case studies.

Illustrative types of theories. In general, to overcome the barriers to theory development, you should try to prepare for your case study by doing such things as reviewing the literature related to what you would like to study (also see Cooper, 1984), discussing your topic and ideas with colleagues or teachers, and asking yourself challenging questions about what you are studying, why you are proposing to do the study, and what you hope to learn as a result of the study.

As a further reminder, you should be aware of the full range of theories that might be relevant to your study. For instance, note that the MIS example illustrates MIS "implementation" theory and that this is but one type of theory that can be the subject of study. Other types of theories for you to consider include

- ◆ individual theories—for example, theories of individual development, cognitive behavior, personality, learning and disability, individual perception, and interpersonal interactions;
- ◆ group theories—for example, theories of family functioning, informal groups, work teams, supervisory-employee relations, and interpersonal networks;
- ◆ organizational theories—for example, theories of bureaucracies, organizational structure and functions, excellence in organizational performance, and interorganizational partnerships; and
- ◆ societal theories—for example, theories of urban development, international behavior, cultural institutions, technological development, and marketplace functions.

Other examples cut across these illustrative types. Decision-making theory (Carroll & Johnson, 1992), for instance, can involve individuals, organizations, or social groups. As another example, a common topic of case studies is the evaluation of publicly supported programs, such as federal, state, or local programs. In this situation, the development of a theory of how a program is supposed to work is essential to the design of the evaluation. In this situation, Bickman (1987) reminds us that the theory needs to distinguish between the substance of the program (e.g., how to make education more effective) and the process of program implementation (e.g., how to install an effective program). The distinction would avoid situations where policy makers might want to know the desired substantive remedies (e.g., findings about a newly effective curriculum) but where an evaluation unfortunately focused on managerial issues (e.g., the need to hire a good project director). Such a mismatch can be avoided by giving closer attention to the substantive theory.

Generalizing from case study to theory. Theory development does not only facilitate the data collection phase of the ensuing case study. The appropriately developed theory also is the level at which the generalization of the case study results will occur. This role of theory has been characterized throughout this book as "analytic generalization" and has been contrasted with another way of generalizing results, known as "statistical generalization." Understanding the distinction between these two types of generalization may be your most important challenge in doing case studies.

Let us first take the more commonly recognized way of generalizing—*statistical* generalization—although it is the less relevant one for doing case studies. In statistical generalization, an inference is made about a population (or universe) on the basis of empirical data collected about a sample from that universe. This is shown as a Level One inference in Figure 2.2.[1] This method of generalizing is commonly recognized because research investigators have ready access to quantitative formulas for determining the confidence with which generalizations can be made, depending mostly upon the size and internal variation within the universe and sample. Moreover, this is the most common way of generalizing when doing surveys (e.g., Fowler, 1988; Lavrakas, 1987) or analyzing archival data.

A fatal flaw in doing case studies is to conceive of statistical generalization as the method of generalizing the results of your case study. This is because your cases are not "sampling units" and should not be chosen for this reason. Rather, individual case studies are to be selected as a laboratory investigator selects the topic of a new experiment. Multiple cases, in this sense, resemble multiple experiments. Under these circumstances, the mode of generalization is *analytic* generalization, in which a previously developed theory is used as a template with which to compare the empirical results of the case study.[2] If two or more cases are shown to support the same theory, replication may be

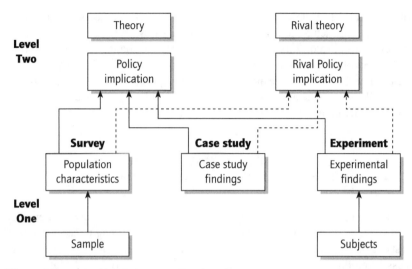

Figure 2.2   Making Inferences: Two Levels

claimed. The empirical results may be considered yet more potent if two or more cases support the same theory but do not support an equally plausible, *rival* theory. Graphically, this type of generalization is shown as a Level Two inference in Figure 2.2.

Analytic generalization can be used whether your case study involves one or several cases, which shall be later referenced as single-case or multiple-case studies. Furthermore, the logic of replication and the distinction between statistical and analytic generalization will be covered in greater detail in the discussion of multiple-case study designs. The main point at this juncture is that you should try to aim toward analytic generalization in doing case studies, and you should avoid thinking in such confusing terms as "the sample of cases" or the "small sample size of cases," as if a single-case study were like a single respondent in a survey or a single subject in an experiment. In other words, in terms of Figure 2.2, you should aim for Level Two inferences when doing case studies.

Because of the importance of this distinction between the two ways of generalizing, you will find repeated examples and discussion throughout the remainder of this chapter as well as in Chapter 5.

Summary. This subsection has suggested that a complete research design, covering the four components described earlier, in fact requires the development of a theoretical framework for the case study that is to be conducted. Rather than resisting such a requirement, a good case study investigator should make the effort to develop this theoretical framework, no matter whether the study is to be explanatory, descriptive, or exploratory. The use of theory, in doing case studies, is an immense aid in defining the appropriate research design and data collection. The same theoretical orientation also becomes the main vehicle for generalizing the results of the case study.

<h2 align="center">CRITERIA FOR JUDGING
THE QUALITY OF RESEARCH DESIGNS</h2>

Because a research design is supposed to represent a logical set of statements, you also can judge the quality of any given design according to certain logical tests. Concepts that have been offered for these tests include trustworthiness, credibility, confirmability, and data dependability (U.S. Government Accountability Office, 1990).

Four tests, however, have been commonly used to establish the quality of any empirical social research. Because case studies are one form of such research, the four tests also are relevant to case studies. An important innovation of this book is the identification of several tactics for dealing with these four tests when doing case studies. Figure 2.3 lists the four widely used tests and the recommended case study tactics, as well as a cross-reference to the phase of research when the tactic is to be used. (Each tactic is described in detail in the referenced chapter of this book.)

Because the four tests are common to all social science methods, the tests have been summarized in numerous textbooks (see L. Kidder & Judd, 1986, pp. 26–29):

♦ *Construct validity:* identifying correct operational measures for the concepts being studied

♦ *Internal validity* (for explanatory or causal studies only and not for descriptive or exploratory studies): seeking to establish a causal relationship, whereby certain conditions are believed to lead to other conditions, as distinguished from spurious relationships

♦ *External validity:* defining the domain to which a study's findings can be generalized

♦ *Reliability:* demonstrating that the operations of a study—such as the data collection procedures—can be repeated, with the same results

Each item on this list deserves explicit attention. For case studies, an important revelation is that the several tactics to be used in dealing with these tests

TESTS	Case Study Tactic	Phase of research in which tactic occurs
Construct validity	♦ use multiple sources of evidence ♦ establish chain of evidence ♦ have key informants review draft case study report	data collection data collection composition
Internal validity	♦ do pattern matching ♦ do explanation building ♦ address rival explanations ♦ use logic models	data analysis data analysis data analysis data analysis
External validity	♦ use theory in single-case studies ♦ use replication logic in multiple-case studies	research design research design
Reliability	♦ use case study protocol ♦ develop case study database	data collection data collection

Figure 2.3   Case Study Tactics for Four Design Tests

should be applied throughout the subsequent conduct of the case study, not just at its beginning. Thus, the "design work" for case studies may actually continue beyond the initial design plans.

Construct Validity

This first test is especially challenging in case study research. People who have been critical of case studies often point to the fact that a case study investigator fails to develop a sufficiently operational set of measures and that "subjective" judgments are used to collect the data.[3] Take an example such as studying "neighborhood change"—a common case study topic (e.g., Bradshaw, 1999; Keating & Krumholz, 1999).

Over the years, concerns have arisen over how certain urban neighborhoods have changed their character. Any number of case studies has examined the types of changes and their consequences. However, without any prior specification of the significant, operational events that constitute "change," a reader cannot tell whether the claimed changes in a case study genuinely reflect the events in a neighborhood or whether they happen to be based on an investigator's impressions only.

Neighborhood change can cover a wide variety of phenomena: racial turnover, housing deterioration and abandonment, changes in the pattern of urban services, shifts in a neighborhood's economic institutions, or the turnover from low- to middle-income residents in revitalizing neighborhoods. The choice of whether to aggregate blocks, census tracts, or larger areas also can produce different results (Hipp, 2007).

To meet the test of construct validity, an investigator must be sure to cover two steps:

1. define neighborhood change in terms of specific concepts (and relate them to the original objectives of the study) and

2. identify operational measures that match the concepts (preferably citing published studies that make the same matches).

For example, suppose you satisfy the first step by stating that you plan to study neighborhood change by focusing on trends in neighborhood crime. The second step now demands that you select a specific measure, such as police-reported crime (which happens to be the standard measure used in the FBI Uniform Crime Reports) as your measure of crime. The literature will indicate certain known shortcomings in this measure, mainly that unknown proportions of crimes are not reported to the police. You will then need to discuss how the shortcomings nevertheless will not bias your study of neighborhood crime and hence neighborhood change.

As Figure 2.3 shows, three tactics are available to increase construct validity when doing case studies. The first is the use of *multiple sources of evidence,* in a manner encouraging convergent lines of inquiry, and this tactic is relevant during data collection (see Chapter 4). A second tactic is to establish a *chain of evidence,* also relevant during data collection (also Chapter 4). The third tactic is to have the draft case study report reviewed by key informants (a procedure described further in Chapter 6).

Internal Validity

This second test has been given the greatest attention in experimental and quasi-experimental research (see Campbell & Stanley, 1966; Cook & Campbell, 1979). Numerous "threats" to validity have been identified, mainly dealing with spurious effects. However, because so many textbooks already cover this topic, only two points need to be made here.

First, internal validity is mainly a concern for explanatory case studies, when an investigator is trying to explain how and why event x led to event y. If the investigator incorrectly concludes that there is a causal relationship between x and y without knowing that some third factor—z—may actually have caused y, the research design has failed to deal with some threat to internal validity. Note that this logic is inapplicable to descriptive or exploratory studies (whether the studies are case studies, surveys, or experiments), which are not concerned with this kind of causal situation.

Second, the concern over internal validity, for case study research, extends to the broader problem of making inferences. Basically, a case study involves an inference every time an event cannot be directly observed. An investigator will "infer" that a particular event resulted from some earlier occurrence, based on interview and documentary evidence collected as part of the case study. Is the inference correct? Have all the rival explanations and possibilities been considered? Is the evidence convergent? Does it appear to be airtight? A research design that has anticipated these questions has begun to deal with the overall problem of making inferences and therefore the specific problem of internal validity.

However, the specific tactics for achieving this result are difficult to identify. This is especially true in doing case studies. As one set of suggestions, Figure 2.3 shows that the analytic tactic of *pattern matching,* described further in Chapter 5, is one way of addressing internal validity. Three other analytic tactics, *explanation building, addressing rival explanations,* and *using logic models,* also are described in Chapter 5.

External Validity

The third test deals with the problem of knowing whether a study's findings are generalizable beyond the immediate case study. In the simplest example, if a study of neighborhood change focused on one neighborhood, are the results applicable to another neighborhood? The external validity problem has been a major barrier in doing case studies. Critics typically state that single cases offer a poor basis for generalizing. However, such critics are implicitly contrasting the situation to survey research, in which a sample is intended to generalize to a larger universe. *This analogy to samples and universes is incorrect when dealing with case studies.* Survey research relies on *statistical* generalization, whereas case studies (as with experiments) rely on *analytic* generalization. In analytical generalization, the investigator is striving to generalize a particular set of results to some broader theory (see three examples in BOX 6).

For example, the theory of neighborhood change that led to a case study in the first place is the same theory that will help to identify the other cases to which the results are generalizable. If a study had focused on population transition in an urban neighborhood (e.g., Flippen, 2001), the procedure for selecting a neighborhood for study would have begun with identifying a neighborhood within which the hypothesized transitions were occurring. Theories about transition would then be the domain to which the results could later be generalized.

BOX 6
How Case Studies Can Be Generalized to Theory: Three Examples

6A. The Origins of Social Class Theory

The first example is about the uncovering and labeling of a social class structure based on a case study of a typical American city, *Yankee City* (Warner & Lunt, 1941). This classic case study in sociology made a critical contribution to social stratification theory and an understanding of social differences among "upper," "upper-middle," "middle-middle," "upper-lower," and "lower" classes.

6B. Contributions to Urban Planning Theory

The second example is Jane Jacobs and her famous book, *The Death and Life of Great American Cities* (1961). The book is based mostly on experiences from a single case, New York City. However, the chapter topics, rather than reflecting the single experiences of New York, cover broader theoretical issues in urban planning, such as the role of sidewalks, the role of neighborhood parks, the need for primary mixed uses, the need for small blocks, and the processes of slumming and unslumming. In the aggregate, these issues in fact represent Jacobs's building of a theory of urban planning.

Jacobs's book created heated controversy in the planning profession. As a partial result, new empirical inquiries were made in other locales, to examine one or another facet of her rich and provocative ideas. Her theory, in essence, became the vehicle for examining other cases, and the theory still stands as a significant contribution to the field of urban planning.

6C. A More Contemporary Example

A third example covers a 5-year ethnographic study of a single neighborhood at the edge of Chicago (Carr, 2003). The study shows how the neighborhood successfully thwarted undesirable youth-related crime. The experience, in the author's view, challenged existing theories claiming that strong social ties are crucial to effective neighborhood control. Instead, the author offers newer theories of informal social control that he believes may be especially pertinent to youth crime prevention in contemporary suburban neighborhoods.

The generalization is not automatic, however. A theory must be tested by replicating the findings in a second or even a third neighborhood, where the theory has specified that the same results should occur. Once such direct replications have been made, the results might be accepted as providing strong support for the theory, even though further replications had not been performed. This *replication logic* is the same that underlies the use of experiments (and allows scientists to cumulate knowledge across experiments). The logic will be discussed further in this chapter in the section on multiple-case designs.

Reliability

Most people are probably already familiar with this final test. The objective is to be sure that, if a later investigator followed the same procedures as described by an earlier investigator and conducted the same case study all over again, the later investigator should arrive at the same findings and conclusions. (Note that the emphasis is on doing the *same* case over again, not on "replicating" the results of one case by doing another case study.) The goal of reliability is to minimize the errors and biases in a study.

One prerequisite for allowing this other investigator to repeat an earlier case study is the need to document the procedures followed in the earlier case. Without such documentation, you could not even repeat your own work (which is another way of dealing with reliability). In the past, case study research procedures have been poorly documented, making external reviewers suspicious of the reliability of the case study method.[4] Figure 2.3 indicates two specific tactics to overcome these shortcomings—the use of a *case study protocol* to deal with the documentation problem in detail (discussed in Chapter 3) and the development of a *case study database* (discussed in Chapter 4).

The general way of approaching the reliability problem is to make as many steps as operational as possible and to conduct research as if someone were always looking over your shoulder. Accountants and bookkeepers always are aware that any calculations must be capable of being audited. In this sense, an auditor also is performing a reliability check and must be able to produce the same results if the same procedures are followed. A good guideline for doing case studies is therefore to conduct the research so that an auditor could in principle repeat the procedures and arrive at the same results.

Summary

Four tests may be considered relevant in judging the quality of a research design. In designing and doing case studies, various tactics are available to deal with these tests, though not all of the tactics occur at the formal stage of designing a case study. Some of the tactics occur during the data collection, data analysis, or compositional phases of the research and are therefore described in greater detail in subsequent chapters of this book.

EXERCISE 2.3   Defining the Criteria for Judging the Quality of Research Designs

Define the four criteria for judging the quality of research designs: (a) construct validity, (b) internal validity, (c) external validity, and (d) reliability. Give an example of each type of criterion in a case study you might want to do.

CASE STUDY DESIGNS

These general characteristics of research designs serve as a background for considering the specific designs for case studies. Four types of designs will be discussed, based on a 2 × 2 matrix (see Figure 2.4). The matrix first shows that every type of design will include the desire to analyze contextual conditions in relation to the "case," with the dotted lines between the two signaling that the boundaries between the case and the context are not likely to be sharp. The matrix then shows that single- and multiple-case studies reflect different design situations and that, within these two variants, there also can be unitary or multiple units of analysis. The resulting four types of designs for case studies are (Type 1) single-case (holistic) designs, (Type 2) single-case (embedded)

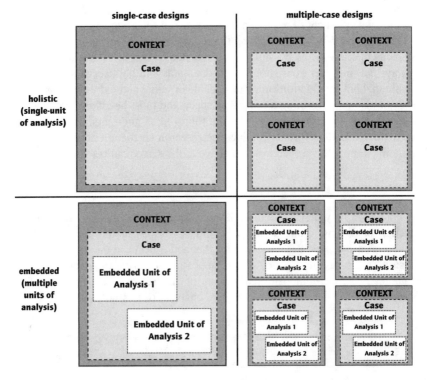

Figure 2.4   Basic Types of Designs for Case Studies
SOURCE: COSMOS Corporation.

designs, (Type 3) multiple-case (holistic) designs, and (Type 4) multiple-case (embedded) designs. The rationale for these four types of designs is as follows.

What Are the Potential Single-Case Designs (Types 1 and 2)?

Rationale for single-case designs. A primary distinction in designing case studies is between *single-* and *multiple*-case designs. This means the need for a decision, prior to any data collection, on whether a single case or multiple cases are going to be used to address the research questions. The single-case study is an appropriate design under several circumstances, and five rationales are given below. Recall that a single-case study is analogous to a single experiment, and many of the same conditions that justify a single experiment also justify a single-case study.

One rationale for a single case is when it represents the *critical case* in testing a well-formulated theory (again, note the analogy to the critical *experiment*). The theory has specified a clear set of propositions as well as the circumstances within which the propositions are believed to be true. A single case, meeting all of the conditions for testing the theory, can confirm, challenge, or extend the theory. The single case can then be used to determine whether a theory's propositions are correct or whether some alternative set of explanations might be more relevant. In this manner, like Graham Allison's comparison of three theories and the Cuban missile crisis (described in Chapter 1, BOX 2), the single case can represent a significant contribution to knowledge and theory building. Such a study can even help to refocus future investigations in an entire field. (See BOX 7 for another example, in the field of organizational innovation.)

A second rationale for a single case is where the case represents an *extreme* case or a *unique* case. Either of these situations commonly occurs in clinical psychology, where a specific injury or disorder may be so rare that any single case is worth documenting and analyzing. For instance, one rare clinical syndrome is the inability of certain clinical patients to recognize familiar faces. Given visual cues alone, such patients are unable to recognize loved ones, friends, pictures of famous people, or (in some cases) their own image in a mirror. This syndrome appears to be due to some physical injury to the brain. Yet the syndrome occurs so rarely that scientists have been unable to establish any common patterns (Yin, 1970, 1978). In such circumstances, the single-case study is an appropriate research design whenever a new person with this syndrome—known as prosopagnosia—is encountered. The case study would document the person's abilities and disabilities, determine the precise nature of the face recognition deficit, but also ascertain whether related disorders exist.

BOX 7
The Critical Case as a Single-Case Study

One rationale for selecting a single-case rather than a multiple-case design is that the single case can represent the critical test of a significant theory. Gross, Bernstein, and Giacquinta (1971) used such a design by focusing on a single school in their book, *Implementing Organizational Innovations* (also see BOX 19B, Chapter 3, p. 110).

The school was selected because it had a prior history of innovation and could not be claimed to suffer from "barriers to innovation." In the prevailing theories, such barriers had been prominently cited as the major reason that innovations failed. Gross et al. (1971) showed that, in this school, an innovation also failed but that the failure could not be attributed to any barriers. Implementation processes, rather than barriers, appeared to account for the failure.

In this manner, the book, though limited to a single case, represented a watershed in organizational innovation theory. Prior to the study, analysts had focused on the identification of barriers to innovation; since the study, the literature has been much more dominated by studies of the implementation process.

Conversely, a third rationale for a single case is the *representative* or *typical* case. Here, the objective is to capture the circumstances and conditions of an everyday or commonplace situation (see BOX 8; also see BOX 14, p. 75). The case study may represent a typical "project" among many different projects, a manufacturing firm believed to be typical of many other manufacturing firms in the same industry, a typical urban neighborhood, or a representative school, as examples. The lessons learned from these cases are assumed to be informative about the experiences of the average person or institution.

A fourth rationale for a single-case study is the *revelatory* case. This situation exists when an investigator has an opportunity to observe and analyze a phenomenon previously inaccessible to social science inquiry, such as Whyte's

---

BOX 8
The Average Case as a Single-Case Study

A famous community case study in sociology, *Middletown*, is about an average American city. The investigators, Robert and Helen Lynd (1929), deliberately chose to study a small town in middle America during the early 20th century (also see BOX 14, p. 75). Their purpose was to show how the transition from an agricultural to an industrial economy occurred in the average town—and thereby to provide a case study about a significant development in all of American history.

(1943/1955) *Street Corner Society,* previously described in Chapter 1, BOX 2A. Another example is Elliot Liebow's (1967) famous case study of unemployed men, *Tally's Corner* (see BOX 9). Liebow had the opportunity to meet the men in an African American neighborhood in Washington, D.C. and to learn about their everyday lives. His observations of and insights into the problems of unemployment formed a significant case study, because few social scientists had previously had the opportunity to investigate these problems, even though the problems were common across the country. When other investigators have similar types of opportunities and can uncover some prevalent phenomenon previously inaccessible to social scientists, such conditions justify the use of a single-case study on the grounds of its revelatory nature.

BOX 9
The Revelatory Case as a Single-Case Study

Another rationale for selecting a single-case rather than a multiple-case design is that the investigator has access to a situation previously inaccessible to scientific observation. The case study is therefore worth conducting because the descriptive information alone will be revelatory.

Such was the situation in Elliot Liebow's (1967) sociological classic, *Tally's Corner.* The book is about a single group of African American men living in a poor, inner-city neighborhood. By befriending these men, the author was able to learn about their lifestyles, their coping behavior, and in particular their sensitivity to unemployment and failure. The book provided insights into a subculture that has prevailed in many U.S. cities for a long period of time, but one that had been only obscurely understood. The single case showed how investigations of such topics could be done, thus stimulating much further research and eventually the development of policy actions.

A fifth rationale for a single-case study is the *longitudinal* case: studying the same single case at two or more different points in time. The theory of interest would likely specify how certain conditions change over time, and the desired time intervals would presumably reflect the anticipated stages at which the changes should reveal themselves.

These five serve as major reasons for conducting a single-case study. There are other situations in which the single-case study may be used as a pilot case that is the first of a multiple-case study. However, in these latter instances, the single-case study cannot be regarded as a complete study on its own.

Whatever the rationale for doing single-case studies (and there may be more than the five mentioned here), a potential vulnerability of the single-case design is that a case may later turn out not to be the case it was thought to be at the outset. Single-case designs therefore require careful investigation of the potential case to minimize the chances of misrepresentation and to maximize the access needed to collect the case study evidence. A fair warning is not to commit yourself to any single-case study until all of these major concerns have been covered.

Holistic versus embedded case studies. The same single-case study may involve *more than one unit of analysis.* This occurs when, within a single case, attention is also given to a subunit or subunits (see BOX 10). For instance, even though a case study might be about a single organization, such as a hospital, the analysis might include outcomes about the clinical services and staff employed by the hospital (and possibly even some quantitative analyses based on the employee records of the staff). In an evaluation study, the single case might be a public program that involves large numbers of funded projects— which would then be the embedded units. In either situation, these embedded units can be selected through sampling or cluster techniques (McClintock, 1985). No matter how the units are selected, the resulting design would be called an *embedded case study design* (see Figure 2.4, Type 2). In contrast, if the case study examined only the global nature of an organization or of a program, a *holistic design* would have been used (see Figure 2.4, Type 1).

These two variants of single-case studies both have their strengths and weaknesses. The holistic design is advantageous when no logical subunits can be identified or when the relevant theory underlying the case study is itself of a holistic nature. Potential problems arise, however, when a global approach allows an investigator to avoid examining any specific phenomenon in operational detail. Thus, a typical problem with the holistic design is that the entire case study may be conducted at an unduly abstract level, lacking sufficiently clear measures or data.

BOX 10
An Embedded, Single-Case Design

Union Democracy (1956) is a highly regarded case study by three eminent academicians— Seymour Martin Lipset, Martin Trow, and James Coleman. The case study is about the inside politics of the International Typographical Union and involves several units of analysis (see "Kinds of Data" table). The main unit was the organization as a whole, the smallest unit was the individual member, and several intermediary units also were important. At each level of analysis, different data collection techniques were used, ranging from historical to survey analysis.

Kinds of Data (BOX 10 Continued)

Unit Being Characterized	Total System — Issues, Data on Occupation; Union Laws; Policies; Historical Data; Convention Reports	Intermediate Units — Locals' Histories and Voting records; Issues on Local Level; size of Locals	Intermediate Units — Shops' Voting Records; Shop Size	Individuals — Interviews with Leaders	Individuals — Interviews of the Sample of Men
ITU as a whole	Structural, environmental, behavioral properties	By inference, communication network (structural)		Structural, environmental, behavioral properties	Distributions of individual properties
Locals	Behavioral properties (militancy, etc.)	Behavioral properties, size	By inference, communication network (structural)		Chapel chairman's attributes; friends' attributes
Shops			Behavioral properties, size		
Other immediate social environment of men	The social climate, by inference from dominant issues and election outcome	The social climate, by inference from dominant issues and election outcome			
Men	By inference, dominant values and interests	By inference: values, interests, and loyalties (e.g., local over international)	By inference: values, interests, loyalties (e.g., to shop over local)	By inference: values	Behavior, background, values, attitudes

SOURCE: Lipset, Trow, & Coleman (1956, p. 422). Reprinted by permission.

A further problem with the holistic design is that the entire nature of the case study may shift, unbeknownst to the researcher, during the course of study. The initial study questions may have reflected one orientation, but as the case study proceeds, a different orientation may emerge, and the evidence begins to address different research questions. Although some people have claimed such flexibility to be a strength of the case study approach, in fact the largest criticism of case studies is based on this type of shift—in which the implemented research design is no longer appropriate for the research questions being asked (see COSMOS Corporation, 1983). Because of this problem, you need to avoid such unsuspected slippage; if the relevant research questions really do change, you should simply start over again, with a new research design. One way to increase the sensitivity to such slippage is to have a set of subunits. Thus, an embedded design can serve as an important device for focusing a case study inquiry.

An embedded design, however, also has its pitfalls. A major one occurs when the case study focuses only on the subunit level and fails to return to the larger unit of analysis. For instance, an evaluation of a program consisting of multiple projects may include project characteristics as a subunit of analysis. The project-level data may even be highly quantitative if there are many projects. However, the original evaluation becomes a project study (i.e., a multiple-case study of different projects) if no investigating is done at the level of the original case—that is, the program. Similarly, a study of organizational climate may involve individual employees as a subunit of study. However, if the data focus only on individual employees, the study will in fact become an employee and not an organizational study. In both examples, what has happened is that the original phenomenon of interest (a program or organizational climate) has become the context and not the target of study.

Summary. Single cases are a common design for doing case studies, and two variants have been described: those using holistic designs and those using embedded units of analysis. Overall, the single-case design is eminently justifiable under certain conditions—where the case represents (a) a critical test of existing theory, (b) a rare or unique circumstance, or (c) a representative or typical case, or where the case serves a (d) revelatory or (e) longitudinal purpose.

A major step in designing and conducting a single case is defining the unit of analysis (or the case itself). An operational definition is needed, and some caution must be exercised—before a total commitment to the whole case study is made—to ensure that the case in fact is relevant to the issues and questions of interest.

Within the single case may still be incorporated subunits of analyses, so that a more complex—or embedded—design is developed. The subunits can often add significant opportunities for extensive analysis, enhancing the insights into the single case. However, if too much attention is given to these subunits, and if the larger, holistic aspects of the case begin to be ignored, the case study itself will have shifted its orientation and changed its nature. If the shift is justifiable, you need to address it explicitly and indicate its relationship to the original inquiry.

What Are the Potential Multiple-Case Designs (Types 3 and 4)?

The same study may contain more than a single case. When this occurs, the study has used a multiple-case design, and such designs have increased in frequency in recent years. A common example is a study of school innovations (such as the use of new curricula, rearranged school schedules, or a new educational technology), in which individual schools adopt some innovation. Each school might be the subject of an individual case study, but the study as a whole covers several schools and in this way uses a multiple-case design.

Multiple- versus single-case designs. In some fields, multiple-case studies have been considered a different "methodology" from single-case studies. For example, both anthropology and political science have developed one set of rationales for doing single-case studies and a second set for doing what have been considered "comparative" (or multiple-case) studies (see Eckstein, 1975; Lijphart, 1975). This book, however, considers single- and multiple-case designs to be variants within the same methodological framework—and no broad distinction is made between the so-called classic (that is, single) case study and multiple-case studies. The choice is considered one of research design, with both being included under the case study method.

Multiple-case designs have distinct advantages and disadvantages in comparison to single-case designs. The evidence from multiple cases is often considered more compelling, and the overall study is therefore regarded as being more robust (Herriott & Firestone, 1983). At the same time, the rationale for single-case designs cannot usually be satisfied by multiple cases. By definition, the unusual or rare case, the critical case, and the revelatory case all are likely to involve only single cases. Moreover, the conduct of a multiple-case study can require extensive resources and time beyond the means of a single student or independent research investigator. Therefore, the decision to undertake multiple-case studies cannot be taken lightly.

Selecting the multiple cases also raises a new set of questions. Here, *a major insight is to consider multiple cases as one would consider multiple experiments*—that is, to follow a "replication" design. This is far different from a mistaken analogy in the past, which incorrectly considered multiple cases to be similar to the multiple respondents in a survey (or to the multiple subjects within an experiment)—that is, to follow a "sampling" design. The methodological differences between these two views are revealed by the different rationales underlying the replication as opposed to sampling designs.

Replication, not sampling logic, for multiple-case studies. The replication logic is analogous to that used in multiple experiments (see Hersen & Barlow, 1976). For example, upon uncovering a significant finding from a single experiment, an ensuing and pressing priority would be to replicate this finding by conducting a second, third, and even more experiments. Some of the replications might attempt to duplicate the exact conditions of the original experiment. Other replications might alter one or two experimental conditions considered unimportant to the original finding, to see whether the finding could still be duplicated. Only with such replications would the original finding be considered robust.

The logic underlying the use of multiple-case studies is the same. Each case must be carefully selected so that it either (a) predicts similar results (a *literal replication*) or (b) predicts contrasting results but for anticipatable reasons (a *theoretical replication*). The ability to conduct 6 or 10 case studies, arranged effectively within a multiple-case design, is analogous to the ability to conduct 6 to 10 experiments on related topics; a few cases (2 or 3) would be literal replications, whereas a few other cases (4 to 6) might be designed to pursue two different patterns of theoretical replications. If all the cases turn out as predicted, these 6 to 10 cases, in the aggregate, would have provided compelling support for the initial set of propositions. If the cases are in some way contradictory, the initial propositions must be revised and retested with another set of cases. Again, this logic is similar to the way scientists deal with conflicting experimental findings.

An important step in all of these replication procedures is the development of a rich, theoretical framework. The framework needs to state the conditions under which a particular phenomenon is likely to be found (a literal replication) as well as the conditions when it is not likely to be found (a theoretical replication). The theoretical framework later becomes the vehicle for generalizing to new cases, again similar to the role played in cross-experiment designs. Furthermore, just as with experimental science, if some of the empirical cases do not work as predicted, modification must be made to the theory. Remember, too, that theories can be practical and not just academic.

For example, one might consider the initial proposition that an increase in using a new technology in school districts will occur when the technology is used for both administrative and instructional applications, but not either alone. To pursue this proposition in a multiple-case study design, 3 or 4 cases might be selected in which both types of applications are present, to determine whether, in fact, technology use did increase over a period of time (the investigation would be predicting a literal replication in these 3 or 4 cases). Three or

4 additional cases might be selected in which only administrative applications are present, with the prediction being little increase in use (predicting a theoretical replication). Finally, 3 or 4 other cases would be selected in which only instructional applications are present, with the same prediction of little increase in use, but for different reasons than the administrative-only cases (another theoretical replication). If this entire pattern of results across these multiple cases is indeed found, the 9 to 12 cases, in the aggregate, would provide substantial support for the initial proposition.

Another example of a multiple-case replication design comes from the field of urban studies (see BOX 11). You also can find examples of three entire case studies, all following a replication design but covering HIV/AIDS prevention, university administration, and the transformation of business firms, in the companion text (Yin, 2003, chaps. 8–10).

This replication logic, whether applied to experiments or to case studies, must be distinguished from the sampling logic commonly used in surveys. The sampling logic requires an operational enumeration of the entire universe or pool of potential respondents and then a statistical procedure for selecting a

---

BOX 11
A Multiple-Case, Replication Design

A common problem in the 1960s and 1970s was how to get good advice to city governments. Peter Szanton's (1981) book, *Not Well Advised*, reviewed the experiences of numerous attempts by university and research groups to collaborate with city officials.

The book is an excellent example of a multiple-case, replication design. Szanton starts with eight case studies, showing how different university groups all failed to help cities. The eight cases are sufficient "replications" to convince the reader of a general phenomenon. Szanton then provides five more case studies, in which nonuniversity groups also failed, concluding that failure was therefore not necessarily inherent in the academic enterprise. Yet a third group of cases shows how university groups have successfully helped business, engineering firms, and sectors other than city government. A final set of three cases shows that those few groups able to help city government were concerned with implementation and not just with the production of new ideas, leading to the major conclusion that city governments may have peculiar needs in receiving but also then putting advice into practice.

Within each of the four groups of case studies, Szanton has illustrated the principle of literal replication. Across the four groups, he has illustrated theoretical replication. This potent case study design can and should be applied to many other topics.

specific subset of respondents to be surveyed. The resulting data from the sample that is actually surveyed are assumed to reflect the entire universe or pool, with inferential statistics used to establish the confidence intervals for which this representation is presumed accurate. The entire procedure is commonly used when an investigator wishes to determine the prevalence or frequency of a particular phenomenon.

Any application of this sampling logic to case studies would be misplaced. First, case studies are not the best method for assessing the prevalence of phenomena. Second, a case study would have to cover both the phenomenon of interest and its context, yielding a large number of potentially relevant variables. In turn, this would require an impossibly large number of cases—too large to allow any statistical consideration of the relevant variables.

Third, if a sampling logic had to be applied to all types of research, many important topics could not be empirically investigated, such as the following problem: Your investigation deals with the role of the presidency of the United States, and you are interested in doing a multiple-case study of a (few) presidents to test your theory about presidential leadership. However, the complexity of your topic means that your choice of a small number of cases could not adequately represent all the 44 presidents since the beginning of the Republic. Critics using a sampling logic might therefore deny the acceptability of your study. In contrast, if you use a replication logic, the study is eminently feasible.

The replication approach to multiple-case studies is illustrated in Figure 2.5. The figure indicates that the initial step in designing the study must consist of theory development, and then shows that case selection and the definition of specific measures are important steps in the design and data collection process. Each individual case study consists of a "whole" study, in which convergent evidence is sought regarding the facts and conclusions for the case; each case's conclusions are then considered to be the information needing replication by other individual cases. Both the individual cases and the multiple-case results can and should be the focus of a summary report. For each individual case, the report should indicate how and why a particular proposition was demonstrated (or not demonstrated). Across cases, the report should indicate the extent of the replication logic and why certain cases were predicted to have certain results, whereas other cases, if any, were predicted to have contrasting results.

An important part of Figure 2.5 is the dashed-line feedback loop. The loop represents the situation where important discovery occurs during the conduct of one of the individual case studies (e.g., one of the cases did not in fact suit the original design). Such a discovery even may require you to reconsider one or more of the study's original theoretical propositions. At this point,

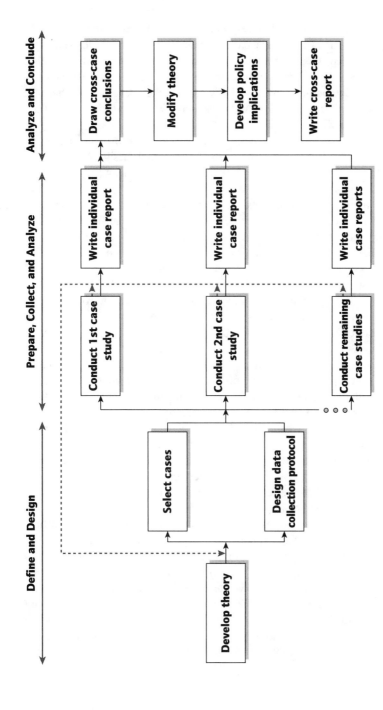

Figure 2.5 Case Study Method

SOURCE: COSMOS Corporation.

Define and Design

Develop theory

Select cases

Design data collection protocol

Prepare, Collect, and Analyze

Conduct 1st case study

Conduct 2nd case study

Conduct remaining case studies

Write individual case report

Write individual case report

Write individual case reports

Analyze and Conclude

Draw cross-case conclusions

Modify theory

Develop policy implications

Write cross-case report

"redesign" should take place before proceeding further. Such redesign might involve the selection of alternative cases or changes in the case study (i.e., data collection) protocol (see Chapter 3). Without such redesign, you risk being accused of distorting or ignoring the discovery, just to accommodate the original design. This condition leads quickly to a further accusation—that you have been selective in reporting your data, to suit your preconceived ideas (i.e., the original theoretical propositions).

Overall, Figure 2.5 depicts a very different logic from that of a sampling design. The logic as well as its contrast with a sampling design may be difficult to follow and is worth extensive discussion with colleagues before proceeding with any multiple case study.

When using a multiple-case design, a further question you will encounter has to do with the *number* of cases deemed necessary or sufficient for your study. However, because a sampling logic should not be used, the typical criteria regarding sample size also are irrelevant. Instead, you should think of this decision as a reflection of the number of case replications—both literal and theoretical—that you need or would like to have in your study.

For the number of literal replications, an appropriate analogy from statistics is the selection of the criterion for establishing the sample size desired to detect an "effect." Designating a "$p < .05$" or "$p < .01$" likelihood of detection as part of a power analysis is not based on any formula but is a matter of discretionary, judgmental choice. Analogously, designating the number of replications depends upon the certainty you want to have about your multiple-case results (as with the higher criterion for establishing the likelihood of detection, the greater certainty lies with the larger number of cases). For example, you may want to settle for two or three literal replications when your theory is straightforward and the issue at hand does not demand an excessive degree of certainty. However, if your theory is subtle or if you want a high degree of certainty, you may press for five, six, or more replications.

For the number of theoretical replications, the important consideration is related to your sense of the importance of rival explanations. The stronger the rivals, the more additional cases you might want, each case showing a different result when some rival explanation had been taken into account. For example, your original hypothesis might be that summer reading programs improve students' reading scores, and you already might have shown this result through several cases that served as literal replications. A rival explanation might be that parents also work more closely with their children during the summer and that this circumstance can account for improved reading scores. You would then find another case, with parent participation but no summer reading program, and in this theoretical replication you would predict that the scores would not improve.

Rationale for multiple-case designs. In short, the rationale for multiple-case designs derives directly from your understanding of literal and theoretical replications. The simplest multiple-case design would be the selection of two or more cases that are believed to be literal replications, such as a set of cases with exemplary outcomes in relation to some evaluation questions, such as "how and why a particular intervention has been implemented smoothly." Selecting such cases requires prior knowledge of the outcomes, with the multiple-case inquiry focusing on how and why the exemplary outcomes might have occurred and hoping for literal (or direct) replications of these conditions from case to case.[5]

More complicated multiple-case designs would likely result from the number and types of theoretical replications you might want to cover. For example, investigators have used a "two-tail" design in which cases from both extremes (of some important theoretical condition, such as good and bad outcomes) have been deliberately chosen. Multiple-case rationales also can derive from the prior hypothesizing of different types of conditions and the desire to have subgroups of cases covering each type. These and other similar designs are more complicated because the study should still have at least two individual cases within each of the subgroups, so that the theoretical replications across subgroups are complemented by literal replications within each subgroup.

Multiple-case studies: Holistic or embedded. The fact that a design calls for multiple-case studies does not eliminate the variation identified earlier with single cases: Each individual case may still be holistic or embedded. In other words, a multiple-case study may consist of multiple holistic cases (see Figure 2.4, Type 3) or of multiple embedded cases (see Figure 2.4, Type 4).

The difference between these two variants depends upon the type of phenomenon being studied and your research questions. In an embedded design, a study even may call for the conduct of a survey at each case study site. For instance, suppose a study is concerned with the impact of the same type of curriculum adopted by different schools. Each school may be the topic of a case study, with the theoretical framework dictating that nine such schools be included as case studies, three to replicate a direct result (literal replication) and six others to deal with contrasting conditions (theoretical replications).

For all nine schools, an embedded design is used because surveys of the students (or, alternatively, examination of students' archival records) are needed to address research questions about the performance of the schools. However, the results of each survey will *not* be pooled across schools. Rather, the survey data will be part of the findings for each individual school, or case. These data may be highly quantitative, focusing on the attitudes and behavior of individual students, and the data will be used along with archival information to interpret the success and operations at the given school. If, in contrast, the survey data are pooled across schools, a replication design is no longer being used. In fact, the study has now become a single-case study, in which all nine schools and their students have now become part of some larger, main unit of analysis. Such a new case study would then require a complete redefinition of the main unit of analysis, with extensive revisions to the original theories and propositions of interest also a likely need.

Summary. This section has dealt with situations in which the same investigation may call for multiple-case studies. These types of designs are becoming more prevalent, but they are more expensive and time-consuming to conduct.

Any use of multiple-case designs should follow a replication, not a sampling logic, and an investigator must choose each case carefully. The cases should serve in a manner similar to multiple experiments, with similar results (a literal replication) or contrasting results (a theoretical replication) predicted explicitly at the outset of the investigation.

The individual cases within a multiple-case study design may be either holistic or embedded. When an embedded design is used, each individual case study may in fact include the collection and analysis of quantitative data, including the use of surveys within each case.

EXERCISE 2.4   Defining a Case Study Research Design

Select one of the case studies described in the BOXES of this book, reviewing the entire case study (not just the material in the BOX). Describe the research design of this case study. How did it justify the relevant evidence to be sought, given the basic research questions to be answered? What methods were used to draw conclusions, based on the evidence? Is the design a single- or multiple-case design? Is it holistic or does it have embedded units of analysis?

MODEST ADVICE IN SELECTING CASE STUDY DESIGNS

Now that you know how to define case study designs and are prepared to carry out design work, three pieces of advice may be offered.

Single- or Multiple-Case Designs?

The first word of advice is that, although all designs can lead to successful case studies, when you have the choice (and resources), multiple-case designs may be preferred over single-case designs. Even if you can do a "two-case"

case study, your chances of doing a good case study will be better than using a single-case design. Single-case designs are vulnerable if only because you will have put "all your eggs in one basket." More important, the analytic benefits from having two (or more) cases may be substantial.

To begin with, even with two cases, you have the possibility of direct replication. Analytic conclusions independently arising from two cases, as with two experiments, will be more powerful than those coming from a single case (or single experiment) alone. Alternatively you may have deliberately selected your two cases because they offered contrasting situations, and you were not seeking a direct replication. In this design, if the subsequent findings support the hypothesized contrast, the results represent a strong start toward theoretical replication—again vastly strengthening your findings compared to those from a single case alone (e.g., Eilbert & Lafronza, 2005; Hanna, 2005; also see BOX 12).

BOX 12
Two, "Two-Case" Case Studies

12A. Contrasting Cases for Community Building

Chaskin (2001) used two case studies to illustrate contrasting strategies for capacity building at the neighborhood level. The author's overall conceptual framework, which was the main topic of inquiry, claimed that there could be two approaches to building community capacity—using a collaborative organization to (a) reinforce existing networks of community organizations or (b) initiate a new organization in the neighborhood. After thoroughly airing the framework on theoretical grounds, the author presents the two case studies, showing the viability of each approach.

12B. Contrasting Strategies for Educational Accountability

In a directly complementary manner, Elmore, Abelmann, and Fuhrman (1997) chose two case studies to illustrate contrasting strategies for designing and implementing educational accountability (i.e., holding schools accountable for the academic performance of their students). One case represented a lower cost, basic version of an accountability system. The other represented a higher cost, more complex version.

In general, criticisms about single-case studies usually reflect fears about the uniqueness or artifactual conditions surrounding the case (e.g., special access to a key informant). As a result, the criticisms may turn into skepticism about your ability to do empirical work beyond having done a single-case study. Having two cases can begin to blunt such criticism and skepticism. Having more than two cases will produce an even stronger effect. In the face of these benefits, having at least two cases should be your goal. If you do use a single-case design, you should be prepared to make an extremely strong argument in justifying your choice for the case.

EXERCISE 2.5 Establishing the Rationale for a Multiple-Case Study
Develop some preliminary ideas about a "case" for your case study. Alternatively, focus on one of the single-case studies presented in the BOXES in this book. In either situation, now think of a companion "case" that might augment the single case. In what ways might the companion case's findings supplement those of the first case? Could the data from the second case fill a gap left by the first case or respond better to some obvious shortcoming or criticism of the first case? Would the two cases together comprise a stronger case study? Could yet a third case make the findings even more compelling?

Closed Designs or Flexible Designs?

Another word of advice is that, despite this chapter's details about design choices, you should not think that a case study's design cannot be modified by new information or discovery during data collection. Such revelations can be enormously important, leading to your altering or modifying your original design.

As examples, in a single-case study, what was thought to be a critical or unique case might have turned out not to be so, after initial data collection had started; ditto a multiple-case study, where what was thought to be parallel cases for literal replication turn out not to be so. With these revelations, you have every right to conclude that your initial design needs to be modified. However, you should undertake any alterations only given a serious caution. The caution is to understand precisely the nature of the alteration: Are you merely selecting different cases, or are you also changing your original theoretical concerns and objectives? The point is that the needed flexibility should not lessen the rigor with which case study procedures are followed.

Mixed Methods Designs: Mixing Case Studies with Other Methods?

Researchers have given increasing attention to "mixed methods research"— a "class of research where the researcher mixes or combines quantitative and qualitative research techniques, methods, approaches, concepts or language into a *single* study" (Johnson & Onwuegbuzie, 2004, p. 17, emphasis added). Confinement to a single study forces the methods being mixed into an integrated mode. The mode differs from the conventional situation whereby different methods are used in *separate* studies that may later be synthesized.

Mixed methods research forces the methods to share the same research questions, to collect complementary data, and to conduct counterpart analyses (e.g., Yin, 2006b)—in short, to follow a mixed methods design. As such, mixed methods research can permit investigators to address more complicated research questions and collect a richer and stronger array of evidence than can be accomplished by any single method alone. Depending upon the nature of your research questions and your ability to use different methods, mixed methods research opens a class of research designs that deserve your consideration.

The earlier discussion of embedded case study designs in fact points to the fact that certain kinds of case studies already represent a form of mixed methods research. The embedded case studies rely on more holistic data collection strategies for studying the main case but then call upon surveys or other more quantitative techniques to collect data about the embedded unit(s) of analysis. In this situation, other research methods are embedded within your case study.

The opposite relationship also can occur. Your case study may be part of a larger, mixed methods study. The main investigation may rely on a survey or other quantitative techniques, and your case study may help to investigate the conditions within one of the entities being surveyed. The contrasting relationships (survey within case or case within survey) are illustrated in Figure 2.6.

At the same time, mixed methods research need not include the use of the case study strategy at all. For instance, much historical work embraces the quantitative analysis of archival records, such as newspapers and other file material. And, in an even broader sense, mixed methods research need not be limited to combinations of quantitative and qualitative methods. For instance, a study could employ a survey to describe certain conditions, complemented by an experiment that tried to manipulate some of those conditions (e.g., Berends & Garet, 2002).

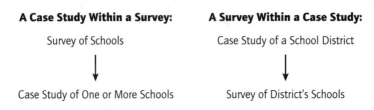

Figure 2.6   Mixed Methods: Two Nested Arrangements

By definition, studies using mixed methods research are more difficult to execute than studies limited to single methods. However, mixed methods research can enable you to address broader or more complicated research questions than case studies alone. As a result, mixing case studies with other methods should be among the possibilities meriting your consideration.

NOTES

1. Figure 2.2 focuses only on the formal research design process, not on data collection activities. For all three types of research (survey, case study, and experiment), data collection techniques might be depicted as the level below Level One in the figure. For example, for case studies, this might include using multiple sources of evidence, as described further in Chapter 4. Similar data collection techniques can be described for surveys or experiments—for example, questionnaire design for surveys or stimulus presentation strategies for experiments.

2. See Gomm, Hammersley, and Foster (2000) for more explanation of *analytic* generalization, though their work uses different labels for the same concept.

3. One of the anonymous reviewers of the third edition of this book pointed out that construct validity also has to do with whether interviewees understand what is being asked of them.

4. For other suggested guidelines for reviewers of case study proposals or manuscripts, see Yin (1999).

5. Strictly quantitative studies that select cases with known outcomes follow the same design and have alternatively been called "case-control," "retrospective," or "case referent" studies (see P. R. Rosenbaum, 2002, p. 7).

REFERENCE TO EXPANDED CASE STUDY
MATERIALS FOR CHAPTER 2

For selected case studies cited in the text of this chapter, two anthologies contain either a more extensive excerpt or the full case study. The table on the next page crosswalks the reference in this book to the location of the excerpt or full rendition.

Chapter 2 Chapter Topic and Page Number	Topics of Illustrative Case Studies	Reference to Lengthier Material
General Approach to Designing Case Studies		
BOX 4, p. 2-6	Exploratory study	None
BOX 5A, p. 2-9	Computers and technology	None
BOX 5B, p. 2-9	Business and industry	CSA-6
p. 2-15 text	Five different case studies	ACSR-1
Criteria for Judging the Quality of Research Designs		
BOX 6A, p. 2-23	Cities and towns	CSA-4
BOX 6B, p. 2-23	Urban planning	None
BOX 6C, p. 2-23	Neighborhoods	None
Case Study Designs		
BOX 7, p. 2-27	Schools	CSA-9
BOX 8, p. 2-28	Cities and towns	CSA-3
BOX 9, p. 2-28	Neighborhoods	None
BOX 10, p. 2-29	Business and industry	CSA-10
BOX 11, p. 2-35	Government agencies	None
p. 2-35 text	Health (HIV/AIDS) care	ACSR-8
p. 2-35 text	University administration	ACSR-9
p. 2-35 text	Business and industry	ASCR-10
Modest Advice in Selecting Case Study Designs		
BOX 12A, p. 2-41	Community organizations	None
BOX 12B, p. 2-41	Schools	None

NOTE: CSA = *Case Study Anthology* (Yin, 2004). ACSR = *Applications of Case Study Research* (Yin, 2003). The number denotes the chapter number in the book.

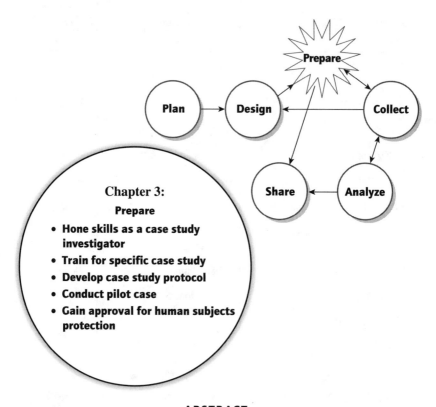

Chapter 3:

Prepare

- **Hone skills as a case study investigator**
- **Train for specific case study**
- **Develop case study protocol**
- **Conduct pilot case**
- **Gain approval for human subjects protection**

ABSTRACT

Preparing to do a case study starts with the prior skills of the investigator and covers the preparation and training for the specific case study (including procedures for protecting human subjects), the development of a case study protocol, the screening of candidate cases to be part of the case study, and the conduct of a pilot case study.

With regard to prior skills, many people incorrectly believe they are sufficiently skilled to do case studies because they think the method is easy to use. In fact, case study research is among the hardest types of research to do because of the absence of routine procedures. Case study investigators therefore need to feel comfortable in addressing procedural uncertainties during the course of a study. Other desirable traits include the ability to ask good questions, "listen," be adaptive and flexible, have a firm grasp of the issues being studied, and know how to avoid bias.

An investigator can prepare to do a high-quality case study through intensive training. A case study protocol should be developed and refined. These procedures are especially desirable if the research is based on a multiple-case design or involves multiple investigators, or both.

3

Preparing to Collect Case Study Evidence

What You Need to Do Before Starting to Collect Case Study Data

Chapters 1 and 2 have shown that doing a case study begins with the research questions to be addressed and the development of a case study design. However, most people associate the "doing" of a case study with the collection of the case study data, and this and the following chapter focus on the data collection activity. This chapter deals with the needed preparation. The next covers the actual data collection techniques.

Preparing for data collection can be complex and difficult. If not done well, the entire case study investigation can be jeopardized, and all of the earlier work—in defining the research questions and designing the case study—will have been for naught.

Good preparation begins with the *desired skills* on the part of the case study investigator. These skills have seldom been the subject of separate attention in the past. Yet, some are critical and can be learned or practiced. Four additional topics also should be a formal part of any case study preparation: *training* for a specific case study, developing a *protocol* for the investigation, *screening* candidate cases, and conducting a *pilot case study*. The protocol is an especially effective way of dealing with the overall problem of increasing the reliability of case studies. However, success with all five topics is needed to ensure that case study data collection will proceed smoothly. All demand a certain amount of patience, which has too frequently been overlooked in the past.

THE CASE STUDY INVESTIGATOR: DESIRED SKILLS

Too many people are drawn to the case study strategy because they believe it is "easy." Many social scientists—especially budding ones—think the case study strategy can be mastered without much difficulty. Their belief is that

Tip: *When am I ready to start collecting the case study data?*

You have just completed designing your case study, following the suggestions in Chapter 2, and you are anxious to start collecting the case study data because time is short, and available data collection opportunities are present. Your readiness, however, should not be defined by external time constraints or conditions. Instead, your "readiness" depends upon your own skill levels for doing case studies, as well as your having completed formal and preparatory procedures prior to collecting actual data.

Have you practiced these skills, and do you think case study research needs to follow formal procedures to prepare for data collection?

they will have to learn only a minimal set of technical procedures; that any of their own shortcomings in formal, analytic skills will be unimportant; and that a case study will allow them simply to "tell it like it is." No belief could be farther from the truth.

In actuality, the demands of a case study on your intellect, ego, and emotions are far greater than those of any other research method. This is because the data collection procedures are *not* routinized. In laboratory experiments or in surveys, for instance, the data collection phase of a research project can be largely, if not wholly, conducted by one (or more) research assistant(s). The assistant is to carry out the data collection activities with a minimum of discretionary behavior, and in this sense, the activity is routinized—and analytically boring.

Conducting case studies offers no such parallel. Rather, a well-trained and experienced investigator is needed to conduct a high-quality case study because of the continuous interaction between the theoretical issues being studied and the data being collected. During data collection, only a more experienced investigator will be able to take advantage of unexpected opportunities rather than being trapped by them—and also will exercise sufficient care against potentially biased procedures.

Unfortunately, there are no tests for distinguishing those persons likely to become good case study investigators from those who are not. Compare this situation to that in mathematics or even a profession such as law. In math, people are able to score themselves for their abilities and to screen themselves from further advancement because they simply cannot carry out higher levels of math problems. To practice law, a person must pass the bar examination in a particular state. Again, many people screen themselves out of the field by failing to pass this test.

No such gatekeepers exist for assessing case study skills. However, a basic list of commonly required skills is as follows:

♦ A good case study investigator should be able to *ask good questions*—and interpret the answers.

♦ An investigator should *be a good "listener"* and not be trapped by her or his own ideologies or preconceptions.

♦ An investigator should *be adaptive and flexible,* so that newly encountered situations can be seen as opportunities, not threats.

♦ An investigator must *have a firm grasp of the issues being studied,* even if in an exploratory mode. Such a grasp reduces the relevant events and information to be sought to manageable proportions.

♦ A person should *be unbiased by preconceived notions,* including those derived from theory. Thus, a person should be sensitive and responsive to contradictory evidence.

Each of these attributes is described below. Any absence of these attributes is remediable, as anyone missing one or more of the skills can work on developing them. But everyone must be honest in assessing her or his capabilities in the first place.

Asking Good Questions

More than with the other research methods discussed in Chapter 1, case studies require an inquiring mind *during* data collection, not just before or after the activity. The ability to pose and ask good questions is therefore a prerequisite for case study investigators. The desired result is for the investigator to create a rich dialogue with the evidence, an activity that encompasses

> pondering the possibilities gained from deep familiarity with some aspect of the world, systematizing those ideas in relation to kinds of information one might gather, checking the ideas in the light of that information, dealing with the inevitable discrepancies between what was expected and what was found by rethinking the possibilities of getting more data, and so on. (Becker, 1998, p. 66)

Case study data collection does follow a formal protocol, but the specific information that may become relevant to a case study is not readily predictable. As you collect case study evidence, you must quickly review the evidence and continually ask yourself why events or facts appear as they do. Your judgments may lead to the immediate need to search for additional evidence. If you are able to ask good questions throughout the data collection process, a good prediction is that you also will be mentally and emotionally exhausted at the end of each day. This depletion of analytic energy is far different from the experience in collecting experimental or survey data—that is, testing "subjects" or administering questionnaires. In these situations, data collection is highly routinized, and the data collector must complete a certain volume of work but exercise minimal discretionary behavior. Furthermore, any substantive review of the evidence does not come until some later time. The result is that such a data collector may become physically exhausted but will have been mentally untested after a day of data collection.

One insight into asking good questions is to understand that research is about questions and not necessarily about answers. If you are the type of person for whom one tentative answer immediately leads to a whole host of new questions, and if these questions eventually aggregate to some significant inquiry about how or why the world works as it does, you are likely to be a good asker of questions.

Being a Good "Listener"

For case studies, "listening" means receiving information through multiple modalities—for example, making keen observations or sensing what might be going on—not just using the aural modality. Being a good listener means being able to assimilate large amounts of new information without bias. As an interviewee recounts an incident, a good listener hears the exact words used by the interviewee (sometimes, the terminology reflects an important orientation), captures the mood and affective components, and understands the context from which the interviewee is perceiving the world.

The listening skill also needs to be applied to the inspection of documentary evidence, as well as to observations of real-life situations. In reviewing documents, listening takes the form of worrying whether there is any important message *between* the lines; any inferences, of course, would need to be corroborated with other sources of information, but important insights may be gained in this way. Poor "listeners" may not even realize that there can be information between the lines. Other listening deficiencies include having a closed mind or simply having a poor memory.

Exercising Adaptiveness and Flexibility

Few case studies will end up exactly as planned. Inevitably, you will have to make minor if not major changes, ranging from the need to pursue an unexpected lead (potentially minor) to the need to identify a new "case" for study (potentially major). The skilled investigator must remember the original purpose of the investigation but then must be willing to adapt procedures or plans if unanticipated events occur (see BOX 13).

BOX 13
Maintaining Flexibility in Designing a Case Study

Peter Blau's study of behavior in large government agencies (*The Dynamics of Bureaucracy*, 1955) is still valued for its insights into the relationship between the formal and informal organization of work groups, even over 50 years later.

Although his study focused on two government agencies, that was not Blau's initial design. As the author notes, he first intended to study a single organization and later switched to a plan to compare two organizations—a public one and a private one (Blau, 1955, pp. 272–273). However, his initial attempts to gain access to a private firm were unsuccessful, and in the meanwhile, he had developed a stronger rationale for comparing two government agencies but of different kinds.

These shifts in the initial plans are examples of the kinds of changes that can occur in the design of a case study. Blau's experience shows how a skilled investigator can take advantage of changing opportunities, as well as shifts in theoretical concerns, to produce a classic case study.

When a shift is made, you must maintain an unbiased perspective and acknowledge those situations in which, in fact, you may have inadvertently begun to pursue a totally new investigation. When this occurs, many completed steps—including the initial design of the case study—must be repeated and redocumented. One of the worst complaints about the conduct of case study research is that investigators change directions without knowing that their original research design was inadequate for the revised investigation, thereby leaving unknown gaps and biases. Thus, the need to balance adaptiveness with *rigor*—but not rigidity—cannot be overemphasized.

Having a Firm Grasp of the Issues Being Studied

The main way of staying on target, of course, is to understand the purpose of the case study investigation in the first place. Each case study investigator must understand the theoretical or policy issues because analytic judgments have to be made throughout the data collection phase. Without a firm grasp of the issues, you could miss important clues and would not know when a deviation was acceptable or even desirable. The point is that case study data collection is not merely a matter of *recording* data in a mechanical fashion, as it is in some other types of research. You must be able to *interpret* the information as it is being collected and to know immediately, for instance, if several sources of information contradict one another and lead to the need for additional evidence—much like a good detective.

In fact, the detective role offers some keen insights into case study fieldwork. Note that the detective arrives on a scene *after* a crime has occurred and is basically being called upon to make *inferences* about what actually transpired. The inferences, in turn, must be based on convergent evidence from witnesses and physical evidence, as well as some unspecifiable element of common sense. Finally, the detective may have to make inferences about multiple crimes, to determine whether the same perpetrator committed them. This last step is similar to the replication logic underlying multiple-case studies.

Avoiding Bias

All of the preceding conditions will be negated if an investigator seeks only to use a case study to substantiate a preconceived position. Case study investigators are especially prone to this problem because they must understand the issues beforehand (see Becker, 1958, 1967). You also may have selected the case study method to enable you (wrongly) to pursue or (worse yet) advocate particular issues.[1] In contrast, the traditional research assistant, though mechanistic and possibly even sloppy, is not likely to introduce a substantive bias into the research.

One test of this possible bias is the degree to which you are open to contrary findings. For example, researchers studying "nonprofit" organizations may be surprised to find that many of these organizations have entrepreneurial and capitalistic motives (even though the organizations don't formally make profits). If such findings are based on compelling evidence, the conclusions of the case study would have to reflect these contrary findings. To test your own tolerance for contrary findings, report your preliminary findings—possibly while still in the data collection phase—to two or three critical colleagues. The colleagues should offer alternative explanations and suggestions for data collection. If the quest for contrary findings can produce documentable rebuttals, the likelihood of bias will have been reduced.

EXERCISE 3.1   Identifying the Skills for Doing Case Studies

Name the various skills that are important for a case study investigator to have. Do you know any people that have been successful in doing case study research? What strengths and weaknesses do they have as research investigators? Are these similar to the ones you have just named?

EXERCISE 3.2   Analyzing Your Own Skills for Doing Case Studies

What distinctive skills do you believe equip you to do a case study? Have you done previous studies requiring the collection and analysis of original data? Have you done any fieldwork, and if so, in what ways are you a good "listener" or an observant person? If you identify some case study skills that you still might need to strengthen, how would you go about the task?

PREPARATION AND TRAINING FOR A SPECIFIC CASE STUDY

Human Subjects Protection

Some time between the completion of your design and the start of your data collection, you will need to show how you plan to protect the human subjects in your case study. You will need to obtain formal approval for your plan. Such approval should not merely be viewed as an oversight process, because you should always conduct all of your research with the highest ethical standard.

The specific need for protecting human subjects comes from the fact that nearly all case studies, like those covered by this book, are about contemporary human affairs. In this single manner, you and other social scientists differ from scientists who study physical, chemical, or other nonhuman systems or from historians who may be studying the "dead past." The study of "a contemporary phenomenon in its real-life context" obligates you to important ethical practices akin to those followed in medical research.

As part of the protection, you are responsible for conducting your case study with special care and sensitivity—going beyond the research design and other technical considerations covered throughout this book. The care usually involves

◆ gaining *informed consent* from all persons who may be part of your case study, by alerting them to the nature of your case study and formally soliciting their volunteerism in participating in the study;

◆ protecting those who participate in your study from any *harm,* including avoiding the use of any *deception* in your study;

◆ protecting the *privacy and confidentiality* of those who participate so that, as a result of their participation, they will not be unwittingly put in any undesirable position, even such as being on a roster to receive requests to participate in some future study, whether conducted by you or anyone else; and

◆ taking special precautions that might be needed to protect *especially vulnerable groups* (for instance, research involving children).

Exactly how you exercise the needed care and sensitivity will vary, depending on your case study. General guidance comes from your own professional ethics. Professional research associations also promulgate their own standards for doing human subjects research, not just case studies (e.g., Joint Committee on Standards for Educational Evaluation, 1981). Most important, however, your institutional setting will have its own expectations, whether you are part of a university or of an independent research organization, and you need to follow its specific guidance.

In particular, every institution now has an Institutional Review Board (IRB). The board is charged with reviewing and approving all human subjects research before such research can proceed. The board's review will cover the objectives of your study and how you plan to protect the human subjects that may be part of the study. Note that your interactions with the specific human subjects in your study take place through both direct contact (as in interviews) and the potential use of personal records (as in client records). Case studies present a more challenging situation than when using other research methods because these interactions are not necessarily as structured as with other methods (such as in administering a closed-ended questionnaire). The board will want to know such information as how you plan to interact with those being studied, the protocols or data collection instruments you are planning to use, and how you will ensure such protections as informed consent and confidentiality.

As a result, the most imperative step before proceeding with your case study is to seek out the IRB at your institution, follow its guidance, and obtain its approval. The IRB's concerns will vary from institution to institution and IRB to IRB. Do not hesitate to speak with a member or two of the IRB informally and ahead of time, to gain insight into the review process and its expectations.

Case Study Training as a Seminar Experience

Training also is a necessary step in doing case study research. The timing of the training, relative to the timing for seeking human subjects approval, will not always be linear. You need to have some data collection plans before seeking approval, but, as pointed out below, the finalization of the plans cannot occur until after the approval has been granted. The training activities described below may therefore take place over an extended period of time, as in a regular seminar.

For case study research, the key to understanding the needed training is to understand that every case study investigator must be able to operate as a "senior" investigator. Once you have started collecting data, you should think of yourself as an independent investigator who cannot rely on a rigid formula to guide your inquiry. You must be able to make intelligent decisions throughout the data collection process.

In this sense, training for a case study investigation actually begins with the definition of the questions being addressed and the development of the case study design. If these steps have been satisfactorily conducted, as described in Chapters 1 and 2, only minimal further effort may be needed, especially if there is only a single case study investigator.

However, it often happens that a case study investigation must rely on a *case study team,*[2] for any of three reasons:

1. a single case calls for intensive data collection at the same site, requiring a "team" of investigators (see BOX 14);

2. a case study involves multiple cases, with different persons being needed to cover each site or to rotate among the sites (Stake, 2006, p. 21); or

3. a combination of the first two conditions.

Under these circumstances, all team members should have contributed to the development of a draft case study protocol. This draft would then have been the version submitted for IRB approval, with the IRB-approved version subsequently being considered the final version of the protocol.

BOX 14
The Logistics of Field Research, Circa 1924–1925

Arranging schedules and gaining access to relevant sources of evidence are important to the *management* of a case study. The modern researcher may feel that these activities have only emerged with the growth of "big" social science during the 1960s and 1970s.

In a famous field study done decades ago, however, many of the same management techniques already had been practiced. The two principal investigators and their staff secretary opened a local office in the city they were studying. This office was used by other project staff for extended periods of time. From this vantage point, the research team participated in local life, examined documentary materials, compiled local statistics, conducted interviews, and distributed and collected questionnaires. This extensive fieldwork resulted 5 years later in the publication of the now-classic study of small-town America, *Middletown* (1929), by Robert and Helen Lynd (also see BOX 8, Chapter 2, p. 48).

When multiple investigators or team members participate in the same case study, all need to learn to be "senior" investigators. Training takes the form of a seminar rather than didactic instruction. As in a seminar, much time has to be allowed for reading, preparing for the training, and holding the training. (See Figure 3.1 for an agenda of an illustrative training session.)

Preparatory Readings: Should include the original case study proposal, if any; a field-oriented methodological text; several works on the substance of the case study; and sample case studies (reports or publications) from previous case study research

Session 1: Discussion of the Purpose of the Case Study, the Main Research Questions, and the Selection of the Case(s)

Session 2: Review of the Case Study Protocol

    A. Discussion of relevant theoretical frameworks and literature

    B. Development or review of hypothetical logic model, if relevant

    C. In-depth discussion of protocol topics (discuss importance of topic and possible types of evidence to be collected in relation to each topic)

    D. Anticipated topics to be covered in the eventual case study report (helps to create consensus over the end goals)

Session 3: Methodological Review

    A. Arrangement of site visit (sample confirmation letter to site)

    B. Fieldwork procedures (discuss methodological principles)

    C. Use of evidence (review types of evidence and need for convergence)

    D. Note taking and other field practices

    E. Follow-up activities (sample thank you note)

    F. Project schedule, including key deadlines

Figure 3.1   Multisession Agenda for Case Study Training

Typically, the seminar will cover all phases of the planned case study investigation, including readings on the subject matter, the theoretical issues that led to the case study design, and case study methods and tactics. You might review examples of tools used in other case studies (see BOX 15), to add to the methodological portion of the training.

The goal of the training is to have all participants understand the basic concepts, terminology, and methodological issues relevant to the study. Each team member needs to know

- why the study is being done,
- what evidence is being sought,

BOX 15
Reviewing the Tools and Methods Used in
Other Case Studies, Circa the 21st Century

Web sites have provided new opportunities to access the tools and methods used in other case studies. For example, in online versions of articles, academic journals may reproduce supplementary materials that might not have appeared in the printed version of the article. For one case study, the supplementary materials included the formal case study protocol, case study coding book, evidentiary tables linking claims to sections of the case study database, and a list of documents in the case study database (Randolph & Eronen, 2007).

♦ what variations can be anticipated (and what should be done if such variations occur), and

♦ what would constitute supportive or contrary evidence for any given proposition.

Discussions, rather than lectures, are the key part of the training effort, to ensure that the desired level of understanding has been achieved.

This seminar approach to case study training can be contrasted to the training for other types of data collection—for example, group training for survey interviewers. The survey training does involve discussions, but it mainly emphasizes the questionnaire items or terminology to be used and takes place over an intensive but short period of time. Moreover, the survey training may not cover the global or conceptual concerns of the study, as interviewers may not need to have any broader understanding beyond the mechanics of the survey instrument. Survey training rarely involves any outside reading about the substantive issues, and the survey interviewer generally does not know how the survey data are to be analyzed or what issues are to be investigated. Such an approach may feed the strengths of doing surveys but would be insufficient for case study training.

Protocol Development and Review

The next subsection will say more about the *content* of the case study protocol. However, a legitimate and desirable training task is the understanding of the protocol by all of the case study investigators.

To reinforce such an understanding, each investigator or team member may be assigned one portion of the substantive topics covered by the protocol. Each investigator is then responsible for reviewing the appropriate reading materials related to the assigned portion, adding any other information that may be relevant, and leading a discussion that clarifies that portion of the protocol's questions. In this manner, such an arrangement should ensure that each team member has mastered the content of the protocol.

Problems to Be Addressed

The training also has the purpose of uncovering problems within the case study plan or with the research team's capabilities. If such problems do emerge, one consolation is that they will be more troublesome if they are not recognized until later, after the data collection begins. Good case study investigators should therefore press to be certain, during the training period, that potential problems are brought into the open.

The most obvious problem is that the training may reveal flaws in the case study design or even the initial definition of the study questions. If this occurs, you must be willing to make the necessary revisions, even if more time and effort are necessary. Sometimes, the revisions will challenge the basic purpose of the investigation, as in a situation in which the original objective may have been to investigate a technological phenomenon, such as the use of personal computers, but in which the case study really turns out to be about an organizational phenomenon, such as poor supervision. Any revisions, of course, also may lead to the need to review a slightly different literature and to recast the entire study and its audience. You also should check your IRB's procedures to see whether it will need to conduct a new human subjects review. Despite these unexpected developments, changing the basic premise of your case study is fully warranted if the training has demonstrated the unrealistic (or uninteresting) nature of the original plan.

A second problem is that the training may reveal incompatibilities among the investigating team—and in particular, the fact that some of the team members may not share the orientation of the project or its sponsors. In one multiple-case study of community organizations, for instance, team members varied in their beliefs regarding the efficacy of such organizations (U.S. National Commission on Neighborhoods, 1979). When such biases are discovered, one way of dealing with the contrary orientations is to suggest to the team that contrary evidence will be respected if it is collected and verifiable. A team member still has the choice, of course, of continuing to participate in the study or deciding to drop out.

A third problem is that the training may reveal some impractical time deadlines or expectations regarding available resources. For instance, a case study may have assumed that 20 persons were to be contacted for open-ended interviews during a site visit, as part of the data collection. The training may have revealed, however, that the time needed for meeting with these persons is likely to be much longer than anticipated. Under such circumstances, any expectation for interviewing 20 persons would have to depend on revising the original data collection schedule.

Finally, the training may uncover some positive features, such as the fact that two or more team members have complementary skills and are able to work productively together. Such rapport and productivity during the training session may readily extend to the actual data collection period and may therefore suggest certain pairings for the fieldwork teams. In general, the training should have the effect of creating group norms for the ensuing data collection activity. This norm-building process is more than an amenity; it will help ensure supportive reactions, should unexpected problems arise during the data collection.

EXERCISE 3.3   Conducting Training for Doing a Case Study

Describe the major ways in which the preparation and training to do a case study project are *different* from those for doing projects using other types of research strategies (e.g., surveys, experiments, histories, and archival analysis). Develop a training agenda to prepare for a case study you might be considering, in which two or three persons are to collaborate.

THE CASE STUDY PROTOCOL

A case study protocol has only one thing in common with a survey questionnaire: Both are directed at a single data point—either a single case (even if the case is part of a larger, multiple-case study) or a single respondent.

Beyond this similarity are major differences. The protocol is more than a questionnaire or instrument. First, the protocol contains the instrument but also contains the procedures and general rules to be followed in using the protocol. Second, the protocol is directed at an entirely different party than that of a survey questionnaire, explained below. Third, having a case study protocol is desirable under all circumstances, but it is essential if you are doing a multiple-case study.

The protocol is a major way of increasing the *reliability* of case study research and is intended to guide the investigator in carrying out the data collection from a single case (again, even if the single case is one of several in a multiple-case study). Figure 3.2 gives a *table of contents* from an illustrative protocol, which was used in a study of innovative law enforcement practices supported by federal funds. The practices had been defined earlier through a

A. Introduction to the Case Study and Purpose of Protocol

   1. Case study questions, hypotheses, and propositions

   2. Theoretical framework for the case study (*reproduces the logic model*)

   3. Role of protocol in guiding the case study investigator (*notes that the protocol is a standardized agenda for the investigator's line of inquiry*)

B. Data Collection Procedures

   1. Names of sites to be visited, including contact persons

   2. Data collection plan (*covers the type of evidence to be expected, including the roles of people to be interviewed, the events to be observed, and any other documents to be reviewed when on site*)

   3. Expected preparation prior to site visits (*identifies specific information to be reviewed and issues to be covered, prior to going on site*)

C. Outline of Case Study Report

   1. The law enforcement practice in operation

   2. Innovativeness of the practice

   3. Outcomes from the practice, to date

   4. Law enforcement agency context and history pertaining to the practice

   5. Exhibits to be developed: chronology of events covering the implementation and outcomes of the practice at this site; logic model for the practice; arrays or presenting outcome or other data; references to relevant documents; list of persons interviewed

D. Case Study Questions (see Figure 3.3 for a detailed question)

   1. The practice in operation and its innovativeness

     a. Describe the practice in detail, including the deployment of personnel and technologies, if any.

     b. What is the nature, if any, of collaborative efforts across communities or jurisdictions that have been needed to put the practice into place?

     c. How did the idea for the practice start?

     d. Was there a planning process, and how did it work? What were the original goals and target populations or areas for the practice?

Figure 3.2 (Continued)

---

    e. In what ways is the practice innovative, compared to other practices of the same kind or in the same jurisdiction?

    f. Describe whether the practice has been supported from the jurisdiction's regular budget or as a result of funding from an external source.

2. Evaluation

    a. What is the design for evaluating the practice, and who is doing the evaluation?

    b. What part of the evaluation has been implemented?

    c. What are the outcome measures being used, and what outcomes have been identified to date?

    d. What rival explanations have been identified and explored, for attributing the outcomes to the investment of the federal funds?

Figure 3.2   Table of Contents of Protocol for Conducting Case Studies of Innovative Law Enforcement Practices

careful screening process (see later discussion in this chapter for more detail on "screening case study nominations"). Furthermore, because data were to be collected from 18 such cases as part of a multiple-case study, the information about any given case could not be collected in great depth, and thus the number of the case study questions was minimal.

As a general matter, a case study protocol should have the following sections:

♦ an overview of the case study project (project objectives and auspices, case study issues, and relevant readings about the topic being investigated),

♦ field procedures (presentation of credentials, access to the case study "sites," language pertaining to the protection of human subjects, sources of data, and procedural reminders),

♦ case study questions (the specific questions that the case study investigator must keep in mind in collecting data, "table shells" for specific arrays of data, and the potential sources of information for answering each question—see Figure 3.3 for an example), and

♦ a guide for the case study report (outline, format for the data, use and presentation of other documentation, and bibliographical information).

A quick glance at these topics will indicate why the protocol is so important. First, it keeps you targeted on the topic of the case study. Second, preparing the

---

Define a practice put into place at the school 2 or more years ago, aimed directly at improving school instruction; does the practice have a name?

- ◆ Operationalize the practice by placing the actions and events into a logic model framework; collect information about the chronology of these actions and events, as well as their causal relations.

- ◆ Collect data related to the nature and extent of any improvements for the relevant period of time—for example,
  - o Raised expectations or consensus over goals
  - o Improved educational standards or tightened academic requirements
  - o Increased quality of the teaching staff
  - o Increased participation by parents in their child's learning
  - o Student performance (e.g., enrollment in specific courses, attendance, or results from achievement tests)

Figure 3.3   Illustrative Protocol Question (from a Study of School Practices)

protocol forces you to anticipate several problems, including the way that the case study reports are to be completed. This means, for instance, that you will have to identify the *audience* for your case study report even before you have conducted your case study. Such forethought will help to avoid mismatches in the long run.

The table of contents of the illustrative protocol in Figure 3.2 reveals another important feature of the case study report: In this instance, the desired report starts by calling for a description of the innovative practice being studied (see item C1 in Figure 3.2)—and only later covers the agency context and history pertaining to the practice (see item C4). This choice reflects the fact that most investigators write too extensively on history and background conditions. While these are important, the description of the subject of the study—the innovative practice—needs more attention.

Each section of the protocol is discussed next.

Overview of the Case Study Project

The overview should cover the background information about the project, the substantive issues being investigated, and the relevant readings about the issues.

As for background information, every project has its own context and perspective. Some projects, for instance, are funded by government agencies having a general mission and clientele that need to be remembered in conducting the research. Other projects have broader theoretical concerns or are offshoots of earlier research studies. Whatever the situation, this type of background information, in summary form, belongs in the overview section.

A procedural element of this background section is a statement about the project which you can present to anyone who may want to know about the project, its purpose, and the people involved in conducting and sponsoring the project. This statement can even be accompanied by a letter of introduction, to be sent to all major interviewees and organizations that may be the subject of study. (See Figure 3.4 for an illustrative letter.) The bulk of the overview, however, should be devoted to the substantive issues being investigated. This may include the rationale for selecting the case(s), the propositions or hypotheses being examined, and the broader theoretical or policy relevance of the inquiry. For all of these topics, relevant readings should be cited, and the essential reading materials should be made available to everyone on the case study team.

A good overview will communicate to the informed reader (that is, someone familiar with the general topic of inquiry) the case study's purpose and setting. Some of the materials (such as a summary describing the project) may be needed for other purposes anyway, so that writing the overview should be seen as a doubly worthwhile activity. In the same vein, a well-conceived overview even may later form the basis for the background and introduction to the final case study report.

Field Procedures

Chapter 1 has previously defined case studies as studies of events within their *real-life* context. This has important implications for defining and designing the case study, which have been discussed in Chapters 1 and 2.

For data collection, however, this characteristic of case studies also raises an important issue, for which properly designed field procedures are essential. You will be collecting data from people and institutions in their everyday situations, not within the controlled confines of a laboratory, the sanctity of a library, or the structured limitations of a survey questionnaire. In a case study, you must therefore learn to integrate real-world events with the needs of the data collection plan. In this sense, you do not have the control over the data collection environment as others might have in using the other research methods discussed in Chapter 1.

Note that in a laboratory experiment, human "subjects" are solicited to enter into the laboratory—an environment controlled nearly entirely by the research investigator. The subject, within ethical and physical constraints, must follow the

```
                NATIONAL COMMISSION ON NEIGHBORHOODS
                   2000 K Street, N.W., Suite 350
                       Washington, D.C. 20006
                          202-632-5200


                                              May 30, 1978

      To Whom It May Concern:

            This is to introduce
      a highly qualified individual with wide experience
      in the field of neighborhood revitalization and com-
      munity organization.               has been engaged
      by the National Commission on Neighborhoods to join
      a team of experts now undertaking a series of 40-50
      case studies commissioned by our Task Force on Gover-
      nance.

            Ultimately, by means of this case study
      approach, the Commission hopes to identify and docu-
      ment answers to such questions as: What enables some
      neighborhoods to survive, given the forces, attitudes
      and investment policies (both public and private)
      working against them? What preconditions are neces-
      sary in order to expand the number of neighborhoods
      where successful revitalization, benefiting existing
      residents, is possible? What can be done to promote
      these preconditions?

            This letter is directed to community leaders,
      administrative staff and city officials. We must ask
      you to give your time, experience and patience to our
      interviewers. Your cooperation is most essential if
      the case studies are to successfully guide and support
      the final policy recommendations which the Commission
      must forward to the President and to Congress.

            On behalf of all twenty members of the Commission,
      I wish to express our gratitude for your assistance.
      Should you wish to be entered on our mailing list for
      the Commission newsletter and final report, our inter-
      viewer will be glad to make the proper arrangements.

            Again, thank you very much.

                              Sincerely,

                              /signed/
                              Senator Joseph F. Timilty
                              Chairman
```

Figure 3.4   Illustrative Letter of Introduction

investigator's instructions, which carefully prescribe the desired behavior. Similarly, the human "respondent" to a survey questionnaire cannot deviate from the agenda set by the questions. Therefore, the respondent's behavior also is constrained by the ground rules of the investigator. Naturally, the subject or respondent who does not wish to follow the prescribed behaviors may freely drop out of the experiment or survey. Finally, in the historical archive, pertinent documents may not always be available, but the investigator can inspect what exists at his or her own pace and at a time convenient to her or his schedule. In all three situations, the research investigator closely controls the formal data collection activity.

Doing case studies involves an entirely different situation. For interviewing key persons, you must cater to the interviewee's schedule and availability, not your own. The nature of the interview is much more open-ended, and an interviewee may not necessarily cooperate fully in sticking to your line of questions. Similarly, in making observations of real-life activities, you are intruding into the world of the subject being studied rather than the reverse; under these conditions, you are the one who may have to make special arrangements, to be able to act as an observer (or even as a participant-observer). As a result, your behavior—and not that of the subject or respondent—is the one likely to be constrained.

This contrasting process of doing data collection leads to the need to have explicit and well-planned field procedures encompassing guidelines for "coping" behaviors. Imagine, for instance, sending a youngster to camp; because you do not know what to expect, the best preparation is to have the resources to be prepared. Case study field procedures should be the same way.

With the preceding orientation in mind, the field procedures of the protocol need to emphasize the major tasks in collecting data, including

♦ gaining access to key organizations or interviewees;

♦ having sufficient resources while in the field—including a personal computer, writing instruments, paper, paper clips, and a preestablished, quiet place to write notes privately;

♦ developing a procedure for calling for assistance and guidance, if needed, from other case study investigators or colleagues;

♦ making a clear schedule of the data collection activities that are expected to be completed within specified periods of time; and

♦ providing for unanticipated events, including changes in the availability of interviewees as well as changes in the mood and motivation of the case study investigator.

These are the types of topics that can be included in the field procedures section of the protocol. Depending upon the type of study being done, the specific procedures will vary.

The more operational these procedures are, the better. To take but one minor issue as an example, case study data collection frequently results in the accumulation of numerous documents at the field site. The burden of carrying such bulky documents can be reduced by two procedures. First, the case study team may have had the foresight to bring large, prelabeled envelopes, to mail the documents back to the office rather than carry them. Second, field time may have been set aside for perusing the documents and then going to a local copier facility and copying only the few relevant pages of each document—and then returning the original documents to the informants at the field site. These and other operational details can enhance the overall quality and efficiency of case study data collection.

A final part of this portion of the protocol should carefully describe the procedures for protecting human subjects. First, the protocol should repeat the rationale for the IRB-approved field procedures. Then, the protocol should include the "scripted" words or instructions for the team to use in obtaining informed consent or otherwise informing case study interviewees and other participants of the risks and conditions associated with the research.

Case Study Questions

The heart of the protocol is a set of substantive questions reflecting your actual line of inquiry. Some people may consider this part of the protocol to be the case study "instrument." However, two characteristics distinguish case study questions from those in a survey instrument. (Refer back to Figure 3.3 for an illustrative question from a study of a school program; the complete protocol included dozens of such questions.)

General orientation of questions. First, the questions are posed *to you, the investigator,* not to an interviewee. In this sense, the protocol is directed at an entirely different party than a survey instrument. The protocol's questions, in essence, are your reminders regarding the information that needs to be collected, and why. In some instances, the specific questions also may serve as prompts in asking questions during a case study interview. However, the main purpose of the protocol's questions is to keep the investigator on track as data collection proceeds.

Each question should be accompanied by a list of likely sources of evidence. Such sources may include the names of individual interviewees, documents, or observations. This crosswalk between the questions of interest and the likely sources of evidence is extremely helpful in collecting case study data. Before arriving on the case study scene, for instance, a case study investigator can quickly review the major questions that the data collection should cover.

(Again, these questions form the structure of the inquiry and are not intended as the literal questions to be asked of any given interviewee.)

Levels of questions. Second, the questions in the case study protocol should distinguish clearly among different types or levels of questions. The potentially relevant questions can, remarkably, occur at any of five levels:

Level 1: questions asked of specific interviewees;

Level 2: questions asked of the individual case (these are the questions in the case study protocol to be answered by the investigator during a single case, even when the single case is part of a larger, multiple-case study);

Level 3: questions asked of the pattern of findings across multiple cases;

Level 4: questions asked of an entire study—for example, calling on information beyond the case study evidence and including other literature or published data that may have been reviewed; and

Level 5: normative questions about policy recommendations and conclusions, going beyond the narrow scope of the study.

Of these five levels, you should concentrate heavily on Level 2 for the case study protocol.

The difference between Level 1 and Level 2 questions is highly significant. The two types of questions are most commonly confused because investigators think that their questions of inquiry (Level 2) are synonymous with the specific questions they will ask in the field (Level 1). To disentangle these two levels in your own mind, think again about a detective, especially a wily one. The detective has in mind what the course of events in a crime might have been (Level 2), but the actual questions posed to any witness or suspect (Level 1) do not necessarily betray the detective's thinking. The *verbal* line of inquiry is different from the *mental* line of inquiry, and this is the difference between Level 1 and Level 2 questions. For the case study protocol, explicitly articulating the Level 2 questions is therefore of much greater importance than any attempt to identify the Level 1 questions.

In the field, keeping in mind the Level 2 questions while simultaneously articulating Level 1 questions in conversing with an interviewee is not easy. In a like manner, you can lose sight of your Level 2 questions when examining a detailed document that will become part of the case study evidence (the common revelation occurs when you ask yourself, "Why am I reading this document?"). To overcome these problems, successful participation in the earlier seminar training helps. Remember that being a "senior" investigator means maintaining a working knowledge of the entire case study inquiry. The (Level 2) questions in the case study protocol embody this inquiry.

The other levels also should be understood clearly. A cross-case question, for instance (Level 3), may be whether the larger school districts among your cases are more responsive than smaller school districts or whether complex bureaucratic structures make the larger districts more cumbersome and less responsive. However, this Level 3 question should not be part of the protocol for collecting data from the single case, because the single case only can address the responsiveness of a single school district. The Level 3 question cannot be addressed until the data from all the single cases (in a multiple-case study) are examined. Thus, only the multiple-case analysis can cover Level 3 questions. Similarly, the questions at Levels 4 and 5 also go well beyond any individual case study, and you should note this limitation if you include such questions in the case study protocol. Remember: *The protocol is for the data collection from a single case (even when part of a multiple-case study) and is not intended to serve the entire project.*

Undesired confusion between unit of data collection and unit of analysis. Related to the distinction between Level 1 and Level 2 questions, a more subtle and serious problem can arise in articulating the questions in the case study protocol. The questions should cater to the unit of analysis of the case study, which may be at a different level from the unit of data collection of the case study. Confusion will occur if, under these circumstances, the data collection process leads to an (undesirable) distortion of the unit of analysis.

The common confusion begins because the data collection sources may be individual people (e.g., interviews with individuals), whereas the unit of analysis of your case study may be a collective (e.g., the organization to which the individual belongs)—a frequent design when the case study is about an organization, community, or social group. Even though your data collection may have to rely heavily on information from individual interviewees, your conclusions cannot be based entirely on interviews as a source of information (you would then have collected information about individuals' reports about the organization, not necessarily about organizational events as they actually had occurred). In this example, the protocol questions therefore need to be about the organization, not the individual.

However, the reverse situation also can be true. Your case study may be about an individual, but the sources of information can include archival records (e.g., personnel files or student records) from an organization. In this situation, you also would want to avoid basing your conclusions about the individual from the organizational sources of information only. In this example, the protocol questions therefore need to be about the individual, not the organization.

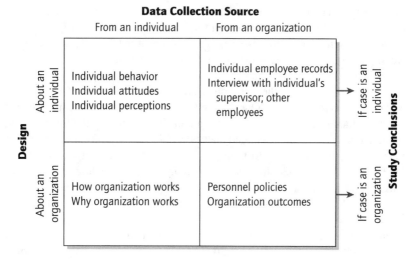

Figure 3.5   Design versus Data Collection: Different Units of Analysis

Figure 3.5 illustrates these two situations, where the unit of analysis for the case study is different from the unit of data collection.

Other data collection devices. The protocol questions also can include empty "table shells" (for more detail, see Miles & Huberman, 1994). These are the outlines of a table, defining precisely the "rows" and "columns" of a data array—but in the absence of having the actual data. In this sense, the table shell indicates the data to be collected, and your job is to collect the data called forth by the table. Such table shells help in several ways. First, the table shells force you to identify exactly what data are being sought. Second, they ensure that parallel information will be collected at different sites, where a multiple-case design is being used. Finally, the table shells aid in understanding what will be done with the data once they have been collected.

Guide for the Case Study Report

This element is generally missing in most case study plans. Investigators neglect to think about the outline, format, or audience for the case study report until after the data have been collected. Yet, some planning at this preparatory stage—admittedly out of sequence in the typical conduct of most research—means that a tentative outline can (and should) appear in the case study protocol. (Such planning accounts for the arrow between "prepare" and "share" in the figure at the outset of this chapter.)

Again, one reason for the traditional, linear sequence is related to practices with other research methods. One does not worry about the report from an experiment until after the experiment has been completed, because the format of the report and its likely audience already have been dictated by the conventional formats of academic journals. Most reports of experiments follow a similar outline: the posing of the research questions and hypotheses; a description of the research design, apparatus, and data collection procedures; the presentation of the data collected; the analysis of the data; and a discussion of findings and conclusions.

Unfortunately, case study reports do not have such a uniformly acceptable outline. Nor, in many instances, do case study reports end up in journals (Feagin et al., 1991, pp. 269–273). For this reason, each investigator must be concerned, throughout the conduct of a case study, with the design of the final case study report. The problem is not easy to deal with.

In addition, the protocol also can indicate the extent of documentation for the case study report. Properly done, the data collection is likely to lead to large amounts of documentary evidence, in the form of published reports, publications, memoranda, and other documents collected about the case. What is to be done with this documentation, for later presentation? In most studies, the documents are filed away and seldom retrieved. Yet, this documentation is an important part of the "database" for a case study (see Chapter 4) and should not be ignored until after the case study has been completed. One possibility is to have the case study report include an annotated bibliography in which each of the available documents is itemized. The annotations would help a reader (or the investigator, at some later date) to know which documents might be relevant for further inquiry.

In summary, to the extent possible, the basic outline of the case study report should be part of the protocol. This will facilitate the collection of relevant data, in the appropriate format, and will reduce the possibility that a return visit to the case study site will be necessary. At the same time, the existence of such an outline should not imply rigid adherence to a predesigned protocol. In fact, case study plans can change as a result of the initial data collection, and you are encouraged to consider these flexibilities—if used properly and without bias—to be an advantage of the case study method.

EXERCISE 3.4   Developing a Case Study Protocol

Select some phenomenon in need of explanation from the everyday life of your university or school (past or present). Illustrative topics might be, for example, why the university or school changed some policy or how it makes decisions about its curriculum requirements. For these illustrative topics (or some topics of your own choosing), design a case study protocol to collect the information needed to make an adequate explanation. What would be your main research questions or propositions? What specific sources of data would you seek (e.g., persons to be interviewed, documents to be sought, and field observations to be made)? Would your protocol be sufficient in guiding you through the entire process of doing your case study?

SCREENING THE CANDIDATE "CASES" FOR YOUR CASE STUDY

Another preparatory step is the final selection of the case(s) to be part of your case study. Sometimes, the selection is straightforward because you have chosen to study a unique case whose identity has been known from the outset of your inquiry. Or, you already may know the case you will study because of some special arrangement or access that you have. However, at other times, there may be many qualified case study candidates, and you must choose your final single case or array of multiple cases from among them. The goal of the screening procedure is to be sure that you identify the final cases properly prior to formal data collection. The worst scenario would occur when, after having started formal data collection, the case turns out not to be viable or to represent an instance of something other than what you had intended to study.

When you have only a score or so (20 to 30) of possible candidates that can serve as your cases (whether these candidates are "sites" or individuals or some other entity depends on your unit of analysis), the screening may consist of querying people knowledgeable about each candidate. You even may collect limited documentation about each candidate. To be avoided, at all costs, is an extensive screening procedure that effectively becomes a "mini" case study of every candidate case. Prior to collecting the screening data, you should have defined a set of operational criteria whereby candidates will be deemed qualified to serve as cases. If doing a single-case study, choose the case that is likely, all other things being equal, to yield the best data. If doing a multiple-case study, select cases that best fit your (literal or theoretical) replication design.

When the eligible number of candidates is larger, a two-stage screening procedure is warranted. The first stage should consist of collecting relevant quantitative data about the entire pool, from some archival source (e.g., statistical databases about individual schools or firms). You may have to obtain the archival data from some central source (e.g., a federal, state, or local agency or a national association). Once obtained, you should define some relevant criteria for either stratifying or reducing the number of candidates. The goal is to reduce the number of candidates to 20 to 30 and then to conduct the second screening stage, which consists of carrying out the procedure in the previous paragraph. Such a two-stage procedure was followed in a case study of local economic development, and the experience is fully reported in the companion text (Yin, 2003, chap. 6, pp. 9–14).

In completing the screening process, you may want to revisit your earlier decision about the total number of cases to be studied. Regardless of any resource constraints, if multiple candidates are qualified to serve as cases, the larger the number you can study, the better.

THE PILOT CASE STUDY

Pilot cases may be conducted for several reasons unrelated to the criteria for selecting the final cases in the case study design. For example, the informants at a pilot site may be unusually congenial and accessible, or the site may be geographically convenient or may have an unusual amount of documentation and data. One other possibility is that a pilot case represents a most complicated case, compared to the likely real cases, so that nearly all relevant data collection issues will be encountered in the pilot case.

A pilot case study will help you to refine your data collection plans with respect to both the content of the data and the procedures to be followed. In this regard, it is important to note that a *pilot test* is not a *pretest*. The pilot case is more formative, assisting you to develop relevant lines of questions—possibly even providing some conceptual clarification for the research design as well. In contrast, the pretest is the occasion for a formal "dress rehearsal," in which the data collection plan is used as the final plan as faithfully as possible. As a result, the pilot test might preferably occur before seeking final approval from an IRB, as discussed earlier in this chapter.

The pilot case study can be so important that more resources may be devoted to this phase of the research than to the collection of data from any of the actual cases. For this reason, several subtopics are worth further discussion: the selection of pilot cases, the nature of the inquiry for the pilot cases, and the nature of the reports from the pilot cases.

Selection of Pilot Cases

In general, convenience, access, and geographic proximity can be the main criteria for selecting a pilot case or cases. This will allow for a less structured and more prolonged relationship between yourself and the case than might occur in the "real" cases. The pilot case can then assume the role of a "laboratory" in detailing your protocol, allowing you to observe different phenomena from many different angles or to try different approaches on a trial basis.

One study of technological innovations in local services (Yin, 2003, pp. 6–9) actually had seven pilot cases, each focusing on a different type of technology. Four of the cases were located in the same metropolitan area as the research team's and were visited first. Three of the cases, however, were located in different cities and were the basis for a second set of visits. The cases were not chosen because of their distinctive technologies or for any other substantive reason. The main criterion, besides proximity, was the fact that access to the cases was made easy by some prior personal contact on the part of the research team. Finally, the interviewees in the cases also were congenial to the notion that the investigators were at an early stage of their research and would not have a fixed agenda.

In return for serving as a pilot case, the main informants usually expect to receive some feedback from you about their case. Your value to them is as an external observer, and you should be prepared to provide such feedback. To do so, even though you should already have developed a draft protocol representing the topics of interest to your case study, you should adapt parts of the protocol to suit the informants' needs. You should then conduct the pilot case by following (and pilot-testing) your formal field procedures. Under no circumstance should the pilot case be the occasion for an overly informal or highly personalized inquiry.

Scope of the Pilot Inquiry

Nevertheless, the scope of the inquiry for the pilot case can be much broader and less focused than the ultimate data collection plan. Moreover, the inquiry can cover both substantive and methodological issues.

In the above-mentioned example, the research team used the seven pilot cases to improve its conceptualization of different types of technologies and their related organizational effects. The pilot studies were done prior to the selection of specific technologies for the final data collection—and prior to the final articulation of the study's theoretical propositions. Thus, the pilot data provided considerable insight into the basic issues being studied. This information was used in parallel with an ongoing review of relevant literature, so that the final research design was informed both by prevailing theories and by a fresh set of empirical observations. The dual sources of information help to ensure that the actual study reflected significant theoretical or policy issues as well as questions relevant to contemporary cases.

Methodologically, the work on the pilot cases can provide information about relevant field questions and about the logistics of the field inquiry. In the technology pilot cases, one important logistical question was whether to observe the technology in action first or to collect information about the prevalent organizational issues first. This choice interacted with a further question about the deployment of the field team: If the team consisted of two or more persons, what assignments required the team to work together and what assignments could be completed separately? Variations in these procedures were tried during the pilot case studies, the trade-offs were acknowledged, and eventually a satisfactory procedure was developed for the formal data collection plan.

Reports from the Pilot Cases

The pilot case reports are mainly of value to the investigators and need to be written clearly, even if in the form of memoranda. One difference between the pilot reports and the actual case study reports is that the pilot reports should be explicit about the lessons learned for both research design and field procedures. The pilot reports might even contain subsections on these topics.

If more than a single pilot case is planned, the report from one pilot case also can indicate the modifications to be attempted in the next pilot case. In other words, the report can contain the agenda for the ensuing pilot case. If enough pilot cases are done in this manner, the final agenda may actually become a good prototype for the final case study protocol.

EXERCISE 3.5   Selecting a Case for Doing a Pilot Study

Define the desired features for a pilot case, as a prelude to a new case study research project. How would you go about contacting and using such a case? Describe why you might want only one pilot case, as opposed to two or more pilot cases.

SUMMARY

This chapter has reviewed the preparations for data collection. Depending upon the scope of a case study—whether single or multiple cases will be involved or whether single or multiple investigators will be involved—the preparatory tasks will be correspondingly straightforward or complex.

The major topics have been the desired skills of the case study investigator, the preparation and training of the case study investigators for a specific case study, the nature of the case study protocol, the screening of candidate cases, and the role and purpose of a pilot case study. Every case study should follow these different steps to varying degrees, depending upon the specific inquiry.

As with the management of other affairs, the expertise with which these activities are conducted will improve with practice. Thus, one desirable sequence is for you to complete a relatively straightforward case study before attempting to do a more complex one, from a managerial standpoint. With the successful completion of each case study, these preparatory tasks may even become second nature. Furthermore, if the same case study team has conducted several different studies together, the team will work with increasing efficiency and professional satisfaction with each ensuing case study.

NOTES

1. Thacher (2006) argues forcefully in support of what he calls "normative" case studies. In such studies, the investigators do use case studies to advocate specific issues, at the risk of being challenged about the fairness of their data. Such risks may be best left to very senior investigators but are not recommended for those with less experience in doing case studies, much less novices.

2. The difference between having a single case study investigator and needing multiple investigators can create a significantly different orientation to the entire case study method. The classic single investigators have frequently been brilliant and creative—quickly and intuitively adapting to new conditions during data collection or finding newly appealing patterns during data analysis. With multiple investigators, such talents may have to be curbed because of the need for consistency across investigators, but the good discipline is rewarded by minimizing the likelihood of introducing bias into the case study.

REFERENCE TO EXPANDED CASE STUDY
MATERIALS FOR CHAPTER 3

For selected case studies cited in the text of this chapter, two anthologies contain either a more extensive excerpt or the full case study. The table below crosswalks the reference in this book to the location of the excerpt or full rendition.

Chapter 3 Chapter Topic and Page Number	Topics of Illustrative Case Studies	Reference to Lengthier Material
The Case Study Investigator: Desired Skills		
BOX 13, p. 3-6	Government agencies	None
Preparation and Training for a Specific Case Study		
BOX 14, p. 3-12	Cities and towns	CSA-3
BOX 15, p. 3-12	Social services	None
The Case Study Protocol	None	
Screening the Candidate "Cases" for Your Case Study		
p. 3-28 text	Local economic development	ACSR, pp. 9–14
The Pilot Case Study		
p. 3-29 text	Computers and technology	ACSR, pp. 6–9

NOTE: CSA = *Case Study Anthology* (Yin, 2004). ACSR = *Applications of Case Study Research* (Yin, 2003). The number denotes the chapter number in the book.

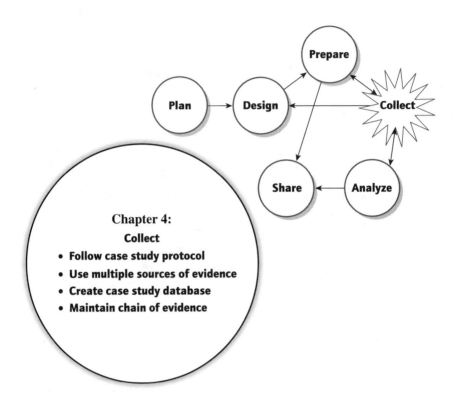

Chapter 4:

Collect

- **Follow case study protocol**
- **Use multiple sources of evidence**
- **Create case study database**
- **Maintain chain of evidence**

ABSTRACT

Case study evidence may come from six sources: documents, archival records, interviews, direct observation, participant-observation, and physical artifacts. Using these six sources calls for mastering different data collection procedures. Throughout, a major objective is to collect data about actual human events and behavior. This objective differs from (but complements) the typical survey objective of capturing perceptions, attitudes, and verbal reports about events and behavior (rather than direct evidence about the events and behavior).

In addition to the attention given to the six sources, some overriding principles are important to any data collection effort in doing case studies. These include the use of (a) multiple sources of evidence (evidence from two or more sources, converging on the same facts or findings), (b) a case study database (a formal assembly of evidence distinct from the final case study report), and (c) a chain of evidence (explicit links among the questions asked, the data collected, and the conclusions drawn). The incorporation of these principles into a case study will increase its quality substantially.

4

Collecting Case Study Evidence

The Principles You Should Follow in
Working with Six Sources of Evidence

Case study evidence can come from many sources. This chapter discusses six of them: documentation, archival records, interviews, direct observation, participant-observation, and physical artifacts. Each source is associated with an array of data or evidence. One purpose of this chapter is to review the six sources briefly. A second purpose is to convey three essential data collection principles, regardless of the sources used.

Supporting textbooks. You may find the six sources of evidence all potentially relevant, even in doing the same case study. For this reason, having them briefly reviewed, all in one place, may be helpful. For any given source of evidence, extensive further detail is available in numerous methodological textbooks and articles. Therefore, you also may want to check out some of these texts, especially if any single source of evidence is especially important to your case study. However, choosing among the texts and other works will require some searching and careful selection.

First, at an earlier time, guidance on collecting data relevant for case studies was available under three rubrics. One was "fieldwork" (e.g., Murphy, 1980; Wax, 1971) and a second was "field research" (e.g., Bouchard, 1976; Schatzman & Strauss, 1973). The third was "social science methods" more broadly (e.g., L. Kidder & Judd, 1986; Webb, Campbell, Schwartz, Sechrest, & Grove, 1981). Under these rubrics, the books also could cover the logistics of planning and conducting the fieldwork (e.g., Fiedler, 1978). The array of data collection techniques included under these rubrics was relevant to doing case studies, although none focused on case studies. The texts are still valuable because they are easy to use and discuss the basic data collection procedures to be followed. Unfortunately, the texts are probably increasingly hard to locate.

Second, recent texts are more readily available, but your choices are more complicated. Individual texts usually only cover some of the sources of evidence (e.g., single interviews, focus group interviews, and field observations)

Tip: *How much time and effort should I devote to collecting the case study data? How do I know whether I'm finished collecting the data?*

Unlike other methods, there is no clear cut-off point. You should try to collect enough data so that (a) you have confirmatory evidence (evidence from two or more different sources) for most of your main topics, and (b) your evidence includes attempts to investigate major rival hypotheses or explanations.

What do you think are some of the cut-off points for other methods, and why wouldn't they work in doing case study research?

---

but not the others (e.g., archival and documentary sources), thereby losing the flavor of the entire blend of multiple sources. Furthermore, the texts also may not suit your needs because they may have a dominant substantive or disciplinary orientation, such as (a) clinical research or research on primary care settings (e.g., Crabtree & Miller, 1999), (b) program evaluations (e.g., Patton, 2002), or (c) social work research (e.g., A. Rubin & Babbie, 1993). Yet other texts may not have such an orientation, but they may focus on only a single source of evidence, such as field interviewing (e.g., H. J. Rubin & Rubin, 1995), doing participant-observation (e.g., Jorgensen, 1989), or using documentary evidence (e.g., Barzun & Graff, 1985). In general, contemporary texts appear to have become more specialized, and few span the needed breadth of data collection methods. In particular, few texts combine data collection through communicative and observational means (i.e., interviews and direct observations, including the use of videotapes) with data collection through documentary and archival sources.

Third, books that might at first appear to be comprehensive methodological texts also cover many topics in addition to data collection and, as a result, only devote a fraction of their entire text to data collection procedures (e.g., 1 of 11 chapters in Creswell, 2007, and 1 of 26 chapters in Silverman, 2000). Other books that do have a truly comprehensive range and that do discuss data collection techniques in greater detail are nevertheless designed to serve more as reference works than as textbooks to be used by individual investigators (e.g., Bickman & Rog, 2000).

Given these variations, you must overcome the complex if not fragmented nature of the methodological marketplace represented by these various texts. To do so will make your own data collection procedures even better.

Supporting principles. In addition to your need to be familiar with the data collection procedures using the six different sources of evidence, you also need to continue addressing the design challenges enumerated in Chapter 2: construct validity, internal validity, external validity, and reliability. For this reason, this chapter gives much emphasis to its second purpose, the discussion of three principles of data collection.

These principles have been neglected in the past and are discussed at length: (a) using multiple, not just single, sources of evidence; (b) creating a case study database; and (c) maintaining a chain of evidence. The principles are extremely important for doing high-quality case studies, are relevant to all six types of sources of evidence, and should be followed whenever possible. In particular, the principles, as noted in Chapter 2 (see Figure 2.5), will help to deal with the problems of construct validity and reliability.

EXERCISE 4.1   Using Evidence

Select and obtain one of the case studies cited in the BOXES of this book. Go through the case study and identify five "facts" important to the case study. For each fact, indicate the source or sources of evidence, if any, used to define the fact. In how many instances was there more than a single source of evidence?

SIX SOURCES OF EVIDENCE

The sources of evidence discussed here are the ones most commonly used in doing case studies: documentation, archival records, interviews, direct observations, participant-observation, and physical artifacts. However, you should be aware that a complete list of sources can be quite extensive—including films, photographs, and videotapes; projective techniques and psychological testing; proxemics; kinesics; "street" ethnography; and life histories (Marshall & Rossman, 1989).

A useful overview of the six major sources considers their comparative strengths and weaknesses (see Figure 4.1). You should immediately note that no single source has a complete advantage over all the others. In fact, the various sources are highly complementary, and a good case study will therefore want to use as many sources as possible (see the later discussion in this chapter on "multiple sources of evidence").

Documentation

Except for studies of preliterate societies, documentary information is likely to be relevant to every case study topic.[1] This type of information can take many forms and should be the object of explicit data collection plans. For instance, consider the following variety of documents:

SOURCE OF EVIDENCE	Strengths	Weaknesses
Documentation	◆ Stable—can be reviewed repeatedly ◆ Unobtrusive—not created as a result of the case study ◆ Exact—contains exact names, references, and details of an event ◆ Broad coverage—long span of time, many events, and many settings	◆ Retrievability—can be difficult to find ◆ Biased selectivity, if collection is incomplete ◆ Reporting bias—reflects (unknown) bias of author ◆ Access—may be deliberately withheld
Archival records	◆ *[Same as those for documentation]* ◆ Precise and usually quantitative	◆ *[Same as those for documentation]* ◆ Accessibility due to privacy reasons
Interviews	◆ Targeted—focuses directly on case study topics ◆ Insightful—provides perceived causal inferences and explanations	◆ Bias due to poorly articulated questions ◆ Response bias ◆ Inaccuracies due to poor recall ◆ Reflexivity—interviewee gives what interviewer wants to hear
Direct observations	◆ Reality—covers events in real time ◆ Contextual—covers context of "case"	◆ Time-consuming ◆ Selectivity—broad coverage difficult without a team of observers ◆ Reflexivity—event may proceed differently because it is being observed ◆ Cost—hours needed by human observers
Participant-observation	◆ *[Same as above for direct observations]* ◆ Insightful into interpersonal behavior and motives	◆ *[Same as above for direct observations]* ◆ Bias due to participant-observer's manipulation of events
Physical artifacts	◆ Insightful into cultural features ◆ Insightful into technical operations	◆ Selectivity ◆ Availability

Figure 4.1   Six Sources of Evidence: Strengths and Weaknesses

♦ letters, memoranda, e-mail correspondence, and other personal documents, such as diaries, calendars, and notes;

♦ agendas, announcements and minutes of meetings, and other written reports of events;

♦ administrative documents—proposals, progress reports, and other internal records;

♦ formal studies or evaluations of the same "case" that you are studying; and

♦ news clippings and other articles appearing in the mass media or in community newspapers.

These and other types of documents all are increasingly available through Internet searches. The documents are useful even though they are not always accurate and may not be lacking in bias. In fact, documents must be carefully used and should not be accepted as literal recordings of events that have taken place. Few people realize, for instance, that even the "verbatim" transcripts of official U.S. Congress hearings have been deliberately edited—by the congressional staff and others who may have testified—before being printed in final form. In another field, historians working with primary documents also must be concerned with the validity of a document.

For case studies, the most important use of documents is to corroborate and augment evidence from other sources. First, documents are helpful in verifying the correct spellings and titles or names of organizations that might have been mentioned in an interview. Second, documents can provide other specific details to corroborate information from other sources. If the documentary evidence is contradictory rather than corroboratory, you need to pursue the problem by inquiring further into the topic. Third, you can make inferences from documents—for example, by observing the distribution list for a specific document, you may find new questions about communications and networking within an organization. However, you should treat inferences only as clues worthy of further investigation rather than as definitive findings because the inferences could later turn out to be false leads.

Because of their overall value, documents play an explicit role in any data collection in doing case studies. Systematic searches for relevant documents are important in any data collection plan. For example, prior to field visits, an Internet search can produce invaluable information. During field visits, you should allot time for using local libraries and other reference centers whose documents, such as back issues of periodicals, may not be available electronically. You should also arrange access to examine the files of any organizations being studied, including a review of documents that may have been put into cold storage. The scheduling of such retrieval activities is usually a flexible matter, independent of other data collection activities, and the search can usually be conducted at your convenience. For this reason, there is little excuse for omitting a thorough review of documentary evidence. Among such evidence, news accounts are excellent sources for covering certain topics, such as the two in BOXES 16 and 17.

BOX 16
Combining Personal Participation with
Extensive Newspaper Documentation

Improving educational conditions—especially for urban schools in the United States—has become one of the biggest challenges for the 21st century. How the Houston, Texas, system dealt with constrained fiscal resources, diverse student populations, and local political constituencies is the topic of an exciting and riveting case study by Donald McAdams (2000). McAdams benefits from having been a member of the system's school board for three elected, 4-year terms. He writes as a storyteller, not a social science analyst. At the same time, the book contains numerous references to local news articles to corroborate events. The result is one of the most readable but also well-documented case studies that readers will encounter.

BOX 17
Comparing Evidence from Two Archival Sources to
Cover the Same Community Events

One of the most inflammatory community events in the 1990s came to be known as the "Rodney King crisis." White police officers were serendipitously videotaped in the act of beating an African American man, but a year later, they all were acquitted of any wrongdoing. The acquittal sparked a major civil disturbance, in which 58 people were killed, 2,000 injured, and 11,000 arrested.

A case study of this crisis deliberately drew from two different newspapers—the major daily for the metropolitan area and the most significant newspaper for the area's African American community (R. N. Jacobs, 1996). For the pertinent period surrounding the crisis, the first newspaper produced 357 articles and the second (a weekly, not daily, publication) 137 articles. The case study traces the course of events and shows how the two papers constructed different understandings of the crisis, illustrating the potential biases of documentary evidence and the need to address such biases.

At the same time, many people have been critical of the potential overreliance on documents in case study research. This is probably because the casual investigator may mistakenly assume that all kinds of documents—including proposals for projects or programs—contain the unmitigated truth. In fact, important in reviewing any document is to understand that it was written for some specific purpose and some specific audience *other than* those of the case study being done. In this sense, the case study investigator is a vicarious observer, and the documentary evidence reflects a communication among other parties attempting to achieve some other objectives. By constantly trying to identify these objectives, you are less likely to be misled by documentary evidence and more likely to be correctly critical in interpreting the contents of such evidence.[2]

A newer problem has arisen because of the abundance of materials available through Internet searches. You may get lost in reviewing such materials and actually waste a lot of time on them. Note, however, that the problem is not that different from having an overabundance of numeric data about your case, as might be available from sources such as the U.S. census (also see discussion of archival records, next) if you were doing a neighborhood study. In both situations, you need to have a strong sense of your case study inquiry and focus on the most pertinent information. One suggestion is to sort or triage the materials (documents or numeric data) by their apparent centrality to your inquiry. Then, spend more time reading or reviewing what appears central, and leave aside other, less important materials for later reading or review. The procedure will not be perfect, but it will permit you to keep moving to other case study tasks.

Archival Records

For many case studies, archival records—often taking the form of computer files and records as in the U.S. census data just mentioned—also may be relevant. Examples of archival records include

- ◆ "public use files" such as the U.S. census and other statistical data made available by federal, state, and local governments;
- ◆ service records, such as those showing the number of clients served over a given period of time;
- ◆ organizational records, such as budget or personnel records;
- ◆ maps and charts of the geographical characteristics of a place; and
- ◆ survey data, such as data previously collected about a site's employees, residents, or participants.

These and other archival records can be used in conjunction with other sources of information in producing a case study. However, unlike documentary evidence, the usefulness of these archival records will vary from case study to case study. For some studies, the records can be so important that they can become the object of extensive retrieval and quantitative analysis (for example, see a multiple-case study of 20 universities, in Yin, 2003, chap. 9). In other studies, they may be of only passing relevance.

When archival evidence has been deemed relevant, an investigator must be careful to ascertain the conditions under which it was produced as well as its accuracy. Sometimes, the archival records can be highly quantitative, but numbers alone should not automatically be considered a sign of accuracy. Nearly every social scientist, for instance, is aware of the pitfalls of using the FBI's Uniform Crime Reports—or any other archival records based on crimes reported by law enforcement agencies. The same general word of caution made earlier with documentary evidence therefore also applies to archival evidence: Most archival records were produced for a specific purpose and a specific audience other than the case study investigation, and these conditions must be fully appreciated in interpreting the usefulness and accuracy of the records.

Interviews

One of the most important sources of case study information is the interview. Such an observation may be surprising because of the usual association between interviews and the survey method. However, interviews also are essential sources of case study information. The interviews will be guided conversations rather than structured queries. In other words, although you will be pursuing a consistent line of inquiry, your actual stream of questions in a case study interview is likely to be fluid rather than rigid (H. J. Rubin & Rubin, 1995).

Note that this means that, throughout the interview process, you have two jobs: (a) to follow your own line of inquiry, as reflected by your case study protocol, and (b) to ask your actual (conversational) questions in an unbiased manner that also serves the needs of your line of inquiry (see distinction between "Level 1" and "Level 2" questions in Chapter 3). For instance, you may want (in your line of inquiry) to know "why" a particular process occurred as it did. Becker (1998, pp. 58–60), however, has pointed to the important difference in actually posing a "why" question to an informant (which, in his view, creates defensiveness on the informant's part) in contrast to posing a "how" question—the latter in fact being his preferred way of addressing any "why" question in an actual conversation. Thus, case study interviews require you to operate on two levels at the same time: satisfying the needs of your line of inquiry (Level 2 questions) while simultaneously putting forth "friendly" and "nonthreatening" questions in your open-ended interviews (Level 1 questions).

One type of case study interview is an *in-depth interview*. You can ask key respondents about the facts of a matter as well as their opinions about events. In some situations, you may even ask the interviewee to propose her or his own insights into certain occurrences and may use such propositions as the basis for further inquiry. The "interview" may therefore take place over an extended period of time, not just a single sitting. The interviewee also can suggest other persons for you to interview, as well as other sources of evidence.

The more that an interviewee assists in this manner, the more that the role may be considered one of an "informant" rather than a respondent. Key informants are often critical to the success of a case study. Such persons provide the case study investigator with insights into a matter and also can initiate access to corroboratory or contrary sources of evidence. Such a person, named "Doc," played an essential role in the conduct of the famous case study presented in *Street Corner Society* (Whyte, 1943/1955; also see BOX 2A, Chapter 1, p. 7). Similar key informants have been noted in other case studies. Of course, you need to be cautious about becoming overly dependent on a key informant, especially because of the interpersonal influence—frequently subtle—that the informant may have over you. A reasonable way of dealing with this pitfall again is to rely on other sources of evidence to corroborate any insight by such informants and to search for contrary evidence as carefully as possible.

A second type of case study interview is a *focused interview* (Merton, Fiske, & Kendall, 1990), in which a person is interviewed for a short period of time— an hour, for example. In such cases, the interviews may still remain openended and assume a conversational manner, but you are more likely to be following a certain set of questions derived from the case study protocol.

For example, a major purpose of such an interview might simply be to corroborate certain facts that you already think have been established (but not to ask about other topics of a broader, open-ended nature). In this situation, the specific questions must be carefully worded, so that you appear genuinely naive about the topic and allow the interviewee to provide a fresh commentary about it; in contrast, if you ask leading questions, the corroboratory purpose of the interview will not have been served. Even so, you need to exercise caution when different interviewees appear to be echoing the same thoughts—corroborating each other but in a conspiratorial way.[3] Further probing is needed. One way is to test the sequence of events by deliberately checking with persons known to hold different perspectives. If one of the interviewees fails to comment, even though the others tend to corroborate one another's versions of what took place, the good case study investigator will even jot this down in the case study notes, citing the fact that a person was asked but declined to comment, as done in good journalistic accounts.

Yet a third type of interview entails more structured questions, along the lines of a formal *survey*. Such a survey could be designed as part of an embedded case study (see Chapter 2) and produce quantitative data as part of the case study evidence (see BOX 18). This situation would be relevant, for instance, if you were doing a case study of an urban design project and surveyed a group of designers about the project (e.g., Crewe, 2001) or if you did a case study of an organization that included a survey of workers and managers. This type of survey would follow both the sampling procedures and the instruments used in regular surveys, and it would subsequently be analyzed in a similar manner. The difference would be the survey's role in relation to other sources of evidence. For example, residents' perceptions of neighborhood decline or improvement would not necessarily be taken as a measure of actual decline or improvement but would be considered only one component of the overall assessment of the neighborhood.

BOX 18
A Case Study Encompassing a Survey

Hanna (2000) used a variety of sources of data, including a survey, to conduct a case study of an urban-rural estuarine setting. In this setting, an integrated resource management program was established to help manage environmental and economic planning issues. The case study focused on the estuarine setting, including its description and the policies and public participation that appeared to affect it. Within the case study, participants in the policy process served as an embedded unit of analysis. Hanna surveyed these individuals, and the survey data were presented with statistical tests as part of the single-case study.

Overall, interviews are an essential source of case study evidence because most case studies are about human affairs or behavioral events. Well-informed interviewees can provide important insights into such affairs or events. The interviewees also can provide shortcuts to the prior history of such situations, helping you to identify other relevant sources of evidence.

At the same time, even though your interviews may focus on behavioral events because they are the key ingredients of your case study, the interviews should always be considered *verbal reports* only. As such, even in reporting about such events or explaining how they occurred, the interviewees' responses are subject to the common problems of bias, poor recall, and poor or inaccurate articulation. Again, a reasonable approach is to corroborate interview data with information from other sources.

Sometimes, you will be interested in an interviewee's opinions or attitudes, apart from explaining behavioral events. Corroborating these opinions or attitudes against other sources would not be relevant, as in dealing with behavioral events. You still may want to get a feeling for the prevalence of the opinions or attitudes by comparing them with those of others, but the more you do this, the more you are moving toward a conventional survey and should follow survey procedures and precautions.

A common question about doing interviews is whether to record them. Using recording devices is a matter of personal preference. Audiotapes certainly provide a more accurate rendition of any interview than any other method. However, a recording device should not be used when (a) an interviewee refuses permission or appears uncomfortable in its presence, (b) there is no specific plan for transcribing or systematically listening to the contents of the electronic record—a process that takes enormous time and energy, (c) the investigator is clumsy enough with mechanical devices that the recording creates distractions during the interview itself, or (d) the investigator thinks that the recording device is a substitute for "listening" closely throughout the course of an interview.

Direct Observation

Because a case study should take place in the natural setting of the "case," you are creating the opportunity for direct observations. Assuming that the phenomena of interest have not been purely historical, some relevant behaviors or environmental conditions will be available for observation. Such observations serve as yet another source of evidence in a case study.

The observations can range from formal to casual data collection activities. Most formally, observational instruments can be developed as part of the case study protocol, and the fieldworker may be asked to assess the occurrence of certain types of behaviors during certain periods of time in the field (see the two examples in BOX 19). This can involve observations of meetings, sidewalk activities, factory work, classrooms, and the like. Less formally, direct observations might be made throughout a field visit, including those occasions during which other evidence, such as that from interviews, is being collected. For instance, the condition of buildings or work spaces will indicate something about the climate or impoverishment of an organization; similarly, the location or the furnishings of an interviewee's office may be one indicator of the status of the interviewee within an organization.

BOX 19
Using Observational Evidence

19A. Reporting Field Observations

"Clean rooms" are a key part of the manufacturing process for producing semiconductor chips. Among other features, employees wear "bunny suits" of lint-free cloth and handle extremely small components in these rooms. In their case study of high-tech working life, *Silicon Valley Fever*, Rogers and Larsen (1984) used observational evidence to show how employees adapted to the working conditions in these clean rooms, adding that, at the time, most of the employees were women while most of the supervisors were men.

19B. Combining Field Observations with Other Types of Case Study Evidence

Case studies need not be limited to a single source of evidence. In fact, most of the better case studies rely on a variety of sources.

One example of a case study that used such a variety is a book by Gross et al. (1971) covering events in a single school (also see BOX 7, Chapter 2, p. 48). The case study included an observational protocol for measuring the time that students spent on various tasks but also relied on a structured survey of a larger number of teachers, open-ended interviews with a smaller number of key persons, and a review of organizational documents. Both the observational and survey data led to quantitative information about attitudes and behavior in the school, whereas the open-ended interviews and documentary evidence led to qualitative information.

All sources of evidence were reviewed and analyzed together, so that the case study's findings were based on the convergence of information from different sources, not quantitative or qualitative data alone.

Observational evidence is often useful in providing additional information about the topic being studied. If a case study is about a new technology or a school curriculum, for instance, observations of the technology or curriculum at work are invaluable aids for understanding the actual uses of the technology or curriculum or any potential problems being encountered. Similarly, observations of a neighborhood or of an organizational unit add new dimensions for understanding either the context or the phenomenon being studied. The observations can be so valuable that you may even consider taking photographs at the case study site. At a minimum, these photographs will help to convey important case characteristics to outside observers (see Dabbs, 1982). Note, however, that in some situations—such as photographing students in public schools—you will need written permission before proceeding.

A common procedure to increase the reliability of observational evidence is to have more than a single observer making an observation—whether of the formal or the casual variety. Thus, when resources permit, a case study investigation should allow for the use of multiple observers.

Participant-Observation

Participant-observation is a special mode of observation in which you are not merely a passive observer. Instead, you may assume a variety of roles within a case study situation and may actually participate in the events being studied. In urban neighborhoods, for instance, these roles may range from having casual social interactions with various residents to undertaking specific functional activities within the neighborhood (see Yin, 1982a). The roles for different illustrative studies in neighborhoods and organizations have included

- being a resident in a neighborhood that is the subject of a case study (see BOX 20);
- taking some other functional role in a neighborhood, such as serving as a storekeeper's assistant;
- serving as a staff member in an organizational setting; and
- being a key decision maker in an organizational setting.

BOX 20
Participant-Observation in a Neighborhood
Near "Street Corner Society"

Participant-observation has been a method used frequently to study urban neighborhoods. One such study of subsequent fame was conducted by Herbert Gans, who wrote *The Urban Villagers* (1962), a study about "group and class in the life of Italian-Americans."

Gans's methodology is documented in a separate chapter of his book, titled "On the Methods Used in This Study." He notes that his evidence was based on six approaches: the use of the neighborhood's facilities, attendance at meetings, informal visiting with neighbors and friends, formal and informal interviewing, the use of informants, and direct observation. Of all these sources, the "participation role turned out to be most productive" (pp. 339–340). This role was based on Gans's being an actual resident, along with his wife, of the neighborhood he was studying. The result is a classic statement of neighborhood life undergoing urban renewal and change, and a stark contrast to the stability found in a nearby neighborhood, as covered in Whyte's (1943/1955) *Street Corner Society* some 20 years earlier (also see BOX 2A, Chapter 1, p. 7).

The participant-observation technique has been most frequently used in anthropological studies of different cultural or social groups. The technique also can be used in more everyday settings, such as a large organization (see BOX 21; also see BOX 16, earlier) or informal small groups.

BOX 21
A Participant-Observer Study in an "Everyday" Setting

Eric Redman provides an insider's account of how Congress works in his well-regarded case study, *The Dance of Legislation* (1973). The case study traces the introduction and passage of the legislation that created the National Health Service Corps during the 91st Congress in 1970.

Redman's account, from the vantage point of an author who was on the staff of one of the bill's main supporters, Senator Warren G. Magnuson, is well written and easy to read. The account also provides the reader with great insight into the daily operations of Congress—from the introduction of a bill to its eventual passage, including the politics of a lame-duck session when Richard Nixon was president.

The account is an excellent example of participant-observation in a contemporary setting. It contains information about insiders' roles that few persons have been privileged to share. The subtle legislative strategies, the overlooked role of committee clerks and lobbyists, and the interaction between the legislative and executive branches of government are all re-created by the case study, and all add to the reader's general understanding of the legislative process.

Participant-observation provides certain unusual opportunities for collecting case study data, but it also involves major problems. The most distinctive opportunity is related to your ability to gain access to events or groups that are otherwise inaccessible to a study. In other words, for some topics, there may be no way of collecting evidence other than through participant-observation. Another distinctive opportunity is the ability to perceive reality from the viewpoint of someone "inside" the case study rather than external to it. Many have argued that such a perspective is invaluable in producing an "accurate" portrayal of a case study phenomenon. Finally, other opportunities arise because you may have the ability to manipulate minor events—such as convening a meeting of a group of persons in the case. Only through participant-observation can such manipulation occur, as the use of documents, archival records, and interviews, for instance, assumes a passive investigator. The manipulations will not be as precise as those in experiments, but they can produce a greater variety of situations for the purposes of collecting data.

The major problems related to participant-observation have to do with the potential biases produced (see Becker, 1958). First, the investigator has less ability to work as an external observer and may, at times, have to assume positions or advocacy roles contrary to the interests of good social science practice. Second, the participant-observer is likely to follow a commonly known phenomenon and become a supporter of the group or organization being studied, if such support did not already exist. Third, the participant role may simply require too much attention relative to the observer role. Thus, the participant-observer may not have sufficient time to take notes or to raise questions about events from different perspectives, as a good observer might. Fourth, if the organization or social group being studied is physically dispersed, the participant-observer may find it difficult to be at the right place at the right time, either to participate in or to observe important events.

These trade-offs between the opportunities and the problems have to be considered seriously in undertaking any participant-observation study. Under some circumstances, this approach to case study evidence may be just the right approach; under other circumstances, the credibility of a whole case study project can be threatened.

Physical Artifacts

A final source of evidence is a physical or cultural artifact—a technological device, a tool or instrument, a work of art, or some other physical evidence. Such artifacts may be collected or observed as part of a case study and have been used extensively in anthropological research.

Physical artifacts have less potential relevance in the most typical kind of case study. However, when relevant, the artifacts can be an important component in the overall case. For example, one case study of the use of personal computers in the classroom needed to ascertain the nature of the actual use of the machines. Although use could be directly observed, an artifact—the computer printout—also was available. Students displayed these printouts as the finished product of their work and maintained notebooks of their printouts. Each printout showed the type of schoolwork that had been done as well as the date and amount of computer time used to do the work. By examining the printouts, the case study investigators were able to develop a broader perspective concerning all of the classroom applications over the length of a semester, far beyond that which could be directly observed in the limited time of a field visit.

Summary

This section has reviewed six commonly used sources of case study evidence. The procedures for collecting each type of evidence must be developed and mastered independently to ensure that each source is properly used. Not all sources will be relevant for all case studies. However, the trained case study investigator should be acquainted with the procedures associated with using each source of evidence—or have colleagues who have the needed expertise and who can work as members of the case study team.

EXERCISE 4.2   Identifying Specific Types of Evidence

Name a case study topic you would like to study. For some aspect of this topic, identify the specific type of evidence that would be relevant—for example, if a document, what kind of document? If an interview, what respondent and what questions? If an archival record, what records and what variables?

THREE PRINCIPLES OF DATA COLLECTION

The benefits from these six sources of evidence can be maximized if you follow three principles. These principles are relevant to all six sources and, when used properly, can help to deal with the problems of establishing the construct validity and reliability of the case study evidence. The three are as follows.

Principle 1: Use Multiple Sources of Evidence

Any of the preceding sources of evidence can and have been the sole basis for entire studies. For example, some studies have relied only on participant-observation but have not examined a single document; similarly, numerous studies have relied on archival records but have not involved a single interview.

This isolated use of sources may be a function of the independent way that sources have typically been conceived—as if an investigator should choose the single most appropriate source or the one with which she or he is most familiar. Thus, on many an occasion, investigators have announced the design of a new study by identifying both the problem to be studied and the prior selection of a *single* source of evidence—such as "interviews"—as the focus of the data collection effort.

Triangulation: Rationale for using multiple sources of evidence. The approach to individual sources of evidence as just described, however, is not recommended for conducting case studies. On the contrary, a major strength of case study data collection is the opportunity to use many different sources of evidence (see BOX 22 and BOX 19B, earlier, for examples of such studies). Furthermore, the need to use multiple sources of evidence far exceeds that in other research methods, such as experiments, surveys, or histories. Experiments, for instance, are largely limited to the measurement and recording of actual behavior in a laboratory and generally do not include the systematic use of survey or verbal information. Surveys tend to be the opposite, emphasizing verbal information but not the measurement or recording of individual behavior. Finally, histories are limited to events in the "dead" past and therefore seldom have any contemporary sources of evidence, such as direct observations of a phenomenon or interviews with key actors.

BOX 22
A Case Study Combining Personal Experience
with Extensive Field Research

Most people across the country by now have heard of Head Start. Its development and growth into one of the most successful federal programs is traced by Zigler and Muenchow (1992). Their book is exceptionally insightful, possibly because it is based on Zigler's personal experiences with the program, beginning with his role as its first director. However, the book also calls on other independent sources of evidence, with the coauthor contributing historical and field research, including interviews of more than 200 persons associated with Head Start. All of these multiple sources of evidence are integrated into a coherent if not compelling case study of Head Start. The result is a winning combination: a most readable but also well-documented book.

Of course, each of these strategies can be modified, creating hybrid strategies in which multiple sources of evidence are more likely to be relevant. An example of this is the evolution of "oral history" studies in the past several decades. Such studies involve extensive interviews with key leaders who have retired, on the stipulation that the interview information will not be reported until after the leader's death. Later, the historian will join the interview data with the more conventional array of historical evidence. Nevertheless, such a modification of the traditional methods does not alter the fact that the case study inherently deals with a wide variety of evidence, whereas the other methods do not.

The use of multiple sources of evidence in case studies allows an investigator to address a broader range of historical and behavioral issues. However, the most important advantage presented by using multiple sources of evidence is the development of *converging lines of inquiry,* a process of triangulation and corroboration emphasized repeatedly in the previous section of this chapter. Thus, any case study finding or conclusion is likely to be more convincing and accurate if it is based on several different sources of information, following a corroboratory mode (see BOX 23).

BOX 23
Triangulating from Multiple Sources of Evidence

Basu, Dirsmith, and Gupta (1999) conducted a case study of the federal government's audit agency, the U.S. Government Accountability Office. Their case was theory oriented and examined the relationship between an organization's actual work and the image it presents to external parties (the finding was that they are loosely coupled). The case study used an impressive array of sources of evidence—an extended period of field observations, with diaries; interviews of 55 persons; and reviews of historical accounts, public records, administrators' personal files, and news articles—all triangulating on the same set of research questions.

Patton (2002) discusses four types of triangulation in doing evaluations—the triangulation

1. of data sources (*data triangulation*),
2. among different evaluators (*investigator triangulation*),
3. of perspectives to the same data set (*theory triangulation*), and
4. of methods (*methodological triangulation*).

The present discussion pertains only to the first of these four types (*data triangulation*), encouraging you to collect information from multiple sources but aimed at corroborating the same fact or phenomenon. In pursuing such corroboratory strategies, Figure 4.2 distinguishes between two conditions—when you have really triangulated the data (upper portion) and when you have multiple sources as part of the same study but that nevertheless address *different* facts (lower portion). When you have really triangulated the data, the events or facts of the case study have been supported by more than a single source of evidence; when you have used multiple sources but not actually triangulated the data, you typically have analyzed each source of evidence separately and have compared the conclusions from the different analyses—but not triangulated the data.

With data triangulation, the potential problems of *construct validity* also can be addressed because the multiple sources of evidence essentially provide

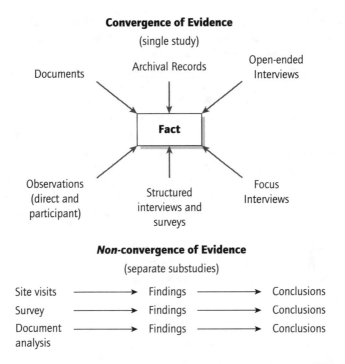

Convergence of Evidence
(single study)

Documents   Archival Records   Open-ended Interviews

Fact

Observations (direct and participant)   Structured interviews and surveys   Focus Interviews

***Non*-convergence of Evidence**
(separate substudies)

Site visits   ⟶   Findings   ⟶   Conclusions
Survey   ⟶   Findings   ⟶   Conclusions
Document analysis   ⟶   Findings   ⟶   Conclusions

Figure 4.2   Convergence and Nonconvergence of Multiple Sources of Evidence

multiple measures of the same phenomenon. Not surprisingly, one analysis of case study methods found that those case studies using multiple sources of evidence were rated more highly, in terms of their overall quality, than those that relied on only single sources of information (see COSMOS Corporation, 1983).

Prerequisites for using multiple sources of evidence. At the same time, the use of multiple sources of evidence imposes a greater burden, hinted at earlier, on yourself or any other case study investigator. First is that the collection of data from multiple sources is more expensive than if data were only collected from a single source (Denzin, 1978, p. 61). Second and more important, each investigator needs to know how to carry out the full variety of data collection techniques. For example, a case study investigator may have to collect and analyze documentary evidence as in history, to retrieve and analyze archival records as in economics or operations research, and to design and conduct surveys as in survey research. If any of these techniques is used improperly, the opportunity to address a broader array of issues, or to establish converging lines of inquiry, may be lost. This requirement for mastering multiple data collection techniques therefore raises important questions regarding the training and expertise of the case study investigator.

Unfortunately, many graduate training programs emphasize one type of data collection activity over all others, and the successful student is not likely to have a chance to master the others. To overcome such conditions, you should seek other ways of obtaining the needed training and practice. One such way is to work in a multidisciplinary research organization rather than being limited to a single academic department. Another way is to analyze the methodological writings of a variety of social scientists (see Hammond, 1968) and to learn of the strengths and weaknesses of different data collection techniques as they have been practiced by experienced scholars. Yet a third way is to design different pilot studies that will provide an opportunity for practicing different techniques.

No matter how the experience is gained, every case study investigator should be well versed in a variety of data collection techniques so that a case study can use multiple sources of evidence. Without such multiple sources, an invaluable advantage of the case study strategy will have been lost. Worse, what started out as a case study may turn into something else. For example, you might overly rely on open-ended interviews as your data, giving insufficient attention to documentary or other evidence to corroborate the interviews. If you then complete your analysis and study, you probably will have done an "interview" study, similar to surveys that are entirely based on verbal reports that come from open-ended interviews—but you would not have done a case study. In this interview study, your text would constantly have to point out the self-reported nature of your data, using such phrases as "as reported by the interviewees," "as stated in the interviews," or "she/he reported that. . . ." and the like.

EXERCISE 4.3   Seeking Converging Evidence

Name a particular incident that occurred recently in your everyday life. How would you go about establishing the "facts" of this incident, if you wanted now (in retrospect) to demonstrate what had happened? Would you interview any important persons (including yourself)? Would there have been any artifacts or documentation to rely on?

Principle 2: Create a Case Study Database

A second principle has to do with the way of organizing and documenting the data collected for case studies. Here, case studies have much to borrow from the practices followed by the other research methods defined in Chapter 1. Their documentation commonly consists of two *separate* collections:

1. the data or evidentiary base and
2. the report of the investigator, whether in article, report, or book form.

With the advent of computer files, the distinction between these two collections has been made even clearer. For example, investigators doing psychological, survey, or economic research may exchange data files and other electronic documentation that contain only the actual database—for example, behavioral responses or test scores in psychology, itemized responses to various survey questions, or economic indicators. The database then can be the subject of separate, secondary analysis, independent of any reports by the original investigator.

However, with case studies, the distinction between a separate database and the case study report has not yet become an institutionalized practice. Too often, the case study data are synonymous with the narrative presented in the case study report, and a critical reader has no recourse if he or she wants to inspect the raw data that led to the case study's conclusions. The case study report may not have presented adequate data, and without a case study database, the raw data may not be available for independent inspection. A major exception to this is where ethnographic studies have separated and stored data on their fieldwork, to make these data available to new research investigators. The practice is sufficiently important, however, that every case study project should strive to develop a formal, presentable database, so that in principle, other investigators can review the evidence directly and not be limited to the written case study reports. In this manner, a case study database markedly increases the *reliability* of the entire case study.

The lack of a formal database for most case studies is a major shortcoming of case study research and needs to be corrected. There are numerous ways of accomplishing the task, as long as you and other investigators are aware of the need and are willing to commit the additional effort required to build the database. At the same time, the existence of an adequate database does not preclude the need to present sufficient evidence within the case study report itself (to be discussed further in Chapter 6). Every report should still contain enough data so that the reader of the report can draw independent conclusions about the case study.

Nevertheless, the problem of initially establishing a case study database has not been recognized by most of the books on field methods. Thus, the subsections below represent an extension of the current state of the art. The problem of developing the database is described in terms of four components: notes, documents, tabular materials, and narratives.

Case study notes. For case studies, your own notes are likely to be the most common component of a database. These notes take a variety of forms. The notes may be a result of your interviews, observations, or document analysis. The notes may be handwritten, typed, on audiotapes, or in word-processing or other electronic files, and they may be assembled in the form of a diary, on index cards, or in some less organized fashion.

Regardless of their form or content, these case study notes must be stored in such a manner that other persons, yourself included, can retrieve them efficiently at some later date. Most commonly, the notes can be organized according to the major subjects—as outlined in the case study protocol—covered by a case study; however, any classificatory system will do, as long as the system is usable by an outside party. Only in this manner will the notes be available as part of the case study database.

This identification of the notes as part of the case study database does not mean, however, that you need to spend excessive amounts of time in rewriting interviews or making extensive editorial changes to make the notes presentable. Building such a formal case record, by editing and rewriting the notes, may be a misplaced priority. Any such editing should be directed at the case study report itself, not at the notes. The only essential characteristics of the notes are that they be organized, categorized, complete, and available for later access.

Case study documents. Many documents relevant to a case study will be collected during the course of a study. Chapter 3 indicated that the disposition of these documents should be covered in the case study protocol and suggested that one helpful way is to have an annotated bibliography of these documents. Such annotations would again facilitate storage and retrieval, so that later investigators can inspect or share the database.

The single, unique characteristic of these documents is that they are likely to require a large amount of physical storage space, unless you trouble to make portable document format (PDF) copies and store them electronically. In addition, the documents may be of varying importance to the database, and you may want to establish a primary file and a secondary file for such documents. The main objective, again, is to make the documents readily retrievable for later inspection or perusal. In those instances in which the documents have been relevant to specific interviews, one additional cross-reference is to have the interview notes cite the documents.

Tabular materials. The database may consist of tabular materials, either collected from the site being studied or created by the research team. Such materials also need to be organized and stored to allow for later retrieval.

The materials may include survey and other quantitative data. For example, a survey may have been conducted at one or more of the case study sites as part of an embedded case study. In such situations, the tabular materials may be stored in computer files. As another example, in dealing with archival or observational evidence, a case study may have called for "counts" of various phenomena (see Miles & Huberman, 1994). The documentation of these counts, done by the case study team, also should be organized and stored as part of the database. In brief, any tabular materials, whether based on surveys, observational counts, or archival data, can be treated in a manner similar to the way they are handled when using other research methods.

Narratives. Certain types of narrative, produced by a case study investigator upon completion of all data collection, also may be considered a formal part of the database and not part of the final case study report. The narrative reflects a special practice that should be used more frequently: to have case study investigators compose *open-ended answers to the questions in the case study protocol.* This practice has been used on several occasions in multiple-case studies designed by the author (see BOX 24).

BOX 24
Narratives in the Case Study Database

A series of 12 case studies was done on personal computer use in schools (Yin, 2003, chap. 3). Each case study was based on open-ended answers to about 50 protocol questions concerning matters such as the number and location of the personal computers (an inventory question requiring tabular and narrative responses), the relationship between the computer units and other computational systems within a school district, and the training and coordination provided by the district.

After data collection has finished, the case study investigator's first responsibility was to answer these 50 questions as completely as possible, citing specific sources of evidence in footnotes. These answers were unedited but served as the basis for both the individual case reports and the cross-case analysis. The availability of the database meant that other members of the case study team could determine the events at each site, even before the case study reports were completed.

In such a situation, each answer represents your attempt to integrate the available evidence and to converge upon the facts of the matter or their tentative interpretation. The process is actually an analytic one and is the start of the case study analysis. The format for the answers may be considered analogous to that of a comprehensive "take-home" exam, used in academic courses. You the investigator are the respondent, and your goal is to cite the relevant evidence—whether from interviews, documents, observations, or archival evidence—in composing an adequate answer. The main purpose of the open-ended answer is to document the connection between specific pieces of evidence and various issues in the case study, generously using footnotes and citations.

The entire set of answers can be considered part of the case study database. You, along with any other interested party, can then use this database to compose the actual case study report. Or, if no reports are composed concerning the individual cases (see Chapter 6 for such situations), the answers can serve as the database for the subsequent cross-case analysis. Again, because the answers are part of the database and not of the final report, you should not spend much time trying to make the answers presentable. In other words, you need not perform the standard editing and copyediting chores. (However, for an example of a case study that was written entirely in the form of narrative answers to the protocol questions and in which such editing was done, see Yin 2003, chap. 2.) The most important attribute of good answers is that they indeed connect the pertinent issues—through adequate citations—to specific evidence.

> **EXERCISE 4.4   Practicing the Development of a Database**
>
> For the topic you covered in Exercise 4.3, write a short report (no more than two double-spaced pages) that adheres to the following outline: Start the report by stating a major question you were attempting to answer (about the facts of the incident recalled from your everyday life). Now provide the answer, citing the evidence you had used (your format should include formal citations and footnotes). Repeat the procedure for another research question (or the questions from your hypothetical case study protocol). Envisage how this question-and-answer sequence might be one of many in your total case study "database."

Principle 3: Maintain a Chain of Evidence

Another principle to be followed, to increase the *reliability* of the information in a case study, is to maintain a chain of evidence. Such a principle is based on a notion similar to that used in forensic investigations.

The principle is to allow an external observer—in this situation, the reader of the case study—to follow the derivation of any evidence from initial research questions to ultimate case study conclusions (see Figure 4.3). Moreover, this external observer should be able to trace the steps in either direction (from conclusions back to initial research questions or from questions to conclusions). As with criminological evidence, the process should be tight enough that evidence presented in "court"—the case study report—is assuredly the same evidence that was collected at the scene of the "crime" during the data collection process.

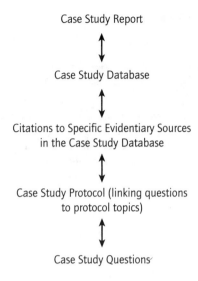

Case Study Report

Case Study Database

Citations to Specific Evidentiary Sources
in the Case Study Database

Case Study Protocol (linking questions
to protocol topics)

Case Study Questions

Figure 4.3   Maintaining a Chain of Evidence

Conversely, no original evidence should have been lost, through carelessness or bias, and therefore fail to receive appropriate attention in considering the "facts" of a case. If these objectives are achieved, a case study also will have addressed the methodological problem of determining construct validity, thereby increasing the overall quality of the case study.

Imagine the following scenario. You have read the conclusions in a case study report and want to know more about the basis for the conclusions. You therefore want to trace the evidentiary process backward.

First, the report itself should have made sufficient citation to the relevant portions of the case study database—for example, by citing specific documents, interviews, or observations. Second, the database, upon inspection, should reveal the actual evidence and also indicate the circumstances under which the evidence was collected—for example, the time and place of an interview. Third, these circumstances should be consistent with the specific procedures and questions contained in the case study protocol, to show that the data collection had followed the procedures stipulated by the protocol. Finally, a reading of the protocol should indicate the link between the content of the protocol and the initial study questions.

In the aggregate, you have therefore been able to move from one part of the case study process to another, with clear cross-referencing to methodological procedures and to the resulting evidence. This is the ultimate "chain of evidence" that is desired.

EXERCISE 4.5   Establishing a Chain of Evidence

State a hypothetical conclusion that might emerge from a case study you are going to do. Now work backward and identify the specific data or evidence that would have supported such a conclusion. Similarly, work backward and define the protocol question that would have led to the collection of this evidence, and then the study question that in turn would have led to the design of the protocol question. Do you understand how this chain of evidence has been formed and how one can move forward or backward in tracing the chain?

SUMMARY

This chapter has reviewed six sources of case study evidence, how evidence can be collected from these sources, and three important principles regarding the data collection process.

The data collection process for case studies is more complex than those used in other research methods. A case study investigator must have a methodological versatility not necessarily required for using other methods and must follow certain formal procedures to ensure *quality control* during the data collection process. The three principles described above are steps in this direction. They are not intended to straitjacket the inventive and insightful investigator. They are intended to make the process as explicit as possible, so that the final results—the data that have been collected—reflect a concern for construct validity and for reliability, thereby becoming worthy of further analysis. How such analysis can be carried out is the subject of the next chapter.

NOTES

1. Limited availability of print materials in low-income communities in the United States—even including signage and materials in schools and public libraries—has been the subject of study (Neuman & Celano, 2001). To the extent of such impoverishment, researchers studying such neighborhoods and their community organizations (or schools) may find the use of documentary sources of evidence also limited.

2. Excellent suggestions regarding the ways of verifying documentary evidence, including the nontrivial problem of determining the actual author of a document, are offered by Barzun and Graff (1985, pp. 109–133). An exemplary quantitative study of the authorship problem is found in Mosteller and Wallace (1984).

3. Such consistent responses are likely to occur when interviewing members of a "closed" institution, such as the residents of a drug treatment program or the teachers in a closely knit school. The apparent conspiracy arises because those being interviewed all are aware of the "socially desirable" responses and appear to be providing corroboratory evidence when in fact they are merely repeating their institution's mantra.

REFERENCE TO EXPANDED CASE STUDY MATERIALS FOR CHAPTER 4

For selected case studies cited in the text of this chapter, two anthologies contain either a more extensive excerpt or the full case study. The table below crosswalks the reference in this book to the location of the excerpt or full rendition.

Chapter 4 Chapter Topic and Page Number	Topics of Illustrative Case Studies	Reference to Lengthier Material
Six Sources of Evidence		
BOX 16, p. 4-7	Schools	CSA-19
BOX 17, p. 4-7	Cities and towns	CSA-13
p. 4-8 text	University administration	ACSR-9
BOX 18, p. 4-12	Urban planning	None
BOX 19A, p. 4-14	Computers and technology	CSA-12
BOX 19B, p. 4-14	Schools	CSA-9
BOX 20, p. 4-15	Neighborhoods	None
BOX 21, p. 4-16	Government agencies	None
Three Principles of Data Collection		
BOX 22, p. 4-20	Health care	CSA-15
BOX 23, p. 4-20	Government agencies	None
BOX 24, p. 4-27	Computers in schools	ACSR-3
p. 4-28 text	Neighborhoods	ACSR-2

NOTE: CSA = *Case Study Anthology* (Yin, 2004). ACSR = *Applications of Case Study Research* (Yin, 2003). The number denotes the chapter number in the book.

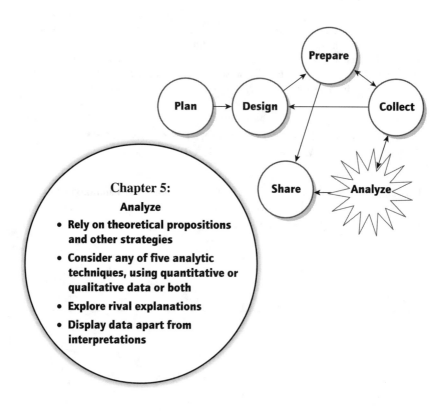

Chapter 5:

Analyze

- **Rely on theoretical propositions and other strategies**
- **Consider any of five analytic techniques, using quantitative or qualitative data or both**
- **Explore rival explanations**
- **Display data apart from interpretations**

ABSTRACT

Data analysis consists of examining, categorizing, tabulating, testing, or otherwise recombining evidence, to draw empirically based conclusions. Analyzing case study evidence is especially difficult because the techniques still have not been well defined. To overcome this circumstance, every case study analysis should follow a general analytic strategy, defining priorities for what to analyze and why. Four strategies are relying on theoretical propositions, developing case descriptions, using both quantitative and qualitative data, and examining rival explanations. Using various computer aids to manipulate your data will not substitute for the absence of a general analytic strategy.

Any of these strategies can be used in practicing five specific techniques for analyzing case studies: pattern matching, explanation building, time-series analysis, logic models, and cross-case synthesis. With appropriately fine-grained data, the analyses can incorporate statistical models, such as regression or structural equation models. Throughout, a persistent challenge is to produce high-quality analyses, which require attending to *all* the evidence collected, displaying and presenting the evidence separate from any interpretation, and considering alternative interpretations.

5

Analyzing Case Study Evidence

How to Start Your Analysis, Your Analytic Choices, and How They Work

AN ANALYTIC STRATEGY: MORE THAN FAMILIARITY WITH ANALYTIC TOOLS

Need for an Analytic Strategy

Introduction. The analysis of case study evidence is one of the least developed and most difficult aspects of doing case studies. Too many times, investigators start case studies without having the foggiest notion about how the evidence is to be analyzed (despite Chapter 3's recommendation that the analytic approaches be considered when developing the case study protocol). Such investigations easily become stalled at the analytic stage; this author has known colleagues who have simply ignored their case study data for month after month, not knowing what to do with the evidence.

Because of the problem, the experienced case study investigator is likely to have great advantages over the novice at the analytic stage. Unlike statistical analysis, there are few fixed formulas or cookbook recipes to guide the novice. Instead, much depends on an investigator's own style of rigorous empirical thinking, along with the sufficient presentation of evidence and careful consideration of alternative interpretations.

Investigators and especially novices do continue to search for formulas, recipes, or tools, hoping that familiarity with these devices will produce the needed analytic result. The tools are important and can be useful, but they are usually most helpful if you know what to look for (i.e., have an overall analytic strategy), which unfortunately returns you back to your original problem, if you hadn't noticed.

Computer-assisted tools. For instance, computer-assisted routines with prepackaged software such as Atlas.ti, HyperRESEARCH, NVivo, or The Ethnograph

Tip: *How do I start analyzing my case study data?*

You might start with questions (e.g., the questions in your case study protocol) rather than with the data. Start with a small question first, then identify your evidence that addresses the question. Draw a tentative conclusion based on the weight of the evidence, also asking how you should display the evidence so that readers can check your assessment. Continue to a larger question and repeat the procedure. Keep going until you think you have addressed your main research question(s).

Could you have started with the data instead of the questions?

all are examples of *c*omputer-*a*ssisted *q*ualitative *d*ata *a*nalysis *s*oftware (CAQDAS—e.g., Fielding & Lee, 1998). The software has become more diverse and functional over the past decade. Essentially, the tools can help you code and categorize large amounts of narrative text, as might have been collected from open-ended interviews or from large volumes of written materials, such as newspaper articles. Guidance on coding skills and techniques also has improved (e.g., Boyatzis, 1998).

Key to your understanding of the value of these packages are two words: *assisted* and *tools*. The software will not do any analysis for you, but it may serve as an able assistant and reliable tool. For instance, if you enter your textual data and then define an initial set of codes, one or another of the various software packages will readily locate in the textual data all words and phrases matching these codes, count the incidence or occurrence of the words or codes, and even conduct Boolean searches to show when and where multiple combinations are found together. You can do this process iteratively, gradually building more complex categories or groups of codes. However, unlike statistical analyses, you cannot use the software's outputs themselves as if they were the end of your analysis.

Instead, you will need to study the outputs to determine whether any meaningful patterns are emerging. Quite likely, any patterns—such as the frequency of codes or code combinations—will still be conceptually more primitive (lower) than the initial "how" and "why" research questions that might have led to your case study in the first place. In other words, developing a rich and full explanation or even a good description of your case, in response to your initial "how" or "why" questions, will require much post-computer thinking and analysis on your part.

Backtracking, you also will need to have clarified the reasons for defining the initial codes or subsequent codes, as well as connecting them to your original research design (you, not the software, created them). In what ways do the codes or concepts accurately reflect the meaning of the retrieved words and phrases, and why? Answering these questions requires your own analytic rationale.

Under some circumstances, the computerized functions can nevertheless be extremely helpful. The minimal conditions include when (a) the words or verbal reports represent verbatim records and are the central part of your case study evidence and (b) you have a large collection of such data. Such conditions commonly occur in research using *grounded theory* strategies (e.g., Corbin & Strauss, 2007), where the surfacing of a new concept or theme can be highly valuable. However, even under the best of circumstances, nearly all scholars express strong caveats about any use of computer-assisted tools: You must still be prepared to be the main analyst and to direct the tools; they are the assistant, not you.

Most case studies pose a more serious challenge in efforts to use computer-assisted tools: Verbatim records such as interviewees' responses are likely to be only part of the total array of case study evidence. The case study will typically be about complex events and behavior, occurring within a possibly more complex, real-life context. Unless you convert all of your evidence—including your field notes and the archival documents you might have collected—into the needed textual form, computerized tools cannot readily handle this more diverse array of evidence. Yet, as emphasized in Chapter 4, such an array should represent an important strength of your case study. For a diverse set of evidence, you therefore need to develop your own analytic strategies.

A helpful starting point is to "play" with your data. One set of analytic manipulations has been comprehensively described and summarized by Miles and Huberman (1994) and includes

- ♦ Putting information into different arrays
- ♦ Making a matrix of categories and placing the evidence within such categories
- ♦ Creating data displays—flowcharts and other graphics—for examining the data
- ♦ Tabulating the frequency of different events
- ♦ Examining the complexity of such tabulations and their relationships by calculating second-order numbers such as means and variances
- ♦ Putting information in chronological order or using some other temporal scheme

These are indeed useful and important manipulations and can put the evidence in some preliminary order. Moreover, conducting such manipulations is one way of overcoming the stalling problem mentioned earlier. Without a broader strategy, however, you are still likely to encounter many false starts and potentially waste large chunks of your time. Furthermore, if after playing with the data, a general strategy does not emerge (or if you are not facile in playing with the data to begin with), the entire case study analysis is likely to be in jeopardy.

Any preliminary manipulations, such as the preceding, or any use of computer-assisted tools therefore cannot substitute for having a general analytic strategy in the first place. Put another way, all empirical research studies, including case studies, have a "story" to tell. The story differs from a fictional account because it embraces your data, but it remains a story because it must have a beginning, end, and middle. The needed analytic strategy is your guide to crafting this story, and only rarely will your data do the crafting for you.

Once you have a strategy, the tools may turn out to be extremely useful (or irrelevant). The strategy will help you to treat the evidence fairly, produce compelling analytic conclusions, and rule out alternative interpretations. The strategy also will help you to use tools and make manipulations more effectively and efficiently. Four such strategies are described below, after which five specific techniques for analyzing case study data are reviewed. These strategies or techniques are not mutually exclusive. You can use any number of them in any combination. A continued alert is to be aware of these choices *before* collecting your data, so that you can be sure your data will be analyzable.

Four General Strategies

Relying on theoretical propositions. The first and most preferred strategy is to follow the theoretical propositions that led to your case study. The original objectives and design of the case study presumably were based on such propositions, which in turn reflected a set of research questions, reviews of the literature, and new hypotheses or propositions.

The propositions would have shaped your data collection plan and therefore would have given priorities to the relevant analytic strategies. One example, from a study of intergovernmental relationships, followed the proposition that federal funds have redistributive dollar effects but also create new organizational changes at the local level (Yin, 1980). The basic proposition—the creation of a "counterpart bureaucracy" in the form of local planning organizations, citizen action groups, and other new offices within a local government itself, but all attuned to specific federal programs—was traced in case studies of several cities. For each city, the purpose of the case study was to show how the formation and modification in local organizations occurred *after* changes in related federal programs and how these local organizations acted on behalf of the federal programs even though they might have been components of local government.

This proposition is an example of a theoretical orientation guiding the case study analysis. Clearly, the proposition helps to focus attention on certain data and to ignore other data. (A good test is to decide what data you might cite if you had only 5 minutes to defend a proposition in your case study.) The proposition also helps to organize the entire case study and to define alternative explanations to be examined. Theoretical propositions stemming from "how" and "why" questions can be extremely useful in guiding case study analysis in this manner.

Developing a case description. A second general analytic strategy is to develop a descriptive framework for organizing the case study. This strategy is less preferable than relying on theoretical propositions but serves as an alternative when you are having difficulty making the first strategy work. For instance, you actually (but undesirably) may have collected a lot of data without having settled on an initial set of research questions or propositions. Studies started this way inevitably encounter challenges at their analytic phase.

Sometimes, the original and explicit purpose of the case study may have been a descriptive one. This was the objective of the famous sociological study *Middletown* (Lynd & Lynd, 1929), which was a case study of a small midwestern city. What is interesting about *Middletown,* aside from its classic value as a rich and historic case, is its compositional structure, reflected by its chapters:

- Chapter I: Getting a Living
- Chapter II: Making a Home
- Chapter III: Training the Young
- Chapter IV: Using Leisure
- Chapter V: Engaging in Religious Practices
- Chapter VI: Engaging in Community Activities

These chapters cover a range of topics relevant to community life in the early 20th century, when Middletown was studied. Note how the descriptive framework organizes the case study analysis but also assumes that data were collected about each topic in the first place. In this sense, you should have thought (at least a little) about your descriptive framework before designing your data collection instruments. As usual, the ideas for your framework should have come from your initial review of literature, which may have revealed gaps or topics of interest to you, spurring your interest in doing a case study. Another suggestion is to note the structure of existing case studies (e.g., by examining the original versions of those cited in the BOXES throughout this book) and at least to observe their tables of contents as an implicit clue to different descriptive approaches.

In other situations, the original objective of the case study may not have been a descriptive one, but a descriptive approach may help to identify the appropriate causal links to be analyzed—even quantitatively. BOX 25 gives an example of a case study that was concerned with the complexity of implementing a local public works program in Oakland, California. Such complexity, the investigators realized, could be *described* in terms of the multiplicity of decisions, by public officials, that had to occur in order for implementation to succeed. This descriptive insight later led to the enumeration, tabulation, and hence quantification of the various decisions. In this sense, the descriptive approach was used to identify (a) an embedded unit of analysis (see Chapter 2) and (b) an overall pattern of complexity that ultimately was used in a causal sense to "explain" why implementation had failed.

BOX 25
Quantifying the Descriptive Elements of a Case Study

Pressman and Wildavsky's (1973) book, *Implementation: How Great Expectations in Washington Are Dashed in Oakland,* is regarded as one of the breakthrough contributions to the study of implementation (Yin, 1982b). This is the process whereby some programmatic activity—an economic development project, a new curriculum in a school, or a crime prevention program, for example—is installed in a specific setting (e.g., organization or community). The process is complex and involves numerous individuals, organizational rules, social norms, and mixtures of good and bad intentions.

Can such a complex process also be the subject of quantitative inquiry and analysis? Pressman and Wildavsky (1973) offer one innovative solution. To the extent that successful implementation can be *described* as a sequence of decisions, an analyst can focus part of the case study on the number and types of such decisions or elements.

Thus, in their chapter titled "The Complexity of Joint Action," the authors analyze the difficulties in Oakland: To implement one public works program required a total of 70 sequential decisions—project approvals, negotiation of leases, letting of contracts, and so on. The analysis examined the level of agreement and the time needed to reach agreement at each of the 70 decision points. Given the normal diversity of opinion and slippage in time, the analysis illustrates—in a quantitative manner—the low probability of implementation success.

Using both qualitative and quantitative data. This third strategy may be more attractive to advanced students and scholars and can yield appreciable benefits. Certain case studies can include substantial amounts of quantitative data. If these data are subjected to statistical analyses at the same time that qualitative data nevertheless remain central to the entire case study, you will have successfully followed a strong analytic strategy.

The quantitative data may have been relevant to your case study for at least two reasons. First, the data may cover the behavior or events that your case study is trying to explain—typically, the "outcomes" in an evaluative case study. Second, the data may be related to an embedded unit of analysis within your broader case study. In either situation, the qualitative data may be critical in explaining or otherwise testing your case study's key propositions. So, imagine a case study about a school, a neighborhood, an organization, a community, a medical practice, or some other common case study topic. For these topics, the outcomes of an evaluative case study might be, respectively, student achievement (for the case study about the school), housing prices (for the neighborhood), employees' salaries (for the organization), various crime rates (for the community), or the course of an illness (for the medical practice). Alternatively, the embedded units might be students (or teachers), census blocks (or single-family housing), employees (for the organization), persons arrested (for the community), or patients (for the medical practice).

All of the illustrative outcomes or embedded units can be the occasion for having collected fine-grained quantitative data. Yet, the main case study questions might have been at a higher level: a single school (not its students), the neighborhood (not its housing units), a business firm (not its employees), a community (not its residents), or a new medical practice (not the patients). To explore, describe, or explain events at this higher level, you would have collected and used qualitative data. Thus, your case study would have deliberately used both qualitative and quantitative data.

If you attempt this third strategy, be prepared for the skills you will need. Beyond knowing how to do the case study well, you may have to master certain statistical techniques. Mentioned later in this chapter (but only in passing) are regression discontinuity analyses, hierarchical linear models, and structural equation models. Do you believe that any of them can be part of a case study analysis?

EXERCISE 5.1   Using Quantitative Data in a Case Study

Select one of your own empirical studies—but *not* a case study—in which you analyzed some quantitative data (or choose such a study from the literature). Describe how the data were analyzed in this study. Argue whether this same analysis, virtually in its same form, could be found as one part of a fuller case study analysis. Do you think that quantitative data are less relevant to case studies than qualitative data?

Examining rival explanations. A fourth general analytic strategy, trying to define and test rival explanations, generally works with all of the previous three: Initial theoretical propositions (the first strategy above) might have included rival hypotheses; the contrasting perspectives of participants and stakeholders may produce rival descriptive frameworks (the second strategy); and data from comparison groups may cover rival conditions to be examined as part of using both quantitative and qualitative data (the third strategy).

For instance, the typical hypothesis in an evaluation is that the observed outcomes were the result of an intervention supported by public or foundation funds. The simple or direct rival explanation would be that the observed outcomes were in fact the result of some other influence besides the intervention and that the investment of funds may not actually have been needed. Being aware (ahead of time) of this direct rival, your case study data collection should then have included attempts to collect evidence about the possible "other influences." Furthermore, you should have pursued your data collection about them vigorously—as if you were in fact trying to prove the potency of the other influences rather than rejecting them (Patton, 2002, p. 553; P. R. Rosenbaum, 2002, pp. 8–10). Then, if you had found insufficient evidence, you would less likely be accused of stacking the deck in favor of the original hypothesis.

The direct rival—that the original investment was not the reason for the observed outcomes—is but one of several types of rival explanations. Figure 5.1 classifies and lists many types of rivals (Yin, 2000). For each type, an informal and more understandable descriptor (in the parentheses and quotation marks in Figure 5.1) accompanies the formal social science categorization, making the gist of the rival thinking clearer.

The list reminds us of three "craft" rivals that underlie all of our social science research, and textbooks have given much attention to these craft rivals. However, the list also defines six "real-life" rivals, which have received virtually no attention by other textbooks (nor, unfortunately, do most texts discuss the challenges and benefits of rival thinking or the use of rival explanations). These real-life rivals are the ones that you should carefully identify prior to your data collection (while not ignoring the craft rivals). Some real-life rivals also may not become apparent until you are in the midst of your data collection, and attending to them at that point is acceptable and desirable. Overall, the more rivals that your analysis addresses and rejects, the more confidence you can place in your findings.

Rival explanations were a critical part of several of the case studies already contained in the BOXES cited earlier (e.g., refer to BOXES 1 and 11 in Chapters 1 and 2, respectively). The authors of these case studies used the rivals to drive their entire case study analysis. Additional examples—covering cases of university innovation and of drug abuse prevention but deliberately

TYPE OF RIVAL	Description or Examples
Craft Rivals:	
1. The Null Hypothesis	The observation is the result of chance circumstances only
2. Threats to Validity	e.g., history, maturation, instability, testing, instrumentation, regression, selection, experimental mortality, and selection-maturation interaction
3. Investigator Bias	e.g., "experimenter effect"; reactivity in field research
Real-Life Rivals:	
4. Direct Rival (Practice or Policy)	An intervention ("suspect 2") other than the target intervention ("suspect 1") accounts for the results (*"the butler did it"*)
5. Commingled Rival (Practice or Policy)	Other interventions and the target intervention both contributed to the results (*"it wasn't only me"*)
6. Implementation Rival	The implementation process, not the substantive intervention, accounts for the results (*"did we do it right?"*)
7. Rival Theory	A theory different from the original theory explains the results better (*"it's elementary, my dear Watson"*)
8. Super Rival	A force larger than but including the intervention accounts for the results (*"it's bigger than both of us"*)
9. Societal Rival	Social trends, not any particular force or intervention, account for the results (*"the times they are a-changin'"*)

Figure 5.1   Brief Descriptions of Different Kinds of Rival Explanations

SOURCE: Yin (2000).

focusing on the essence of the evidence about rival explanations—are found in Yin (2003, chaps. 4 and 5).

Summary. The best preparation for conducting case study analysis is to have a general analytic strategy. Four have been described, relying on theoretical propositions, case descriptions, a dual use of both quantitative and qualitative data, and rival explanations. All four strategies underlie the analytic techniques to be described below. Without such strategies (or alternatives to them), case study analysis will proceed with difficulty.

The remainder of this chapter covers the specific analytic techniques, to be used as part of and along with any of the general strategies. The techniques are especially intended to deal with the previously noted problems of developing *internal validity* and *external validity* in doing case studies (see Chapter 2).

EXERCISE 5.2   Creating a General Analytic Strategy

Assume that you have begun analyzing your case study data but still do not have an overall analytic strategy. Instead of staying stalled at this analytic step, move to the next step and speculate how you might organize your (later) case study report into separate chapters or sections. Within each chapter or section, create substantive titles and headings (e.g., instead of "introduction," make the title say what the introduction is about, even if more than a few words are needed). Try different sequences of titles and headings, noting how such differences might dictate the creation of different analytic strategies. Now choose one sequence and start sorting your data into the designated chapters or sections. You should be on your way to analyzing your case study data.

FIVE ANALYTIC TECHNIQUES

None of the analytic techniques should be considered easy to use, and all will need much practice to be used powerfully. Your objective should be to start modestly, work thoroughly and introspectively, and build your own analytic repertoire over time. The reward will eventually emerge in the form of compelling case study analyses and, ultimately, compelling case studies.

Pattern Matching

For case study analysis, one of the most desirable techniques is to use a pattern-matching logic. Such a logic (Trochim, 1989) compares an empirically based pattern with a predicted one (or with several alternative predictions). If the patterns coincide, the results can help a case study to strengthen its *internal validity.*

If the case study is an explanatory one, the patterns may be related to the dependent or the independent variables of the study (or both). If the case study is a descriptive one, pattern matching is still relevant, as long as the predicted pattern of specific variables is defined prior to data collection.

Nonequivalent dependent variables as a pattern. The dependent-variables pattern may be derived from one of the more potent quasi-experimental research designs, labeled a "nonequivalent, dependent variables design" (Cook & Campbell, 1979, p. 118). According to this design, an experiment or quasi-experiment may have multiple dependent variables—that is, a variety of relevant outcomes. For instance, in quantitative health studies, some outcomes may have been predicted to be affected by a treatment, whereas other outcomes may have been predicted *not* to be affected (Rosenbaum, 2002, pp. 210–211). For these studies as well as a case study, the pattern matching occurs in the following manner: If, for each outcome, the initially predicted values have been found, and at the same time alternative "patterns" of predicted values (including those deriving from methodological artifacts, or "threats" to validity) have not been found, strong causal inferences can be made.

For example, consider a single case in which you are studying the effects of a newly decentralized office computer system. Your major proposition is that—because each peripheral piece of equipment can work independently of any server—a certain pattern of organizational changes and stresses will be produced. Among these changes and stresses, you specify the following, based on propositions derived from previous decentralization theory:

♦ employees will create *new applications* for the office system, and these applications will be idiosyncratic to each employee;

♦ traditional *supervisory links* will be threatened, as management control over work tasks and the use of central sources of information will be diminished;

♦ *organizational conflicts* will increase, due to the need to coordinate resources and services across the decentralized units; but nevertheless,

♦ *productivity* will increase over the levels prior to the installation of the new system.

In this example, these four outcomes each represent different dependent variables, and you would assess each with different measures. To this extent, you have a study that has specified *nonequivalent* dependent variables. You also have predicted an overall pattern of outcomes covering each of these variables. If the results are as predicted, you can draw a solid conclusion about the effects of decentralization. However, if the results fail to show the entire pattern as predicted—that is, even if one variable does not behave as predicted—your initial proposition would have to be questioned (see BOX 26 for another example).

BOX 26
Pattern Matching on Each of Multiple Outcomes

Researchers and politicians alike recognize that U.S. military bases, located across the country, contribute significantly to a local economy's housing, employment, and other markets. When such bases close, a corresponding belief is that the community will suffer in some catastrophic (both economic and social) manner.

To test the latter proposition, Bradshaw (1999) conducted a case study of a closure that had occurred in a modestly sized California community. He first identified a series of sectors (e.g., housing sales, civilian employment, unemployment, population turnover and stability, and retail markets) where catastrophic outcomes might have been feared, and he then collected data about each sector before and after the base closure. A pattern-matching procedure, examining the pre-post patterns of outcomes in every sector and also in comparison to other communities and statewide trends, showed that the outcomes were much less severe than anticipated. Some sectors did not even show any decline. Bradshaw also presented evidence to explain the pattern of outcomes, thereby producing a compelling argument for his conclusions.

This first case could then be augmented by a second one, in which another new office system had been installed, but of a centralized nature—that is, the equipment at all of the individual workstations had been networked. Now you would predict a different pattern of outcomes, using the same four dependent variables enumerated above. And now, if the results show that the decentralized system (Case A) had actually produced the predicted pattern and that this first pattern was different from that predicted and produced by the centralized system (Case B), you would be able to draw an even stronger conclusion about the effects of decentralization. In this situation, you have made a *theoretical replication* across cases. (In other situations, you might have sought a *literal replication* by identifying and studying two or more cases of decentralized systems.)

Finally, you might be aware of the existence of certain threats to the validity of this logic (see Cook & Campbell, 1979, for a full list of these threats). For example, a new corporate executive might have assumed office in Case A, leaving room for a counterargument: that the apparent effects of decentralization were actually attributable to this executive's appointment and not to the newly installed office system. To deal with this threat, you would have to identify some subset of the initial dependent variables and show that the pattern would have been different (in Case A) if the corporate executive had been the actual reason for the effects. If you only had a single-case study, this type of procedure would be essential; you would be using the same data to rule out arguments based on a potential threat to validity. Given the existence of a second case, as in our hypothetical example, you also could show that the argument about the corporate executive would not explain certain parts of the pattern found in Case B (in which the absence of the corporate executive should have been associated with certain opposing outcomes). In essence, your goal is to identify all reasonable threats to validity and to conduct repeated comparisons, showing how such threats cannot account for the dual patterns in both of the hypothetical cases.

Rival explanations as patterns. The use of rival explanations, besides being a good general analytic strategy, also provides a good example of pattern matching for *in*dependent variables. In such a situation (for an example, see BOX 27), several cases may be known to have had a certain type of outcome, and your investigation has focused on how and why this outcome occurred in each case.

BOX 27
Pattern Matching for Rival Explanations and
Replicating across Multiple Cases

A common policy problem is to understand the conditions under which new research findings can be made useful to society. This topic was the subject of a multiple-case study (Yin, 2003, chap. 1, pp. 20–22). For nine different cases, the investigators first provided definitive evidence that important research findings had indeed been put into practical use in every case.

The main research inquiry then dealt with "how" and "why" such outcomes had occurred. The investigators compared three theories ("rivals") from the prevailing literature, that (a) researchers select their own topics to study and then successfully disseminate their findings to the practical world (technology "push"), (b) the practical world identifies problems that attract researchers' attention and that then leads to successful problem solving (demand "pull"), and (c) researchers and practitioners work together, customizing an elongated process of problem identification and solution testing ("social interaction"). Each theory predicts a different pattern of rival events that should precede the preestablished outcome. For instance, the demand "pull" theory requires the prior existence of a problem as a prelude to the initiation of a research project, but the same condition is not present in the other two theories.

For the nine cases, the events turned out to match best a combination of the second and third theories. The multiple-case study had therefore pattern-matched the events in each case with different theoretical predictions and also used a replication logic across the cases.

This analysis requires the development of rival theoretical propositions, articulated in operational terms. The desired characteristic of these rival explanations is that each involves a pattern of independent variables that is mutually exclusive: If one explanation is to be valid, the others cannot be. This means that the presence of certain independent variables (predicted by one explanation) precludes the presence of other independent variables (predicted by a rival explanation). The independent variables may involve several or many different types of characteristics or events, each assessed with different measures and instruments. The concern of the case study analysis, however, is with the overall pattern of results and the degree to which the observed pattern matches the predicted one.

This type of pattern matching of independent variables also can be done either with a single case or with multiple cases. With a single case, the successful matching of the pattern to one of the rival explanations would be evidence for concluding that this explanation was the correct one (and that the other explanations were incorrect). Again, even with a single case, threats to validity—basically constituting another group of rival explanations—should be identified and ruled out. Moreover, if this identical result were additionally obtained over multiple cases, *literal replication* of the single cases would have been accomplished, and the cross-case results might be stated even more assertively. Then, if this same result also failed to occur in a second group of cases, due to predictably different circumstances, *theoretical replication* would have been accomplished, and the initial result would stand yet more robustly.

Simpler patterns. This same logic can be applied to simpler patterns, having a minimal variety of either dependent or independent variables. In the simplest case, where there may be only two different dependent (or independent) variables, pattern matching is possible as long as a different pattern has been stipulated for these two variables.

The fewer the variables, of course, the more dramatic the different patterns will have to be to allow any comparisons of their differences. Nevertheless, there are some situations in which the simpler patterns are both relevant and compelling. The role of the general analytic strategy would be to determine the best ways of contrasting any differences as sharply as possible and to develop theoretically significant explanations for the different outcomes.

Precision of pattern matching. At this point in the state of the art, the actual pattern-matching procedure involves no precise comparisons. Whether one is predicting a pattern of nonequivalent dependent variables, a pattern based on rival explanations, or a simple pattern, the fundamental comparison between the predicted and the actual pattern may involve no quantitative or statistical criteria. (Available statistical techniques are likely to be irrelevant because each of the variables in the pattern will probably represent a single data point, and none will therefore have a "variance.") The most quantitative result will likely occur if the study had set preestablished benchmarks (e.g., productivity will increase by 10%) and the value of the actual outcome was then compared to this benchmark.

Low levels of precision can allow for some interpretive discretion on the part of the investigator, who may be overly restrictive in claiming a pattern to have been violated or overly lenient in deciding that a pattern has been matched. You can make your case study stronger by developing more precise measures. In the absence of such precision, an important suggestion is to avoid postulating very subtle patterns, so that your pattern matching deals with gross matches or mismatches whose interpretation is less likely to be challenged.

Explanation Building

A second analytic technique is in fact a special type of pattern matching, but the procedure is more difficult and therefore deserves separate attention. Here, the goal is to analyze the case study data by building an explanation about the case.

As used in this chapter, the procedure is mainly relevant to explanatory case studies. A parallel procedure, for exploratory case studies, has been commonly cited as part of a hypothesis-generating process (see Glaser & Strauss, 1967), but its goal is not to conclude a study but to develop ideas for further study.

Elements of explanations. To "explain" a phenomenon is to stipulate a presumed set of causal links about it, or "how" or "why" something happened. The causal links may be complex and difficult to measure in any precise manner (see BOX 28).

In most existing case studies, explanation building has occurred in narrative form. Because such narratives cannot be precise, the better case studies are the ones in which the explanations have reflected some theoretically significant propositions. For example, the causal links may reflect critical insights into public policy process or into social science theory. The public policy propositions, if correct, can lead to recommendations for future policy actions (see BOX 29A for an example); the social science propositions, if correct, can lead to major contributions to theory building, such as the transition of countries from agrarian to industrial societies (see BOX 29B for an example).

BOX 28
Explanation Building in a Single-Case Study

Why businesses succeed or fail continues to be a topic of popular as well as research interest. Explanations are definitely needed when failure occurs with a firm that, having successfully grown for 30 years, had risen to become the number two computer maker in the entire country and, across all industries, among the top 50 corporations in size. Edgar Schein's (2003) single-case study assumed exactly that challenge and contains much documentation and interview data (also see BOX 46, Chapter 6, p. 188).

Schein, a professor at MIT, had served as a consultant to the firm's senior management during nearly all of its history. His case study tries to explain how and why the company had a "missing gene"—one that appeared critical to the business's survival. The author argues that the gene was needed to overcome the firm's other tendencies, which emphasized the excellent and creative quality of its technical operations. Instead, the firm should have given more attention to its business and marketing operations. The firm might then have overcome its inability to address layoffs that might have pruned deadwood in a more timely manner and set priorities among competing development projects (the firm developed three different PCs, not just one).

BOX 29
Explanation Building in Multiple-Case Studies

29A. A Study of Multiple Communities

In a multiple-case study, one goal is to build a general explanation that fits each individual case, even though the cases will vary in their details. The objective is analogous to creating an overall explanation, in science, for the findings from multiple experiments.

Martha Derthick's (1972) *New Towns In-Town: Why a Federal Program Failed* is a book about a housing program under President Lyndon Johnson's administration. The federal government was to give its surplus land—located in choice inner-city areas—to local governments for housing developments. But after 4 years, little progress had been made at the seven sites—San Antonio, Texas; New Bedford, Massachusetts; San Francisco, California; Washington, D.C.; Atlanta, Georgia; Louisville, Kentucky; and Clinton Township, Michigan—and the program was considered a failure.

Derthick's (1972) account first analyzes the events at each of the seven sites. Then, a general explanation—that the projects failed to generate sufficient local support—is found unsatisfactory because the condition was not dominant at all of the sites.

According to Derthick, local support did exist, but "federal officials had nevertheless stated such ambitious objectives that some degree of failure was certain" (p. 91). As a result, Derthick builds a modified explanation and concludes that "the surplus lands program failed both because the federal government had limited influence at the local level and because it set impossibly high objectives" (p. 93).

29B. A Study of Multiple Societies

An analytic approach similar to Derthick's is used by Barrington Moore (1966) in his history on the *Social Origins of Dictatorship and Democracy*. The book serves as another illustration of explanation building in multiple-case studies, even though the cases are actually historical examples.

Moore's (1966) book covers the transformation from agrarian to industrial societies in six different countries—England, France, the United States, China, Japan, and India—and the general explanation of the role of the upper classes and the peasantry is a basic theme that emerges and that became a significant contribution to the field of history.

Iterative nature of explanation building. The explanation-building process, for explanatory case studies, has not been well documented in operational terms. However, the eventual explanation is likely to be a result of a series of iterations:

- ♦ Making an initial theoretical statement or an initial proposition about policy or social behavior
- ♦ Comparing the findings of *an initial case* against such a statement or proposition
- ♦ Revising the statement or proposition
- ♦ Comparing other details of the case against the revision
- ♦ Comparing the revision to the facts of *a second, third, or more cases*
- ♦ Repeating this process as many times as is needed

In this sense, the final explanation may not have been fully stipulated at the beginning of a study and therefore differs from the pattern-matching approaches previously described. Rather, the case study evidence is examined, theoretical positions are revised, and the evidence is examined once again from a new perspective in this iterative mode.

The gradual building of an explanation is similar to the process of refining a set of ideas, in which an important aspect is again to entertain other *plausible or rival explanations.* As before, the objective is to show how these rival explanations cannot be supported, given the actual set of case study events.

Potential problems in explanation building. You should be forewarned that this approach to case study analysis is fraught with dangers. Much analytic insight is demanded of the explanation builder. As the iterative process progresses, for instance, an investigator may slowly begin to drift away from the original topic of interest. Constant reference to the original purpose of the inquiry and the possible alternative explanations may help to reduce this potential problem. Other safeguards already have been covered by Chapters 3 and 4—that is, the use of a case study protocol (indicating what data were to be collected), the establishment of a case study database for each case (formally storing the entire array of data that were collected, available for inspection by a third party), and the following of a chain of evidence.

EXERCISE 5.3   Constructing an Explanation

Identify some observable changes that have been occurring in your neighborhood (or the neighborhood around your campus). Develop an explanation for these changes and indicate the critical set of evidence you would collect to support or challenge this explanation. If such evidence were available, would your explanation be complete? Compelling? Useful for investigating similar changes in another neighborhood?

Time-Series Analysis

A third analytic technique is to conduct a time-series analysis, directly analogous to the time-series analysis conducted in experiments and quasi-experiments. Such analysis can follow many intricate patterns, which have been the subject of several major textbooks in experimental and clinical psychology with single *subjects* (e.g., see Kratochwill, 1978); the interested reader is referred to such works for further detailed guidance. The more intricate and precise the pattern, the more that the time-series analysis also will lay a firm foundation for the conclusions of the case study.

Simple time series. Compared to the more general pattern-matching analysis, a time-series design can be much simpler in one sense: In time series, there may only be a single dependent or independent variable. In these circumstances, when a large number of data points are relevant and available, statistical tests can even be used to analyze the data (see Kratochwill, 1978).

However, the pattern can be more complicated in another sense because the appropriate starting or ending points for this single variable may not be clear. Despite this problem, the ability to trace changes over time is a major strength of case studies—which are not limited to cross-sectional or static assessments of a particular situation. If the events over time have been traced in detail and with precision, some type of time-series analysis always may be possible, even if the case study analysis involves some other techniques as well (see BOX 30).

BOX 30
Using Time-Series Analysis in a Single-Case Study

In New York City, and following a parallel campaign to make the city's subways safer, the city's police department took many actions to reduce crime in the city more broadly. The actions included enforcing minor violations ("order restoration and maintenance"), installing computer-based crime-control techniques, and reorganizing the department to hold police officers accountable for controlling crime.

Kelling and Coles (1997) first describe all of these actions in sufficient detail to make their potential effect on crime reduction understandable and plausible. The case study then presents time series of the annual rates of specific types of crime over a 7-year period. During this period, crime initially rose for a couple of years and then declined for the remainder of the period. The case study explains how the timing of the relevant actions by the police department matched the changes in the crime trends. The authors cite the plausibility of the actions' effects, combined with the timing of the actions in relation to the changes in crime trends, to support their explanation for the reduction in crime rates in the New York City of that era.

The essential logic underlying a time-series design is the match between the observed (empirical) trend and either of the following: (a) a theoretically significant trend specified before the onset of the investigation or (b) some rival trend, also specified earlier. Within the same single-case study, for instance, two different patterns of events may have been hypothesized over time. This is what D. T. Campbell (1969) did in his now-famous study of the change in Connecticut's speed limit law, reducing the limit to 55 miles per hour in 1955. The predicted time-series pattern was based on the proposition that the new law (an "interruption" in the time series) had substantially reduced the number of fatalities, whereas the other time-series pattern was based on the proposition that no such effect had occurred. Examination of the actual data points— that is, the annual number of fatalities over a period of years before and after the law was passed—then determined which of the alternative time series best matched the empirical evidence. Such comparison of "interrupted time series" within the same case can be used in many different situations.

The same logic also can be used in doing a multiple-case study, with contrasting time-series patterns postulated for different cases. For instance, a case study about economic development in cities may have examined the reasons that a manufacturing-based city had more negative employment trends than those of a service-based city. The pertinent outcome data might have consisted of annual employment data over a prespecified period of time, such as 10 years. In the manufacturing-based city, the predicted employment trend might have been a declining one, whereas in the service-based city, the predicted trend might have been a rising one. Similar analyses can be imagined with regard to the examination of youth gangs over time within individual cities, changes in health status (e.g., infant mortality), trends in college rankings, and many other indicators. Again, with appropriate data, the analysis of the trends can be subjected to statistical analysis. For instance, you can compute "slopes" to cover time trends under different conditions (e.g., comparing student achievement trends in schools with different kinds of curricula) and then compare the slopes to determine whether their differences are statistically significant (see Yin, Schmidt, & Besag, 2006). As another approach, you can use regression discontinuity analysis to test the difference in trends before and after a critical event, such as the passing of a new speed limit law (see D. T. Campbell, 1969).

Complex time series. The time-series designs can be more complex when the trends within a given case are postulated to be more complex. One can postulate, for instance, not merely rising or declining (or flat) trends but some rise followed by some decline within the same case. This type of mixed pattern, across time, would be the beginning of a more complex time series. The relevant statistical techniques would then call for stipulating nonlinear models. As always, the strength of the case study strategy would not merely be in assessing this type of time series but also in having developed a rich explanation for the complex pattern of outcomes and in comparing the explanation with the outcomes.

Greater complexities also arise when a multiple set of variables—not just a single one—are relevant to a case study and when each variable may be predicted to have a different pattern over time. Such conditions can especially be present in embedded case studies: The case study may be about a single case, but extensive data also cover an embedded unit of analysis (see Chapter 2, Figure 2.3). BOX 31 contains two examples. The first (see BOX 31A) was a single-case study about one school system, but hierarchical linear models were used to analyze a detailed set of student achievement data. The second (see

BOX 31B) was about a single neighborhood revitalization strategy taking place in several neighborhoods; the authors used statistical regression models to analyze time trends for the sales prices of single-family houses in the targeted and comparison neighborhoods and thereby to assess the outcomes of the single strategy.

BOX 31
More Complex Time-Series Analyses: Using Quantitative Methods When Single-Case Studies Have an Embedded Unit of Analysis

31A. Evaluating the Impact of Systemwide Reform in Education

Supovitz and Taylor (2005) conducted a case study of Duval County School District in Florida, with the district's students serving as an embedded unit of analysis. A quantitative analysis of the students' achievement scores over a 4-year period, using hierarchical linear models adjusted for confounding factors, showed "little evidence of sustained systemwide impacts on student learning, in comparison to other districts."

The case study includes a rich array of field observations and surveys of principals, tracing the difficulties in implementing new systemwide changes prior to and during the 4-year period. The authors also discuss in great detail their own insights about systemwide reform and the implications for evaluators—that such an "intervention" is hardly self-contained and that its evaluation may need to embrace more broadly the institutional environment beyond the workings of the school system itself.

31B. Evaluating a Neighborhood Revitalization Strategy

Galster, Tatian, and Accordino (2006) do not present their work as a case study. The aim of their study was nevertheless to evaluate a single neighborhood revitalization strategy (as in a single-case study) begun in 1998 in Richmond, Virginia. The article presents the strategy's rationale and some of its implementation history, and the main conclusions are about the revitalization strategy. However, the distinctive analytic focus is on what might be considered an "embedded" unit of analysis: the sales prices of single-family homes. The overall evaluation design is highly applicable to a wide variety of embedded case studies.

To test the effectiveness of the revitalization strategy, the authors used regression models to compare pre- and postintervention (time series) trends between housing prices in targeted and comparison neighborhoods. The findings showed that the revitalization strategy had "produced substantially greater appreciation in the market values of single-family homes in the targeted areas than in comparable homes in similarly distressed neighborhoods."

In general, although a more complex time series creates greater problems for data collection, it also leads to a more elaborate trend (or set of trends) that can strengthen an analysis. Any match of a predicted with an actual time series, when both are complex, will produce strong evidence for an initial theoretical proposition.

Chronologies. The compiling of chronological events is a frequent technique in case studies and may be considered a special form of time-series analysis. The chronological sequence again focuses directly on the major strength of case studies cited earlier—that case studies allow you to trace events over time.

You should not think of the arraying of events into a chronology as a descriptive device only. The procedure can have an important analytic purpose—to investigate presumed causal events—because the basic sequence of a cause and its effect cannot be temporally inverted. Moreover, the chronology is likely to cover many different types of variables and not be limited to a single independent or dependent variable. In this sense, the chronology can be richer and more insightful than general time-series approaches. The analytic goal is to compare the chronology with that predicted by some explanatory theory—in which the theory has specified one or more of the following kinds of conditions:

- Some events must always occur before other events, with the reverse *sequence* being impossible.
- Some events must always be followed by other events, on a *contingency* basis.
- Some events can only follow other events after a prespecified *interval of time.*
- Certain *time periods* in a case study may be marked by classes of events that differ substantially from those of other time periods.

If the actual events of a case study, as carefully documented and determined by an investigator, have followed one predicted sequence of events and not those of a compelling, rival sequence, the single-case study can again become the initial basis for causal inferences. Comparison to other cases, as well as the explicit consideration of threats to internal validity, will further strengthen this inference.

Summary conditions for time-series analysis. Whatever the stipulated nature of the time series, the important case study objective is to examine some relevant "how" and "why" questions about the relationship of events over time, not merely to observe the time trends alone. An interruption in a time series will be the occasion for postulating potential causal relationships; similarly, a chronological sequence should contain causal postulates.

On those occasions when the use of time-series analysis is relevant to a case study, an essential feature is to identify the specific indicator(s) to be traced over time, as well as the specific time intervals to be covered and the presumed temporal relationships among events, *prior to* collecting the actual data. Only as a result of such prior specification are the relevant data likely to be collected in the first place, much less analyzed properly and with minimal bias.

In contrast, if a study is limited to the analysis of time trends alone, as in a descriptive mode in which causal inferences are unimportant, a non–case study strategy is probably more relevant—for example, the economic analysis of consumer price trends over time.

Note, too, that without any hypotheses or causal propositions, chronologies become *chronicles*—valuable descriptive renditions of events but having no focus on causal inferences.

EXERCISE 5.4   Analyzing Time-Series Trends

Identify a simple time series—for example, the number of students enrolled at your university for each of the past 20 years. How would you compare one period of time with another within the 20-year period? If the university admissions policies had changed during this time, how would you compare the effects of such policies? How might this analysis be considered part of a broader case study of your university?

Logic Models

This fourth technique has become increasingly useful in recent years, especially in doing case study evaluations (e.g., Mulroy & Lauber, 2004). The logic model deliberately stipulates a complex chain of events over an extended period of time. The events are staged in repeated cause-effect-cause-effect patterns, whereby a dependent variable (event) at an earlier stage becomes the independent variable (causal event) for the next stage (Peterson & Bickman, 1992; Rog & Huebner, 1992). Evaluators also have demonstrated the benefits when logic models are developed collaboratively—that is, when evaluators and the officials implementing a program being evaluated work together to define a program's logic model (see Nesman, Batsche, & Hernandez, 2007). The process can help a group define more clearly its vision and goals, as well as how the sequence of programmatic actions will (in theory) accomplish the goals.

As an analytic technique, the use of logic models consists of matching empirically observed events to theoretically predicted events. Conceptually, you therefore may consider the logic model technique to be another form of pattern matching. However, because of their sequential stages, logic models deserve to be distinguished as a separate analytic technique from pattern matching.

Joseph Wholey (1979) was at the forefront in developing logic models as an analytic technique. He first promoted the idea of a "program" logic model, tracing events when a public program intervention was intended to produce a certain outcome or sequence of outcomes. The *intervention* could initially produce activities with their own *immediate* outcomes; these immediate outcomes could in turn produce some *intermediate* outcomes; and in turn, the intermediate outcomes were supposed to produce final or *ultimate* outcomes.

To illustrate Wholey's (1979) framework with a hypothetical example, consider a school intervention aimed at improving students' academic performance. The hypothetical intervention involves a new set of classroom activities during an extra hour in the school day (*intervention*). These activities provide time for students to work with their peers on joint exercises (*immediate outcome*). The result of this immediate outcome is evidence of increased understanding and satisfaction with the educational process, on the part of the participating students, peers, and teachers (*intermediate outcome*). Eventually, the exercises and the satisfaction lead to the increased learning of certain key concepts by the students, and they demonstrate their knowledge with higher test scores (*ultimate outcome*).

Going beyond Wholey's (1979) approach and using the strategy of rival explanations espoused throughout this book, an analysis also could entertain rival chains of events, as well as the potential importance of spurious external events. If the data were supportive of the preceding sequence involving the extra hour of schooling, and no rivals could be substantiated, the analysis could claim a causal effect between the initial school intervention and the later increased learning. Alternatively, the conclusion might be reached that the specified series of events was *illogical*—for instance, that the school intervention had involved students at a different grade level than whose learning had been assessed. In this situation, the logic model would have helped to explain a spurious finding.

The program logic model strategy can be used in a variety of circumstances, not just those where a public policy intervention has occurred. A key ingredient is the claimed existence of repeated cause-and-effect sequences of events, all linked together. The links may be qualitative or, with appropriate data involving an embedded unit of analysis, even can be tested with structural equation models (see BOX 32). The more complex the link, the more definitively the case study data can be analyzed to determine whether a pattern match has been made with these events over time. Four types of logic models are discussed next. They mainly vary according to the *unit of analysis* that might be relevant to your case study.

BOX 32
Testing a Logic Model of Reform in a Single School System

An attempted transformation of a major urban school system took place in the 1980s, based on the passage of a new law that decentralized the system by installing powerful local school councils for each of the system's schools.

Bryk, Bebring, Kerbow, Rollow, and Easton (1998) evaluated the transformation, including qualitative data about the system as a whole and about individual schools (embedded units of analysis) in the system. At the same time, the study also includes a major quantitative analysis, taking the form of structural equation modeling with data from 269 of the elementary schools in the system. The path analysis is made possible because the single case (the school system) contains an embedded unit of analysis (individual schools).

The analysis tests a complex logic model whereby the investigators claim that prereform restructuring will produce strong democracy for a school, in turn producing the systemic restructuring of the school, and finally producing innovative instruction. The results, being aggregated across schools, pertain to the collective experience across all of the schools and not to any single school—in other words, the overall transformation of the system (single case) as a whole.

Individual-level logic model. The first type assumes that your case study is about an individual person, with Figure 5.2 depicting the behavioral course of events for a hypothetical youth. The events flow across a series of boxes and arrows reading from left to right in the figure. It suggests that the youth may be at risk for becoming a member of a gang, may eventually join a gang and become involved in gang violence and drugs, and even later may participate in a gang-related criminal offense. Distinctive about this logic model is the series of 11 numbers associated with the various arrows in the figure. Each of the 11 represents an opportunity, through some type of planned intervention (e.g., community or public program), to prevent an individual youth from continuing on the course of events. For instance, community development programs (number 1) might bring jobs and better housing to a neighborhood and reduce the youth's chances of becoming at risk in the first place. How a particular youth might have encountered and dealt with any or all of the 11 possible interventions might be the subject of a case study, with Figure 5.2 helping you to define the relevant data and their analysis.

Firm or organizational-level logic model. A second type of logic model traces events taking place in an individual organization, such as a manufacturing firm. Figure 5.3 shows how changes in a firm (Boxes 5 and 6 in Figure 5.3)

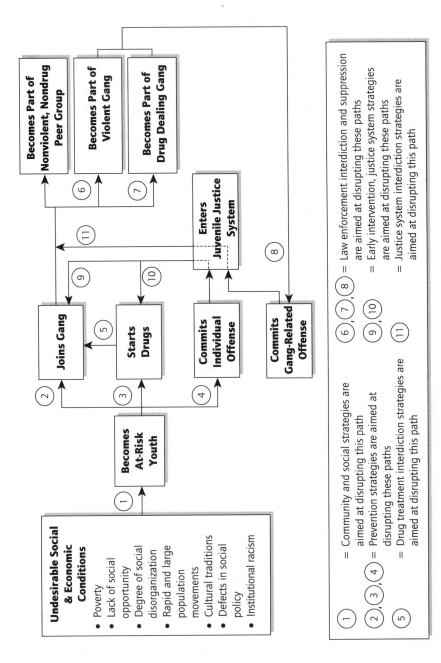

Figure 5.2   Youth Behavior and 11 Possible Interventions

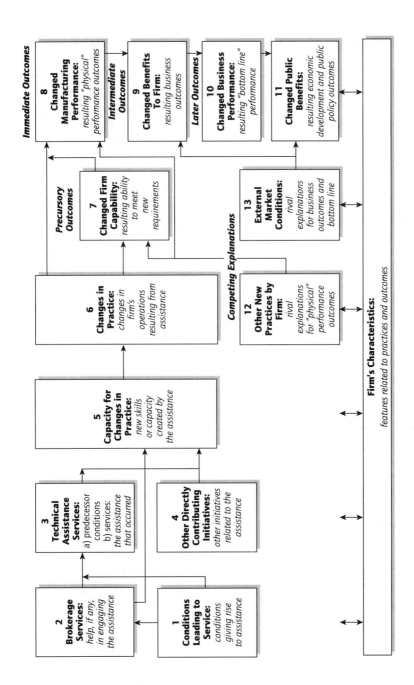

Figure 5.3   Changes in Performance in a Manufacturing Firm

SOURCE: Yin and Oldsman (1995).

are claimed to lead to improved manufacturing (Box 8) and eventually to improved business performance (Boxes 10 and 11). The flow of boxes also reflects a hypothesis—that the initial changes were the result of external brokerage and technical assistance services. Given this hypothesis, the logic model therefore also contains rival or competing explanations (Boxes 12 and 13). The data analysis for this case study would then consist of tracing the actual events over time, at a minimum giving close attention to their chronological sequence. The data collection also should have tried to identify ways in which the boxes were actually linked in real life, thereby corroborating the layout of the arrows connecting the boxes.

An alternative configuration for an organizational-level logic model. Graphically, nearly all logic models follow a linear sequence (e.g., reading from left to right or from top to bottom). In real life, however, events can be more dynamic, not necessarily progressing linearly. One such set of events might occur in relation to the "reforming" or "transformation" of an organization. For instance, business firms may undergo many significant operational changes, and the business's mission and culture (and even name) also may change. The significance of these changes warrants the notion that the entire business has been transformed (see Yin, 2003, chaps. 6 and 10, for a case study of a single firm and then the cross-case analysis of a group of transformed firms). Similarly, schools or school systems can sufficiently alter their way of doing business that "systemic reform" is said to be occurring. In fact, major public initiatives deliberately aim at improving schools by encouraging the reform of entire school systems (i.e., school districts). However, neither the business transformation nor school reform processes are linear, in at least two ways. First, changes may reverse course and not just progress in one direction. Second, the completed transformation or systemic reform is not necessarily an end point implied by the linear logic model (i.e., the final box in the model); continued transform*ing* and reform*ing* may be ongoing processes even over the long haul.

Figure 5.4 presents an alternatively configured, third type of logic model, reflecting these conditions. This logic model tracks all of the main activities in a school system (the initials are decoded in the key to the figure)—over four periods of time (each time interval might represent a 2- or 3-year period of time). Systemic reform occurs when all of the activities are aligned and work together, and this occurs at t_3 in Figure 5.4. At later stages, however, the reform may regress, represented by t_4, and the logic model does not assume that the vacillations will even end at t_4. As a further feature of the logic model, the entire circle at each stage can be positioned higher or lower, representing the level of student performance—the hypothesis being that systemic reform will be associated with the highest performance. The pennants in the middle of the circle indicate the number of schools or classrooms implementing the desired

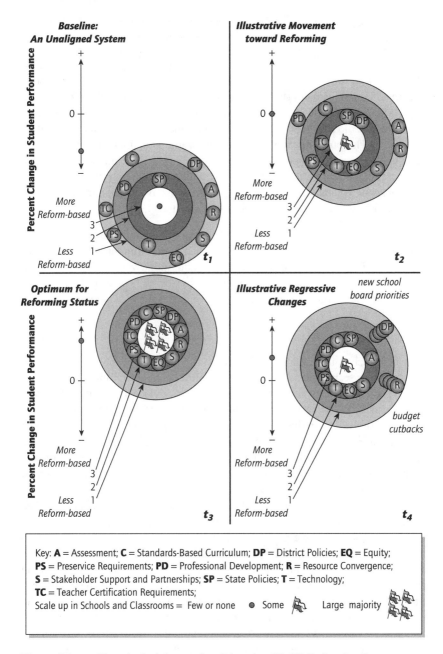

Figure 5.4   Hypothetical States of an Education (K–12) Reforming System

SOURCE: Yin and Davis (2007).

reform practices, and this number also can vacillate. Finally, the logic model contains a "metric," whereby the positioning of the activities or the height of the circle can be defined as a result of analyzing actual data.

Program-level logic model. Returning to the more conventional linear model, Figure 5.5 contains a fourth and final type of logic model. Here, the model depicts the rationale underlying a major federal program, aimed at reducing the incidence of HIV/AIDS by supporting community planning and prevention initiatives. The program provides funds as well as technical assistance to 65 state and local health departments across the country. The model was used to organize and analyze data from eight case studies, including the collection of data on rival explanations, whose potential role also is shown in the model (see Yin, 2003 chap. 8, for the entire multiple-case study).

Summary. Using logic models represents a fourth technique for analyzing case study data. Four types of logic models, applicable to different units of analysis and situations, have been presented. You should define your logic model prior to collecting data and then "test" the model by seeing how well the data support it (see Yin, 2003, for several examples of case studies using logic models).

Cross-Case Synthesis

A fifth technique applies specifically to the analysis of multiple cases (the previous four techniques can be used with either single- or multiple-case studies). The technique is especially relevant if, as advised in Chapter 2, a case study consists of at least two cases (for a synthesis of six cases, see Ericksen & Dyer, 2004). The analysis is likely to be easier and the findings likely to be more robust than having only a single case. BOX 33 presents an excellent example of the important research and research topics that can be addressed by having a "two-case" case study. Again, having more than two cases could strengthen the findings even further.

Cross-case syntheses can be performed whether the individual case studies have previously been conducted as independent research studies (authored by different persons) or as a predesigned part of the same study. In either situation, the technique treats each individual case study as a separate study. In this way, the technique does not differ from other research syntheses—aggregating findings across a series of individual studies (see BOX 34). If there are large numbers of individual case studies available, the synthesis can incorporate quantitative techniques common to other research syntheses (e.g., Cooper & Hedges, 1994) or meta-analyses (e.g., Lipsey, 1992). However, if only a modest number of case studies are available, alternative tactics are needed.

One possibility starts with the creation of word tables that display the data from the individual cases according to some uniform framework. Figure 5.6 has an

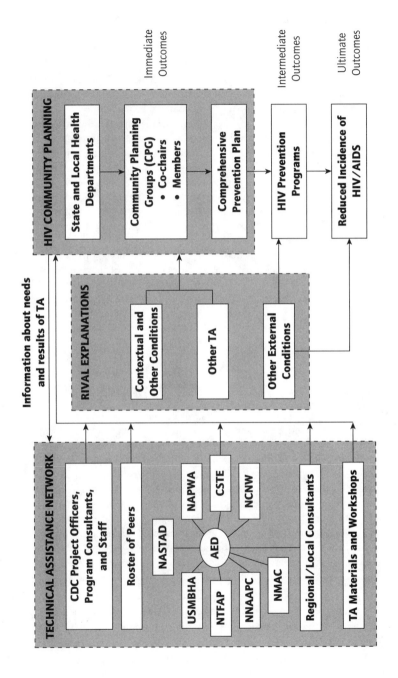

Figure 5.5 Improving Community Planning for HIV/AIDS Prevention
SOURCE: Yin (2003, chap. 8).

157

BOX 33
Using a "Two-Case" Case Study to Test a Policy-Oriented Theory

The international marketplace of the 1970s and 1980s was marked by Japan's prominence. Much of its strength was attributable to the role of centralized planning and support by a special governmental ministry—considered by many to be an unfair competitive edge, compared to the policies in other countries. For instance, the United States was considered to have no counterpart support structures. Gregory Hooks's (1990) excellent case study points to a counterexample frequently ignored by advocates: the role of the U.S. defense department in implementing an industrial planning policy within defense-related industries.

Hooks (1990) provides quantitative data on two cases—the aeronautics industry and the microelectronics industry (the forerunner to the entire computer chip market and its technologies, such as the personal computer). One industry (aeronautics) has traditionally been known to be dependent upon support from the federal government, but the other has not. In both cases, Hooks's evidence shows how the defense department supported the critical early development of these industries through financial support, the support of R&D, and the creation of an initial customer base for the industry's products. The existence of both cases, and not the aeronautics industry alone, makes the author's entire argument powerful and persuasive.

BOX 34
Eleven Program Evaluations and a Cross-"Case" Analysis

Dennis Rosenbaum (1986) collected 11 program evaluations as separate chapters in an edited book. The 11 evaluations had been conducted by different investigators, had used a variety of methods, and were not case studies. Each evaluation was about a different community crime prevention intervention, and some presented ample quantitative evidence and employed statistical analyses. The evaluations were deliberately selected because nearly all had shown positive results. A cross-case analysis was conducted by the present author (Yin, 1986), treating each evaluation as if it were a separate "case." The analysis dissected and arrayed the evidence from the 11 evaluations in the form of word tables. Generalizations about successful community crime prevention, independent of any specific intervention, were then derived by using a replication logic, given that all of the evaluations had shown positive results.

example of such a word table, capturing the findings from 14 case studies of organizational centers, with each center having an organizational partner (COSMOS Corporation, 1998). Of the 14 centers, 7 had received programmatic support and were considered intervention centers; the other 7 were selected as comparison centers. For both types of centers, data were collected about the center's ability to

CENTERS	Characteristics of Co-Location
Intervention Centers:	
1	Partnering staff are located in the same facility as Center 1 and follow Center 1's policies that were in place prior to the partnership. Center 1 receives $25,000 annually from the partnership budget for software and peripherals, and communication and supplies.
2	As a business unit of Center 2, the partnering staff are housed within Center 2's offices. Center 2's parent organization contributes $2,500 for space and $23,375 for indirect expenses annually to the partnership budget.
3	Five partnership offices are co-located with Center 3's staff.
4	Center 4 and its partner share office space.
5	Center 5 staff and the partnering staff are located in the same building, but do not share office space.
6	The two organizations are not co-located.
7	Partnering staff are located in Center 7's offices.
Comparison Centers:	
8	Center 8 and its partner share office space in eight locations statewide.
9	Some sites are co-located.
10	Center 10 and its partner are not co-located.
11	The partnering and center staff share office space.
12	Center 12 and its partner's staff are located in the same building.
13	Center 13 and its partner's staff are located in the same office.
14	Center 14 shares office space with three regional partners.

Figure 5.6   Co-location of Interorganizational Partners (14 Centers and Their Counterpart Organizations)

SOURCE: COSMOS Corporation (1998).

co-locate (e.g., share facilities) with its partnering organization—this being only one of several outcomes of interest in the original study.

The overall pattern in the word table led to the conclusion that the intervention and comparison centers did not differ with regard to this particular outcome. Additional word tables, reflecting other processes and outcomes of interest, were examined in the same way. The analysis of the entire collection of word tables enabled the study to draw cross-case conclusions about the intervention centers and their outcomes.

Complementary word tables can go beyond the single features of a case and array a whole set of features on a case-by-case basis. Now, the analysis can start to probe whether different groups of cases appear to share some similarity and deserve to be considered instances of the same "type" of general case. Such an observation can further lead to analyzing whether the arrayed case studies reflect subgroups or categories of general cases—raising the possibility of a typology of individual cases that can be highly insightful.

An important caveat in conducting this kind of cross-case synthesis is that the examination of word tables for cross-case patterns will rely strongly on argumentative interpretation, not numeric tallies. Chapter 2 has previously pointed out, however, that this method is directly analogous to cross-*experiment* interpretations, which also have no numeric properties when only a small number of experiments are available for synthesis. A challenge you must be prepared to meet as a case study investigator is therefore to know how to develop strong, plausible, and fair arguments that are supported by the data.

PRESSING FOR A HIGH-QUALITY ANALYSIS

No matter what specific analytic strategy or techniques have been chosen, you must do everything to make sure that your analysis is of the highest quality. At least four principles underlie all good social science research (Yin, 1994a, 1994b, 1997, 1999) and require your attention.

First, your analysis should show that you attended to *all the evidence.* Your analytic strategies, including the development of rival hypotheses, must exhaustively cover your key research questions (you can now appreciate better the importance of defining sharp as opposed to vague questions). Your analysis should show how it sought to use as much evidence as was available, and your interpretations should account for all of this evidence and leave no loose ends. Without achieving this standard, your analysis may be vulnerable to alternative interpretations based on the evidence that you had (inadvertently) ignored.

Second, your analysis should address, if possible, *all major rival interpretations.* If someone else has an alternative explanation for one or more of your findings, make this alternative into a rival. Is there evidence to address this rival? If so, what are the results? If not, should the rival be restated as a loose end to be investigated in future studies?

Third, your analysis should address *the most significant aspect* of your case study. Whether it is a single- or multiple-case study, you will have demonstrated your best analytic skills if the analysis focuses on the most important issue (preferably defined at the outset of the case study). By avoiding a detour to a lesser issue, your analysis will be less vulnerable to the possibility that the main issue was being avoided because of possibly negative findings.

Fourth, you should use your own *prior, expert knowledge* in your case study. The strong preference here is for you to demonstrate awareness of current thinking and discourse about the case study topic. If you know your subject matter as a result of your own previous investigations and publications, so much the better.

The case study in BOX 35 was done by a research team with academic credentials as well as strong and relevant practical experience. In their work, the authors demonstrate a care of empirical investigation whose spirit is worth considering in all case studies. The care is reflected in the presentation of the cases themselves, not by the existence of a stringent methodology section whose tenets might not have been fully followed in the actual case study. If you can emulate the spirit of these authors, your case study analysis also will be given appropriate respect and recognition.

BOX 35
Analytic Quality in a Multiple-Case Study of International Trade Competition

The quality of a case study analysis is not dependent solely on the techniques used, although they are important. Equally important is that the investigator demonstrate expertise in carrying out the analysis. This expertise was reflected in Magaziner and Patinkin's (1989) book, *The Silent War: Inside the Global Business Battles Shaping America's Future.*

The authors organized their nine cases in excellent fashion. Across cases, major themes regarding America's competitive advantages (and disadvantages) were covered in a replication design. Within each case, the authors provided extensive interview and other documentation, showing the sources of their findings. (To keep the narrative reading smoothly, much of the data—in word tables, footnotes, and quantitative tabulations—were relegated to footnotes and appendices.) In addition, the authors showed that they had extensive personal exposure to the issues being studied, as a result of numerous domestic and overseas visits.

Technically, a more explicit methodological section might have been helpful. However, the careful and detailed work, even in the absence of such a section, helps to illustrate what all investigators should strive to achieve (also see BOX 5B, Chapter 2, p. 31).

EXERCISE 5.5   Analyzing the Analytic Process

Select and obtain one of the case studies described in the BOXES in this book. Find one of the case study's chapters (usually in the middle of the study) in which evidence is presented, but conclusions also are being made. Describe how this linkage—from cited evidence to conclusions—occurs. Are data displayed in tables or other formats? Are comparisons being made?

SUMMARY

This chapter has presented several ways of analyzing case studies. First, the potential analytic difficulties can be reduced if you have a general strategy for analyzing the data—whether such a strategy is based on theoretical propositions, rival explanations, or descriptive frameworks. In the absence of such strategies, you may have to "play with the data" in a preliminary sense, as a prelude to developing a systematic sense of what is worth analyzing and how it should be analyzed.

Second, given a general strategy, several specific analytic techniques are relevant. Of these, five (pattern matching, explanation building, time-series analysis, logic models, and cross-case syntheses) can be effective in laying the groundwork for high-quality case studies. For all five, a similar replication logic should be applied if a study involves multiple cases. Comparisons to rival propositions and threats to internal validity also should be made within each individual case.

None of these techniques is easy to use. None can be applied mechanically, following any simple cookbook procedure. Not surprisingly, case study analysis is the most difficult stage of doing case studies, and novice investigators are especially likely to have a troublesome experience. Again, one recommendation is to begin with a simple and straightforward case study (or, more preferably, a "two-case" design), even if the research questions are not as sophisticated or innovative as might be desired. Experience gained in completing such straightforward case studies will lead to the ability to tackle more difficult topics in subsequent case studies.

REFERENCE TO EXPANDED CASE STUDY
MATERIALS FOR CHAPTER 5

For selected case studies cited in the text of this chapter, two anthologies contain either a more extensive excerpt or the full case study. The table below crosswalks the reference in this book to the location of the excerpt or full rendition.

Chapter 5 Chapter Topic and Page Number	Topics of Illustrative Case Studies	Reference to Lengthier Material
An Analytic Strategy: More Than Familiarity with Analytic Tools		
BOX 25, p. 5-8	Local economic development	CSA-5
p. 5-114 text	University innovation	ACSR-4
p. 5-114 text	Drug abuse prevention	ACSR-5
Five Specific Analytic Techniques		
BOX 26, p. 5-14	Local economic development	CSA-18
BOX 27, p. 5-15	Making research useful	ACSR, pp. 20–22
BOX 28, p. 5-18	Business and industry	None
BOX 29A, p. 5-18	Local economic development	CSA-8
BOX 29B, p. 5-18	Societies	None
BOX 30, p. 5-21	Crime prevention	CSA-17
BOX 31A, p. 5-23	Schools	None
BOX 31B, p. 5-23	Neighborhoods	None
BOX 32, p. 5-27	Schools	CSA-11
p. 5-29 text	Business and industry	ACSR-6 & 10
p. 5-30 text	Health (HIV/AIDS) care	ACSR-8
p. 5-31 text	Three different case studies	ACSR-6, 8, & 10
BOX 33, p. 5-31	Business and industry	CSA-7
BOX 34, p. 5-32	Crime prevention	None
Pressing for a High-Quality Analysis		
BOX 35, p. 5-34	Business and industry	CSA-6

NOTE: CSA = *Case Study Anthology* (Yin, 2004). ACSR = *Applications of Case Study Research* (Yin, 2003). The number denotes the chapter number in the book.

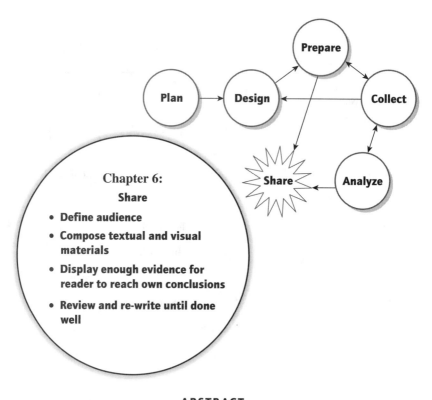

Chapter 6:
Share

- **Define audience**
- **Compose textual and visual materials**
- **Display enough evidence for reader to reach own conclusions**
- **Review and re-write until done well**

ABSTRACT

Reporting a case study means bringing its results and findings to closure. Regardless of the form of the report, similar steps underlie the case study composition: identifying the audience for the report, developing its compositional structure, and having drafts reviewed by others.

Once composed, the case study may be finished—or it may be joined with data collected through other methods, as part of a broader, mixed methods study. Such studies can be advantageous and represent a further challenge in doing case study research.

Whether serving as a finished case study or as part of a mixed methods study, creating a case study report is one of the most challenging aspects of doing case studies. The best general advice is to compose portions of the case study early (e.g., the bibliography and the methodology section), rather than waiting until the end of the data analysis process. As for compositional structures, six alternatives are suggested: linear-analytic, comparative, chronological, theory-building, "suspense," and unsequenced structures. The case study report also presents a choice regarding the disclosure or anonymity of case identities. A final plea is to worry about producing high-quality and not just run-of-the-mill case studies.

6

Reporting Case Studies

How and What to Compose

As a general rule, the compositional phase puts the greatest demands on a case study investigator. The case study report does not follow any stereotypic form, such as a journal article in psychology. Because of this uncertain nature, researchers who do not like to compose may want to question their interest in doing case studies in the first place. Most of the notable case study scholars have been ones who liked to compose and also actually had a flair for writing. Do you?

Of course, most investigators can eventually learn to compose easily and well, and inexperience in composing should not be a deterrent to doing case studies. However, much practice will be needed. Furthermore, to do good case studies, you should want to become good at composing—and not merely put up with it. One indicator of success at this phase of the craft is whether you found term papers easy or difficult to do in high school or college. The more difficult they were, the more difficult it will be to compose a case study report. Another indicator is whether composing is viewed as an opportunity or as a burden. The successful investigator usually perceives the compositional phase as an opportunity—to make a significant contribution to knowledge or practice.

Unfortunately, few people are forewarned about this problem that lies at the end of designing and doing a case study. The smart investigator will begin to compose the case study report even before data collection and analysis have been completed. In general, the compositional phase is so important that you should give it explicit attention throughout the earlier phases of your case study.

Despite this advice, most investigators typically ignore the compositional phase until the very end of their case studies. Under these circumstances, all sorts of "writer's cramps" may appear, and the case study report may become impossible to compose. Thus, a prelude to any case study research may be to consult a textbook covering the writing of research reports more generally (e.g., Barzun & Graff, 1985; Becker, 1986). Such texts offer invaluable reminders for taking notes, making outlines, using plain words, writing clear sentences, establishing a schedule for composing, and combating the common urge not to compose.

> **Tip:** *What's the best way of getting my case study report finished, with the least trouble and time?*
>
> Every investigator differs, so you have to develop your own style and preferences. Improvement occurs with each case study you write. Thus, don't be surprised if your first one is more difficult. One possible strategy is to think about writing "inside-out" and "backwards." Inside-out: Start your report with a table, exhibit, vignette, or quotation to be cited by the narrative of your case study (but don't try to write the narrative yet). In the same manner, now amass all of the tables, exhibits, vignettes, or quotations for your entire report, arraying them in the sequence they are to appear in your report. Backwards: Now start by writing the narrative for the final portion of the case study before the rest, then write the analytic narrative that led to the final portion, and so on.
>
> **If you successfully follow the preceding suggestions, would you be finished, or do you have but a first draft that now needs to be recomposed so that it blends better?**

EXERCISE 6.1   Reducing the Barriers to Composition

Everyone has difficulties in composing reports, whether case studies or not. To succeed at composing, investigators must take specific steps during the conduct of a study to reduce barriers to composition. Name five such steps that you would take—such as starting on a portion of the composition at an early stage. Have you used these five steps in the past?

The purpose of this chapter is not to repeat these general lessons, although they are applicable to case studies. Most of the lessons are important to all forms of research composition, and to describe them here would defeat the purpose of providing information specific to case studies. Instead, the main purpose of this chapter is to highlight those aspects of composition and reporting that are directly related to case studies. These include the following topics, each covered in a separate section:

- targeting case study reports;
- case study reports as part of larger, mixed methods studies;
- illustrative structures for case study compositions;
- procedures to be followed in doing a case study report; and
- in conclusion, speculations on the characteristics of an exemplary case study (extending beyond the report itself and covering the design and content of the case).

One reminder from Chapter 4 is that the case study report should not be the main way of recording or storing the evidentiary base of the case study.

Rather, Chapter 4 advocated the use of a case study database for this purpose (see Chapter 4, Principle 2), and the compositional efforts described in this chapter are primarily intended to serve reporting, and not documentation, objectives.

TARGETING CASE STUDY REPORTS

Giving some initial thought to your likely or preferred audience and reporting formats serves as a good starting point for composing your case study. It can have a more diverse set of potential audiences than most other types of research, including (a) academic colleagues; (b) policy makers, practitioners, community leaders, and other professionals who do not specialize in case study or other social science research; (c) special groups such as a dissertation or thesis committee; and (d) funders of research.[1]

With most research reports, such as reports of experiments, the second audience is not typically relevant, as few would expect the result of a laboratory experiment to be directed to nonspecialists. However, for case studies, this second audience may be a frequent target of the case study report. As another contrast, the third audience would rarely be relevant for some types of research—such as evaluations—because evaluations are not usually suitable as theses or dissertations. However, for case studies, this third audience also is a frequent consumer of the case study report, due to the large number of theses and dissertations in the social sciences that rely on case studies.

Because case studies have more potential audiences than other types of research, one of your essential tasks in designing the overall case study report is to identify the specific audiences for the report. Each audience has different needs, and no single report will serve all audiences simultaneously.

As examples, for *academic colleagues,* the relationships among the case study, its findings, and previous theory or research are likely to be most important (see BOX 36). For *nonspecialists,* the descriptive elements in portraying some real-life situation, as well as the implications for action, are likely to be more important. For a *thesis committee,* mastery of the methodology and theoretical issues, along with an indication of the care with which the research was conducted, is important. Finally, for *research funders,* the significance of the case study findings, whether cast in academic or practical terms, is probably as important as the rigor with which the research was conducted. Successful communication with more than one audience may mean the need for more than one version of a case study report. Investigators should seriously consider catering to such a need (see BOX 37).

BOX 36
Famous Case Study Reprinted

For many years, Philip Selznick's *TVA and the Grass Roots* (1949) has stood as a classic about public organizations. The case has been cited in many subsequent studies of federal agencies, political behavior, and organizational decentralization.

Fully 30 years after its original publication, this case was reprinted in 1980 as part of the Library Reprint Series by the University of California Press, the original publisher. This type of reissuance allows numerous other researchers to have access to this famous case study and reflects its substantial contribution to the field.

BOX 37
Two Versions of the Same Case Study

The city planning office of Broward County, Florida, implemented an office automation system beginning in 1982 ("The Politics of Automating a Planning Office," Standerfer & Rider, 1983). The implementation strategies were innovative and significant—especially in relation to tensions with the county government's computer department. As a result, the case study is interesting and informative, and a popularized version—appearing in a practitioner journal—is fun and easy to read.

Because this type of implementation also covers complex technical issues, the authors made supplementary information available to the interested reader. The popularized version provided a name, address, and telephone number, so that such a reader could obtain the additional information. This type of dual availability of case study reports is but one example of how different reports of the *same* case study may be useful for communicating with different audiences.

EXERCISE 6.2   Defining the Audience

Name the alternative audiences for a case study you might compose. For each audience, indicate the features of the case study report that you should highlight or de-emphasize. Would the same report serve all the audiences, and why?

Communicating with Case Studies

One additional difference between the case study and other types of research is that your case study report can itself be a significant communication device. For many nonspecialists, the description and analysis of a single case often suggests implications about a more general phenomenon.

A related situation, often overlooked, occurs with testimony before a legislative committee. If an elderly person, for instance, testifies about her or his health services before such a committee, its members may assume that they have acquired an understanding of health care for the elderly more generally—based on this "case." Only then might the members be willing to review broader statistics about the prevalence of similar cases. Later, the committee may inquire about the representative nature of the initial case, before proposing new legislation. However, throughout this entire process, the initial "case"—represented by a witness—may have been the essential ingredient in gaining insight into the health care issue in the first place.

In these and other ways, your case study can communicate research-based information about a phenomenon to a variety of nonspecialists. Your case study may even assume the form of a videotape or other multimedia device and not a narrative report (e.g., see Naumes & Naumes, 1999, chap. 10). The usefulness of case studies therefore goes far beyond the role of the typical research report, which is generally addressed to research colleagues rather than nonspecialists. Obviously, descriptive as well as explanatory case studies can be important in this role, and you should not overlook the potential descriptive impact of a well-presented case study (see BOX 38).

BOX 38
Using a Metaphor to Organize Both Theory and Presentation in Another Field

Whether four "countries"—the American colonies, Russia, England, and France—all underwent similar courses of events during their major political revolutions is the topic of Crane Brinton's (1938) famous historical study, *The Anatomy of a Revolution*. Tracing and analyzing these events is done in a descriptive manner, as the author's purpose is not so much to explain the revolutions as to determine whether they followed similar courses (also see BOX 41B, p. 173).

The "cross-case" analysis reveals major similarities: All societies were on the upgrade, economically; there were bitter class antagonisms; the intellectuals deserted their governments; government machinery was inefficient; and the ruling class exhibited immoral, dissolute, or inept behavior (or all three). However, rather than relying solely on this "factors" approach to description, the author also develops the metaphor of a human body suffering from a fever as a way of describing the pattern of events over time. The author adeptly uses the cyclic pattern of fever and chills, rising to a critical point and followed by a false tranquility, to describe the ebb and flow of events in the four revolutions.

Orienting the Case Study Report to an Audience's Needs

Overall, the preferences of the potential audience should dictate the form of your case study report. Although the research procedures and methodology should have followed other guidelines, suggested in Chapters 1 through 5, your report should reflect emphases, detail, compositional forms, and even a length suitable to the needs of the potential audience. The importance of the audience suggests that you might want to collect formal information about what the audiences need and their preferred types of communication (Morris, Fitz-Gibbon, & Freeman, 1987, p. 13). Along these lines, this author has frequently called the attention of thesis or dissertation students to the fact that the thesis or dissertation committee may be their *only* audience. The ultimate report, under these conditions, should attempt to communicate directly with this committee. A recommended tactic is to integrate the committee members' previous research into the thesis or dissertation, creating greater conceptual (and methodological) overlap and thereby increasing the thesis or dissertation's potential communicability to that particular audience.

Whatever the audience, the greatest error you can make is to compose a report from an egocentric perspective. This error will occur if you complete your report without identifying a specific audience or without understanding the specific needs of such an audience. To avoid this error, you should identify the audience, as previously noted. A second and equally important suggestion is to examine prior case study reports that have successfully communicated with this audience. Such earlier reports may offer helpful clues for composing a new report. For instance, consider again the thesis or dissertation student. The student should consult previous dissertations and theses that have passed the academic regimen successfully—or are known to have been exemplary works. The inspection of such works may yield sound information regarding the departmental norms (and reviewers' likely preferences) for designing a new thesis or dissertation.

Formats for Written Case Study Reports

Among written forms of case studies, there are at least four important varieties. The first is the classic single-case study. A single narrative is used to describe and analyze the case. You may augment the narrative with tabular as well as graphic and pictorial displays. Depending upon the depth of the case study, these classic single cases are likely to appear as books, although some of the best discipline-based journals also run rather long articles.

A second type of written product is the multiple-case version of the classic single case. This type of multiple-case report will contain multiple narratives, covering each of the cases singly, usually presented as separate chapters or sections. In addition to these individual case narratives, your report also will contain a chapter or section covering the cross-case analysis and results. Some situations even may call for several cross-case chapters or sections, and the cross-case portion of the final text may justify a volume separate from the individual case narratives (see BOX 39). In these situations, a frequent form of presentation is to have the bulk of the main report contain the cross-case analysis, with the individual cases presented as part of a long appendix to that basic volume.

BOX 39
A Multiple-Case Report

Multiple-case studies often contain both the individual case studies and some cross-case chapters. The composition of such a multiple-case study also may be shared among several authors.

This type of arrangement was used in a study of eight innovations in mathematics and science education, edited by Raizen and Britton (1997). The study, titled *Bold Ventures*, appears in three separate and lengthy volumes (about 250, 350, and 650 pages, respectively). The individual case studies appear in the last two volumes, while the seven chapters in Volume 1 cover cross-case issues. Many different and multiple authors conducted both the individual case studies and the cross-case chapters, although the entire study was orchestrated and coordinated as a single undertaking.

A third type of written product covers either a multiple- or a single-case study but does not contain the traditional narrative. Instead, the composition for each case follows a series of questions and answers, based on the questions and answers in the case study database (see Chapter 4). For reporting purposes, the content of the database is shortened and edited for readability, with the final product still assuming the format, analogously, of a comprehensive examination. (In contrast, the traditional case study narrative may be considered similar to the format of a term paper.) This question-and-answer format may not reflect your full creative talent, but the format helps to avoid the problems of writer's cramps. This is because you can proceed immediately to answer the required set of questions. (Again, the comprehensive exam has a similar advantage over a term paper.)

If you use this question-and-answer format to report a multiple-case study, repeating the same set of questions in covering each individual case study, the advantages are potentially enormous: Your reader(s) need only examine the answers to the same question or questions within each case study to begin making her or his own cross-case comparisons. Because each reader may be interested in different questions, the entire format facilitates the development of a

BOX 40
A Question-and-Answer Format: Case Studies without
the Traditional Narrative

Case study evidence does not need to be presented in the traditional narrative form. An alternative format for presenting the same evidence is to write the narrative in question-and-answer form. A series of questions can be posed, with the answers taking some reasonable length—for example, three or four paragraphs each. Each answer can contain all the relevant evidence and can even be augmented with tabular presentations and citations.

This alternative was followed in 40 case studies of community organizations produced by the U.S. National Commission on Neighborhoods (1979), *People, Building Neighborhoods*. The same question-and-answer format was used in each case, so that the interested reader could do her or his own cross-case analysis by following the same question across all of the cases. The format allowed hurried readers to find exactly the relevant portions of each case. For people offended by the absence of the traditional narrative, each case also called for a summary, unconstrained in its form (but no longer than three pages), allowing the author to exercise her or his more literary talents.

cross-case analysis tailored to the specific interests of its readers (see BOX 40). Yin (2003, chap. 2) contains a complete case study demonstrating this format.

The fourth and last type of written product applies to multiple-case studies only. In this situation, there may be *no* separate chapters or sections devoted to the individual cases. Rather, your entire report may consist of the cross-case analysis, whether purely descriptive or also covering explanatory topics. In such a report, each chapter or section would be devoted to a separate cross-case issue, and the information from the individual cases would be dispersed throughout each chapter or section. With this format, summary information about the individual cases, if not ignored altogether (see BOX 41, as well as Chapter 1, p. 20, BOX 3B), might be presented in abbreviated vignettes.

As a final note, the specific type of case study composition, involving a choice among at least these four alternatives, should be identified during the *design* of the case study. Your initial choice always can be altered, as unexpected conditions may arise, and a different type of composition may become more relevant than the one originally selected. However, early selection will facilitate both the design and the conduct of the case study. Such an initial selection should be part of the case study protocol, alerting you to the likely nature of the final composition and its requirements.

BOX 41
Writing a Multiple-Case Report

In a multiple-case study, the individual case studies need not always be presented in the final manuscript. The individual cases, in a sense, serve only as the evidentiary base for the study and may be cited sporadically in the cross-case analysis (also see BOX 3B, Chapter 1, p. 20).

41A. An Example in Which No Single Cases Are Presented

This approach was used in a book about six federal bureau chiefs, by Herbert Kaufman (1981), *The Administrative Behavior of Federal Bureau Chiefs*. Kaufman spent intensive periods of time with each chief to understand his day-to-day routine. He interviewed the chiefs, listened in on their phone calls, attended meetings, and was present during staff discussions in the chiefs' offices.

The book's purpose, however, was not to portray any single one of these chiefs. Rather, the book synthesizes the lessons from all of them and is organized around such topics as how chiefs decide things, how they receive and review information, and how they motivate their staffs. Under each topic, Kaufman draws appropriate examples from the six cases, but none of the six is presented as a single-case study.

41B. Another Example (from Another Field) in Which No Single Cases Are Presented

A design similar to Kaufman's is used in another field—history—in a famous book by Crane Brinton (1938), *The Anatomy of a Revolution*. Brinton's book is based on four revolutions: the English, American, French, and Russian revolutions (also see BOX 38, p. 169). The book is an analysis and theory of revolutionary periods, with pertinent examples drawn from each of the four "cases"; however, as in Kaufman's book, there is no attempt to present the single revolutions as individual case studies.

CASE STUDY REPORTS AS PART OF LARGER, MIXED METHODS STUDIES

Your completed case study may include data from other methods (e.g., surveys or quantitative analysis of archival data such as health status indicators). In particular, Chapter 2 pointed to the possibility that within a single case might exist embedded units of analysis, which might have been the subject of data collection through these other methods (see Chapter 2, Figure 2.3). In this situation, *the case study encompasses the other methods*, and your completed case study report would incorporate the reporting of the data from these other methods (e.g., see Chapter 4, BOX 18).

A totally different situation occurs when your case study has been deliberately designed to be part of a larger, mixed methods study (Yin, 2006b). In this situation, *the larger study encompasses the case study.* The larger study will contain your completed case study but also should report separately the findings about the data from the other methods. The larger study's overall report would then be based on the pattern of evidence from both the case study and the other methods.

This mixed methods situation deserves a bit more attention so that you will understand its implications for your case study, even though you might not compose your case study report any differently than if it had been a "stand-alone" report. At least three different rationales might have motivated the larger study to use mixed methods.

First, the larger study may have called for mixed methods simply to determine whether converging evidence (triangulation) might be obtained even though different methods had been used (Datta, 1997). In this scenario, your case study would have shared the same initial research questions as those driving the other methods, but you would likely have conducted, analyzed, and reported your case study independently. Part of the larger study's assessment would then be to compare the case study results with those based on the other methods.

Second, the larger study may have been based on a survey or quantitative analysis of archival data—for example, a study of households' financial situations under different income tax conditions. The larger study might then have wanted case studies to illustrate, in greater depth, the experiences of individual families. In this scenario, the questions for your case study might only be surfaced *after* the survey or archival data had been analyzed, and the selection of cases might come from the pool of those surveyed or contained within the archival records. The main implications for your case study effort are that both its timing and direction may depend on the progress and findings of the other inquiries.

Third, the larger study might knowingly have called for case studies to elucidate some underlying process and used another method (such as a survey) to define the prevalence or frequency of such processes. In this scenario of complementarity as opposed to convergence, the case study questions are likely to be closely coordinated with those of the other methods, and the complementary inquiries can occur simultaneously or sequentially. However, the initial analysis and reports from each inquiry should be conducted independently (even though the final analysis may merge findings from all the different methods). BOX 42 contains two examples of larger studies done under this third scenario.

These three different situations show how your case study and its reporting may have to be coordinated within some broader context. Beware that when your case study is not independent, you may have to coordinate deadlines and

---

Box 42
Integrating Case Study and Survey Evidence:
Complementarity of Findings

Multimethod studies can pose complementary questions that are to be addressed by different methods. Most commonly, case studies are used to gain insight into causal processes, whereas surveys provide an indication of the prevalence of a phenomenon. Two studies illustrate this combination.

The first was a study of educational projects funded by the U.S. Department of Education (Berman & McLaughlin, 1974–1978). The study combined case studies of 29 projects with a survey of 293 projects, revealing invaluable information on the implementation process and its outcomes. The second study (Yin, 1981c) combined case studies of 19 sites with a survey of 90 other sites. The findings contributed to understanding the life cycle of technological innovations in local public services.

---

technical directions, and your case study report may not proceed as you might have expected initially. Also assess carefully your willingness and ability to be part of a larger team before making any commitments.

ILLUSTRATIVE STRUCTURES FOR CASE STUDY COMPOSITIONS

The chapters, sections, subtopics, and other components of a report must be organized in some way, and this constitutes your case study report's compositional structure. Attending to such structure has been a topic of attention with other methodologies. For instance, L. Kidder and Judd (1986, pp. 430–431) write of the "hourglass" shape of a report for quantitative studies. Similarly, in ethnography, John Van Maanen (1988) has developed the concept of "tales" for reporting fieldwork results. He identifies several different types of tales: realist tales, confessional tales, impressionist tales, critical tales, formal tales, literary tales, and jointly told tales. These different types may be used in different combinations in the same report.

Alternatives also exist for structuring case study reports. This section suggests six illustrative structures (see Figure 6.1) that may be used with any type of case study formats just described. The illustrations are described mainly in relation to the composition of a single-case study, although the principles are readily translatable into multiple-case reports. As a further note and as indicated in Figure 6.1, the first three are all applicable to descriptive, exploratory, and explanatory case studies. The fourth is applicable mainly to exploratory and explanatory case studies, the fifth to explanatory cases, and the sixth to descriptive cases.

TYPE OF COMPOSITIONAL STRUCTURE	Purpose of Case Study (single- or multiple-case)		
	Explanatory	Descriptive	Exploratory
1. Linear-analytic	X	X	X
2. Comparative	X	X	X
3. Chronological	X	X	X
4. Theory-building	X		X
5. "Suspense"	X		
6. Unsequenced		X	

Figure 6.1   Six Structures and Their Application to Different Purposes of Case Studies

Linear-Analytic Structures

This is a standard approach for composing research reports. The sequence of subtopics starts with the issue or problem being studied and a review of the relevant prior literature. The subtopics then proceed to cover the methods used, the findings from the data collected and analyzed, and the conclusions and implications from the findings.

Most journal articles in experimental science reflect this type of structure, as do many case studies. The structure is comfortable to most investigators and probably is the most advantageous when research colleagues or a thesis or dissertation committee comprise the main audience for a case study. Note that the structure is applicable to explanatory, descriptive, or exploratory case studies. For example, an exploratory case may cover the issue or problem being explored, the methods of exploration, the findings from the exploration, and the conclusions (for further research).

Comparative Structures

A comparative structure repeats the same case study two or more times, comparing alternative descriptions or explanations of the same case. This is best exemplified in Graham Allison's (1971) noted case study on the Cuban missile crisis (see Chapter 1, BOX 1). In this book, the author repeats the "facts" of the case study three times, each time in relation to a different conceptual model. The purpose of the repetition is to show the degree to which the facts fit each model, and the repetitions actually illustrate a pattern-matching technique at work.

A similar approach can be used even if a case study is serving descriptive, and not explanatory, purposes. The same case can be described repeatedly, from different points of view or with different descriptive models, to understand how the case might best be categorized for descriptive purposes—similar to arriving at the correct diagnosis for a clinical patient in psychology. Of course, other variants of the comparative approach are possible, but the main feature is that the entire case study (or the results of a cross-case analysis when doing a multiple-case study) is repeated two or more times, in an overtly comparative mode.

Chronological Structures

Because case studies generally cover events over time, a third type of approach is to present the case study evidence in chronological order. Here, the sequence of chapters or sections might follow the early, middle, and late phases of a case history. This approach can serve an important purpose in doing explanatory case studies because presumed causal sequences must occur linearly over time. If a presumed cause of an event occurs after the event has occurred, one would have reason to question the initial causal proposition.

Whether for explanatory or descriptive purposes, a chronological approach has one pitfall to be avoided: giving disproportionate attention to the early events and insufficient attention to the later ones. Most commonly, an investigator will expend too much effort in composing the introduction to a case, including its early history and background, and leave insufficient time to write about the current status of the case. Yet, much of the interest in the case may be related to the more recent events. Thus, one recommendation when using a chronological structure is to *draft* the case study *backward.* Those chapters or sections that are about the current status of the case should be drafted first, and only after these drafts have been completed should the background to the case be drafted. Once all drafts have been completed, you can then return to the normal chronological sequence in then refining the final version of the case study.

Theory-Building Structures

In this approach, the sequence of chapters or sections will follow some theory-building logic. The logic will depend on the specific topic and theory, but each chapter or section should reveal a new part of the theoretical argument being made. If structured well, the entire sequence and its unfolding of key ideas can produce a compelling and impressive case study.

The approach is relevant to both explanatory and exploratory case studies, both of which can be concerned with theory building. Explanatory cases will be examining the various facets of a causal argument; exploratory cases will be debating the value of further investigating various hypotheses or propositions.

Suspense Structures

This structure inverts the linear-analytic structure described previously. The direct "answer" or outcome of a case study and its substantive significance is, paradoxically, presented in the initial chapter or section. The remainder of the case study—and its most suspenseful parts—are then devoted to the development of an explanation of this outcome, with alternative explanations considered in the ensuing chapters or sections.

This type of approach is relevant mainly to explanatory case studies, as a descriptive case study has no especially important outcome. When used well, the suspense approach is often an engaging compositional structure.

Unsequenced Structures

An unsequenced structure is one in which the sequence of sections or chapters assumes no particular importance. This structure is often sufficient for descriptive case studies, as in the example of *Middletown* (Lynd & Lynd, 1929), cited in Chapters 2 and 3 (BOXES 8 and 14). Basically, one could change the order of the chapters in that book and not alter its descriptive value.

Descriptive case studies of organizations often exhibit the same characteristic. Such case studies use separate chapters or sections to cover an organization's genesis and history, its ownership and employees, its product lines, its formal lines of organization, and its financial status. The particular order in which these chapters or sections is presented is not critical and may therefore be regarded as an unsequenced approach (see BOX 43 for another example).

BOX 43
Unsequenced Chapters, but in a Best-Selling Book

A best-selling book, appealing to both popular and academic audiences, was Peters and Waterman's (1982) *In Search of Excellence*. Although the book is based on more than 60 case studies of America's most successful large businesses, the text contains only the cross-case analysis, each chapter covering an insightful set of general characteristics associated with organizational excellence. However, the particular sequence of these chapters is alterable. The book would have made a significant contribution even if the chapters were in some other order.

If an unsequenced structure is used, the investigator does need to attend to one other problem: a test of completeness. Thus, even though the order of the chapters or sections may not matter, the overall collection does. If certain key topics are left uncovered, the description may be regarded as incomplete. An investigator must know a topic well enough—or have related models of case studies to reference—to avoid such a shortcoming. If a case study fails to present a complete description, the investigator can be accused of having assembled a skewed version of the case—even though the case study was only descriptive.

PROCEDURES IN DOING A CASE STUDY REPORT

Every investigator should have a well-developed set of procedures for analyzing social science data and for composing an empirical report. Numerous texts offer good advice on how you can develop your own customized procedures, including the benefits and pitfalls of using word-processing software (Becker, 1986, p. 160). One common warning is that writing means rewriting—a function not commonly practiced by students and therefore underestimated during the early years of research careers (Becker, 1986, pp. 43–47). The more rewriting, especially in response to others' comments, the better a report is likely to be. In this respect, the case study report is not much different from other research reports.

However, three important procedures pertain specifically to case studies and deserve further mention. The first deals with a general tactic for starting a composition, the second covers the problem of whether to leave the case identities anonymous, and the third describes a review procedure for increasing the *construct validity* of a case study.

When and How to Start Composing

The first procedure is to start composing early in the analytic process. One guide in fact admonishes that "you cannot begin writing early enough" (Wolcott, 1990, p. 20). From nearly the beginning of an investigation, certain sections of your report will always be draftable, and this drafting should proceed even before data collection and analysis have been completed.

For instance, after the literature has been reviewed and the case study has been designed, two sections of a case study report can be drafted: the bibliography and the methodological sections. The *bibliography* always can be augmented later with new citations if necessary, but by and large, the major citations will have been covered in relation to the literature review. This is therefore the time to formalize the references, to be sure that they are complete, and to construct a draft bibliography. If some references are incomplete, the remaining details can be tracked down while the rest of the case study proceeds. This will avoid the usual practice among researchers who do the bibliography last and who therefore spend much clerical time at the very end of their research, rather than attending to the more important (and pleasurable!) tasks of writing, rewriting, and editing.

The *methodological section* also can be drafted at this stage because the major procedures for data collection and analysis should have become part of the case study design. This section may not become a formal part of the final narrative but may be designated as an appendix. Whether part of the text or an appendix, however, the methodological section can and should be drafted at this early stage. You will remember your methodological procedures with greater precision at this juncture.

A third section is the *preliminary literature review* and how it led to or complemented your research questions and the propositions being studied. Because your case study will already have settled on these questions and propositions in order to proceed with protocol development and data collection, much of the connectivity to the literature will be known. Although you may need to revisit this early version after completing your data collection and analysis, having a preliminary draft never hurts.

After data collection but before analysis begins, a fourth section that can be composed covers the *descriptive data about the cases being studied.* Whereas the methodological section should have included the issues regarding the selection of the case(s), the descriptive data should cover qualitative and quantitative information about the case(s). At this stage in the research process, you still may not have finalized your ideas about the type of case study format to be used and the type of structure to be followed. However, the descriptive data are likely to be useful regardless of the format or structure. Furthermore, drafting the descriptive sections, even in abbreviated form, may stimulate your thinking about the overall format and structure.

If you can draft these four sections before analysis has been completed, you will have made a major advance. These sections also may call for substantial documentation (e.g., copies of your final case study protocol), and an opportune time to put such documentation into presentable form (possibly even "camera ready") occurs at this stage of the research. You also will be at an advantage if all details—citations, references, organizational titles, and spellings of people's names—have been accurately recorded during data collection and are integrated into the text at this time (Wolcott, 1990, p. 41).

If these sections are drafted properly, more attention can then be devoted to the analysis itself, as well as to the findings and conclusions. To begin composing early also serves another important psychological function: You may get accustomed to the compositional process as an ongoing (possibly even daily) practice and have a chance to routinize it before the task becomes truly awesome. Thus, if you can identify other sections that can be drafted at these early stages, you should draft them as well.

Case Identities: Real or Anonymous?

Nearly every case study presents an investigator with a choice regarding the anonymity of the case. Should the case study and its informants be accurately identified, or should the names of the entire case and its participants be disguised? Note that the anonymity issue can be raised at two levels: that of the entire case (or cases) and that of an individual person within a case (or cases).

The most desirable option is to disclose the identities of both the case and the individuals, within the constraints for protecting human subjects, discussed in Chapter 3. Disclosure produces two helpful outcomes. First, the reader has the opportunity to recollect any other previous information he or she may have learned about the same case—from previous research or other sources—in reading and interpreting your case study. This ability to become familiar with a new case study in light of prior knowledge is invaluable, similar to the ability to recall previous experimental results when reading about a new set of experiments. Second, the absence of disguised names will make the entire case easier to review, so that footnotes and citations can be checked, if necessary, and appropriate external comments can be solicited about the published case.

Nevertheless, anonymity is necessary on some occasions. The most common rationale occurs when a case study has been on a controversial topic. Anonymity then serves to protect the real case and its real participants. A second occasion occurs when the issuance of the final case report may affect the subsequent actions of those that were studied. This rationale was used in Whyte's (1943/1955) famous case study, *Street Corner Society* (which was about an anonymous neighborhood, "Cornerville").[2] As a third illustrative situation, the purpose of the case study may be to portray an "ideal type," and there may be no reason for disclosing the true identities. This rationale was used by the Lynds in their study *Middletown* (Lynd & Lynd, 1929), in which the names of the small town, its residents, and its industries all were disguised.

On such occasions when anonymity may appear justifiable, however, other compromises should still be sought. First, you should determine whether the anonymity of the individuals alone might be sufficient, thereby leaving the case itself to be identified accurately.

A second compromise would be to name the individuals but to avoid attributing any particular point of view or comment to a single individual, again allowing the case itself to be identified accurately. This second alternative is most relevant when you want to protect the confidentiality of specific individuals. However, the lack of attribution may not always be completely protective— you also may have to disguise the comments so that no one involved in the case can infer the likely source.

For multiple-case studies, a third compromise would be to avoid composing any single-case reports and to report only a cross-case analysis. This last situation would be roughly parallel to the procedure used in surveys, in which the individual responses are not disclosed and in which the published report is limited to the aggregate evidence.

Only if these compromises are impossible should you consider making the entire case study and its informants anonymous. However, anonymity is not to be considered a desirable choice. Not only does it eliminate some important background information about the case, but it also makes the mechanics of composing the case difficult. The case and its components must be systematically converted from their real identities to fictitious ones, and you must make a considerable effort to keep track of the conversions. The cost of undertaking such a procedure should not be underestimated.

> **EXERCISE 6.3   Maintaining Anonymity in Case Studies**
>
> Identify a case study whose "case" has been given a fictitious name (or check some of the boxes in this book for an example). What are the advantages and disadvantages of using such a technique? What approach would you use in reporting your own case study, and why?

Reviewing the Draft Case Study: A Validating Procedure

A third procedure to be followed in doing the case study report is related to the overall quality of the study. The procedure is to have the draft report reviewed, not just by peers (as would be done for any research manuscript) but also by the participants and informants in the case. If the comments are exceptionally helpful, the investigator may even want to publish them as part of the entire case study (see BOX 44).

Such review is more than a matter of professional courtesy. The procedure has been correctly identified as a way of corroborating the essential facts and evidence presented in a case report (Schatzman & Strauss, 1973, p. 134). The informants and participants may still disagree with an investigator's conclusions and interpretations, but these reviewers should not disagree over the actual facts of the case. If such disagreement emerges during the review process, an investigator knows that the case study report is not finished and that such disagreements must be settled through a search for further evidence.

BOX 44
Reviewing Case Studies—and Printing the Comments

A major way of improving the quality of case studies and ensuring their construct validity is to have the draft cases reviewed by those who have been the subjects of study. This procedure was followed to an exemplary degree in a set of five case studies by Alkin, Daillak, and White (1979).

Each case study was about a school district and the way that the district used evaluative information about its students' performance. As part of the analytic and reporting procedure, the draft for each case was reviewed by the informants from the relevant district. The comments were obtained in part as a result of an open-ended questionnaire devised by the investigators for just this purpose. In some instances, the responses were so insightful and helpful that the investigators modified their original material and also printed the responses as part of their book.

With such presentation of supplementary evidence and comments, any reader can reach her or his own conclusions about the adequacy of the cases—an opportunity that has occurred, unfortunately, all too seldom in traditional case study research.

Often, the opportunity to review the draft also produces further evidence, as the informants and participants may remember new materials that they had forgotten during the initial data collection period.

This type of review should be followed even if the case study or some of its components are to remain anonymous. Under this condition, some recognizable version of the draft must be shared with the case study informants or participants. After they have reviewed this draft, and after any differences in facts have been settled, the investigator can disguise the identities so that only the informants or participants will know the true identities. When Whyte (1943/1955) first completed *Street Corner Society,* he followed this procedure by sharing drafts of his book with "Doc," his major informant. He notes,

> As I wrote, I showed the various parts to Doc and went over them with him in detail. His criticisms were invaluable in my revision. (p. 341)

From a methodological standpoint, the corrections made through this process will enhance the accuracy of the case study, hence increasing the *construct validity* of the study. The likelihood of falsely reporting an event should be reduced. In addition, where no objective truth may exist—as when different participants indeed have different renditions of the same event—the procedure should help to identify the various perspectives, which can then be represented in the case study report. At the same time, you need not respond to all the comments made about the draft. For example, you are entitled to your own interpretation of the evidence and should not automatically incorporate your informants' reinterpretations. In this respect, your discretionary options are no different from how you might respond to comments made in the conventional peer review process.

The review of the draft case study by its informants will clearly extend the period of time needed to complete the case study report. Informants, unlike academic reviewers, may use the review cycle as an opportunity to begin a fresh dialogue about various facets of the case, thereby extending the review period even further. You must anticipate these extensions and not use them as an excuse to avoid the review process altogether. When the process has been given careful attention, the potential result is the production of a high-quality case study (see BOX 45).

BOX 45
Formal Reviews of Case Studies

As with any other research product, the review process plays an important role in enhancing and ensuring the quality of the final results. For case studies, such a review process should involve, at a minimum, a review of the draft case study.

One set of case studies that followed this procedure, to an exemplary degree, was sponsored by the U.S. Office of Technology Assessment (1980–1981). Each of 17 case studies, which were about medical technologies, was "seen by at least 20, and some by 40 or more, outside reviewers." Furthermore, the reviewers reflected different perspectives, including those of government agencies, professional societies, consumer and public interest groups, medical practice, academic medicine, and economics and decision sciences.

In one of the case studies, a contrary view of the case—put forth by one of the reviewers—was included as part of the final published version of the case, as well as a response by the case study authors. This type of open printed interchange adds to the reader's ability to interpret the case study's conclusions and therefore to the overall quality of the case study evidence.

EXERCISE 6.4   Anticipating the Difficulties of the Review Process

Case study reports are likely to be improved by having some review by informants—that is, those persons who were the subjects of the study. Discuss the pros and cons of having such reviews. What specific advantage, for quality control purposes, is served? What disadvantages are there? On balance, are such reviews worthwhile?

WHAT MAKES AN EXEMPLARY CASE STUDY?

In all of case study research, one of the most challenging tasks is to define an exemplary case study. Although no direct evidence is available, some speculations seem an appropriate way of concluding this book.[3]

The exemplary case study goes beyond the methodological procedures already highlighted throughout this book. Even if you, as a case study investigator, have followed most of the basic techniques—using a case study protocol, maintaining a chain of evidence, establishing a case study database, and so on—you still may not have produced an *exemplary* case study. The mastering of these techniques makes you a good technician but not necessarily an esteemed social scientist. To take but one analogy, consider the difference between a chronicler and a historian: The former is technically correct but does not produce the insights into human or social processes provided by the latter.

Five general characteristics of an exemplary case study are described below. They are intended to help your case study to be a lasting contribution to research.

EXERCISE 6.5   Defining a Good Case Study

Select a case study that you believe is one of the best you know (again, the selection can be from the BOXES in this book). What makes it a good case study? Why are such characteristics so infrequently found in other case studies? What specific efforts might you make to emulate such a good case study?

The Case Study Must Be Significant

The first general characteristic may be beyond the control of many investigators. If an investigator has access to only a few "cases," or if resources are extremely limited, the ensuing case study may have to be on a topic of only marginal significance. This situation is not likely to produce an exemplary case study. However, where choice exists, the exemplary case study is likely to be one in which

♦ the individual case or cases are unusual and of general public interest,

♦ the underlying issues are nationally important—either in theoretical terms or in policy or practical terms, or

♦ your case meets both of the preceding conditions.

For instance, a single-case study may have been chosen because it was a revelatory case—that is, one reflecting some real-life situation that social scientists had not been able to study in the past. This revelatory case is in itself likely to be regarded as a discovery and to provide an opportunity for doing an exemplary case study. Alternatively, a critical case may have been chosen because of the desire to compare two rival propositions; if the propositions are at the core of a well-known debate in the literature—or reflect major differences in public beliefs—the case study is likely to be significant. Finally, imagine the situation in which both discovery and theory development are found within the same case study, as in a multiple-case study in which each individual case reveals a discovery but in which the replication across cases also adds up to a significant theoretical breakthrough. This situation truly lends itself to the production of an exemplary case study.

In contrast to these promising situations, many students select nondistinctive cases or outmoded theoretical issues as the topics for their case studies. This situation can be avoided, in part, by doing better homework with regard to the existing body of research. Prior to selecting a case study, you should describe, in detail, the contribution to be made, assuming that the intended case study were to be completed successfully. If no satisfactory answer is forthcoming, you might want to plan another case study.

The Case Study Must Be "Complete"

This characteristic is extremely difficult to describe operationally. However, a sense of completeness is as important in doing a case study as it is in defining a complete series of laboratory experiments (or in completing a symphony or finishing a painting). All have the problem of defining the boundaries of the effort, but few guidelines are available.

For case studies, completeness can be characterized in at least three ways. First, the complete case is one in which the boundaries of the case—that is, the distinction between the phenomenon being studied and its context—are given explicit attention. If this is done only mechanically—for example, by declaring at the outset that only arbitrary time intervals or spatial boundaries will be considered—a nonexemplary case study is likely to result. The best way is to show, either through logical argument or the presentation of evidence, that as the analytic periphery is reached, the information is of decreasing relevance to the case study. Such testing of the boundaries can occur throughout the analytic and reporting steps in doing case studies.

A second way involves the collection of evidence. The complete case study should demonstrate convincingly that the investigator expended exhaustive effort in collecting the relevant evidence. The documentation of such evidence need not be placed in the text of the case study, thereby dulling its content. Footnotes, appendices, and the like will do. The overall goal, nevertheless, is to convince the reader that little relevant evidence remained untouched by the investigator, given the boundaries of the case study. This does not mean that the investigator should literally collect all available evidence—an impossible task—but that the critical pieces have been given "complete" attention. Such critical pieces, for instance, would be those representing rival propositions.

A third way concerns the absence of certain artifactual conditions. A case study is not likely to be complete if the study ended only because resources were exhausted, because the investigator ran out of time (when the semester ended), or because she or he faced other, nonresearch constraints. When a time or resource constraint is known at the outset of a study, the responsible investigator should design a case study that can be completed within such constraints, rather than reaching and possibly exceeding his or her limits. This type of design requires much experience and some good fortune. Nevertheless, these are the conditions under which an exemplary case study is likely to be produced. Unfortunately, if in contrast a severe time or resource constraint suddenly emerges in the middle of a case study, it is unlikely that the case study will become exemplary.

The Case Study Must Consider Alternative Perspectives

For explanatory case studies, one valuable approach is the consideration of rival propositions and the analysis of the evidence in terms of such rivals (see Chapter 5). The citing of rival claims or alternative perspectives also should be part of a good abstract for your case study (Kelly & Yin, 2007). Even in doing an exploratory or a descriptive case study, the examination of the evidence from different perspectives will increase the chances that a case study will be exemplary.

For instance, a descriptive case study that fails to account for different perspectives may raise a critical reader's suspicions. The investigator may not have collected all the relevant evidence and only may have attended to the evidence supporting a single point of view. Even if the investigator was not purposefully biased, different descriptive interpretations might not have been entertained, thereby presenting a one-sided case. To this day, this type of problem persists whenever studies of organizations appear to represent the perspectives of management and not workers, or when studies of social groups appear to be insensitive to issues of gender or multiculturalism, or when studies of youth programs appear to represent adult perspectives and ignore those of youths.

To represent different perspectives adequately, an investigator must seek those alternatives that most seriously challenge the assumptions of the case study. These perspectives may be found in alternative cultural views, different theories, variations among the stakeholders or decision makers who are part of the case study, or some similar contrasts. If sufficiently important, the alternative perspectives can appear as alternative renditions covering the same case, using the comparative structure of composition described earlier in this chapter as one of seven possible structures. Less prominently but still invaluable would be the presentation of alternative views as separate chapters or sections of the main case study (see BOX 46).

BOX 46
Adding Alternative Perspectives, Written by a
Case Study's Participants, as Supplements to a Case Study

Edgar Schein's (2003) single-case study tried to explain the demise of a computer firm that had been among the country's top 50 corporations in size (see BOX 28, Chapter 5, p. 142). The contemporary nature of the case study meant that the firm's former executives were still available to offer their own rendition of the firm's fate. Schein supported his own explanation with much documentation and interview data, but he made his case study distinctive in another way: He also included supplementary chapters, each giving a key executive the opportunity to present his own rival explanation.

Many times, if an investigator describes a case study to a critical listener, the listener will immediately offer an alternative interpretation of the facts of the case. Under such circumstances, the investigator is likely to become defensive and to argue that the original interpretation was the only relevant or correct one. In fact, the exemplary case study anticipates these "obvious" alternatives, even advocates their positions as forcefully as possible, and shows—empirically—the basis upon which such alternatives might be rejected.

The Case Study Must Display Sufficient Evidence

Although Chapter 4 encouraged investigators to create a case study database, the critical pieces of evidence for a case study must still be contained within the case study report. The exemplary case study is one that judiciously and effectively presents the most relevant evidence, so that a reader can reach an independent judgment regarding the merits of the analysis.

This selectiveness does not mean that the evidence should be cited in a biased manner—for example, by including only the evidence that supports an investigator's conclusions. On the contrary, the evidence should be presented neutrally, with both supporting and challenging data. The reader should then be able to draw an independent conclusion about the validity of a particular interpretation. The selectiveness is relevant in limiting the report to the most critical evidence and not cluttering the presentation with supportive but secondary information. Such selectiveness takes a lot of discipline among investigators, who usually want to display their entire evidentiary base, in the (false) hope that sheer volume or weight will sway the reader. (In fact, sheer volume or weight will bore the reader.)

Another goal is to present enough evidence to gain the reader's confidence that the investigator "knows" his or her subject. In doing a field study, for instance, the evidence presented should convince the reader that the investigator has indeed been in the field, made penetrating inquiries while there, and has become steeped in the issues about the case. A parallel goal exists in multiple-case studies: The investigator should show the reader that all of the single cases have been treated fairly and that the cross-case conclusions have not been biased by undue attention to one or a few of the entire array of cases.

Finally, the display of adequate evidence should be accompanied by some indication that the investigator attended to the validity of the evidence—in maintaining a chain of evidence, for example. This does not mean that all case studies need to be burdened with methodological treatises. A few judicious footnotes will serve the purpose. Alternatively, some words in the preface of the case study can cover the critical validating steps. Notes to a table or figure also will help. As a negative example, a figure or table that presents evidence without citing its source is an indication of sloppy research and cautions the reader to be more critical of other aspects of the case study. This is not a situation that produces exemplary case studies.

The Case Study Must Be Composed in an Engaging Manner

One last global characteristic has to do with the composition of the case study report. Regardless of the medium used (a written report, an oral presentation, or some other form), the report should be engaging.

For written reports, this means a clear writing style, but one that constantly entices the reader to continue reading. A good manuscript is one that "seduces" the eye. If you read such a manuscript, your eye will not want to leave the page, and you will continue to read paragraph after paragraph, page after page, until exhaustion sets in. Anyone reading good fiction has had this experience. This type of seduction should be the goal in composing any case study report.

The production of such seductive writing calls for talent and experience. The more often that someone has written for the same audience, the more likely that the communication will be effective. However, the clarity of writing also increases with rewriting, which is highly recommended. With the use of electronic writing tools, an investigator has no excuse for shortcutting the rewriting process.

Engagement, enticement, and seduction—these are unusual characteristics of case studies. To produce such a case study requires an investigator to be enthusiastic about the investigation and to want to communicate the results widely. In fact, the good investigator might even think that the case study contains earth-shattering conclusions. This sort of inspiration should pervade the entire investigation and will indeed lead to an exemplary case study.

NOTES

1. Ignored here is a frequent audience for case studies: students taking a course using case studies as a curriculum material. Such use of case studies, as indicated in Chapter 1, is for teaching and not research purposes, and the entire case study strategy might be defined and pursued differently under these conditions.

2. Of course, even when an investigator makes the identity of a case or its participants anonymous, a few other colleagues—sharing the confidence of the investigator—will usually know the real identities. In the case of both *Street Corner Society* and *Middletown*, other sociologists, especially those working in the same academic departments as Whyte and the Lynds, were quite aware of the real identities.

3. The speculations also are based on some empirical findings. As part of an earlier investigation, 21 prominent social scientists were asked to name the best qualities of case studies (see COSMOS Corporation, 1983). Some of these qualities are reflected in this discussion of exemplary case studies.

REFERENCE TO EXPANDED CASE STUDY
MATERIALS FOR CHAPTER 6

For selected case studies cited in the text of this chapter, one anthology contains either a more extensive excerpt or the full case study. The table below crosswalks the reference in this book to the location of the excerpt or full rendition.

Chapter 6 Chapter Topic and Page Number	Topics of Illustrative Case Studies	Reference to Lengthier Material
Targeting Case Study Reports		
BOX 36, p. 6-5	Government agencies	None
BOX 37, p. 6-5	Urban planning	None
BOX 38, p. 6-6	Societies	None
BOX 39, p. 6-8	Innovations	None
BOX 40, p. 6-9	Community organizations	ACSR-2
p. 6-9 text	Community organizations	ACSR-2
BOX 41A, p. 6-9	Leadership	None
BOX 41B, p. 6-9	Societies	None
Case Study Reports as Part of Larger, Mixed Methods Studies		
BOX 42, p. 6-12	Schools	None
Illustrative Structures for Case Study Compositions		
BOX 43, p. 6-17	Business and industry	None
Procedures for Doing a Case Study Report		
BOX 44, p. 6-23	Schools	None
BOX 45, p. 6-24	Health care	None
What Makes an Exemplary Case Study?		
BOX 46, p. 6-29	Business and industry	None

NOTE: ACSR = *Applications of Case Study Research* (Yin, 2003). The number denotes the chapter number in the book.

References

Agranoff, R., & Radin, B. A. (1991). The comparative case study approach in public administration. *Research in Public Administration, 1,* 203–231.

Alkin, M., Daillak, R., & White, P. (1979). *Using evaluations: Does evaluation make a difference?* Beverly Hills, CA: Sage.

Allison, G. T. (1971). *Essence of decision: Explaining the Cuban missile crisis.* Boston: Little, Brown.

Allison, G. T., & Zelikow, P. (1999). *Essence of decision: Explaining the Cuban missile crisis* (2nd ed.). New York: Addison Wesley Longman.

Barzun, J., & Graff, H. (1985). *The modern researcher* (4th ed.). New York: Harcourt Brace Jovanovich.

Basu, O. N., Dirsmith, M. W., & Gupta, P. P. (1999). The coupling of the symbolic and the technical in an institutionalized context. *American Sociological Review, 64,* 506–526.

Becker, H. S. (1958). Problems of inference and proof in participant observation. *American Sociological Review, 23,* 652–660.

Becker, H. S. (1967). Whose side are we on? *Social Problems, 14,* 239–247.

Becker, H. S. (1986). *Writing for social scientists: How to start and finish your thesis, book, or article.* Chicago: University of Chicago Press.

Becker, H. S. (1998). *Tricks of the trade: How to think about your research while you're doing it.* Chicago: University of Chicago Press.

Benbasat, I., Goldstein, D. K., & Mead, M. (1987). The case research strategy in studies of information systems. *MIS Quarterly, 11,* 369–386.

Berends, M., & Garet, M. S. (2002). In (re)search of evidence-based school practices: Possibilities for integrating nationally representative surveys and randomized field trials to inform educational policy. *Peabody Journal of Education, 77*(4), 28–58.

Berman, P., & McLaughlin, M. (1974–1978). *Federal programs supporting educational change* (8 vols.). Santa Monica, CA: RAND.

Bickman, L. (1987). The functions of program theory. In L. Bickman (Ed.), *Using program theory in evaluation* (pp. 5–18). San Francisco: Jossey-Bass.

Bickman, L., & Rog, D. J. (Eds.). (2000). *Handbook of applied research methods.* Thousand Oaks, CA: Sage.

Blau, P. M. (1955). *The dynamics of bureaucracy.* Chicago: University of Chicago Press.

Bonoma, T. V. (1985). Case research in marketing: Opportunities, problems, and a process. *Journal of Marketing Research, 12,* 199–208.

Boruch, R. (2007, October 12). *The flight of error: Scientific questions, evidential answers, and STEM education research.* Presentation at workshop on STEM Education Research Designs: Conceptual and Practical Considerations for Planning Experimental Studies, Arlington, VA, sponsored by the University of California, Irvine.

193

Boruch, R., & Foley, E. (2000). The honestly experimental society. In L. Bickman (Ed.), *Validity & social experimentation: Donald Campbell's legacy* (pp. 193–238). Thousand Oaks, CA: Sage.

Bouchard, T. J., Jr. (1976). Field research methods. In M. D. Dunnette (Ed.), *Industrial and organizational psychology* (pp. 363–413). Chicago: Rand McNally.

Boyatzis, R. E. (1998). *Transforming qualitative information: Thematic analysis and code development.* Thousand Oaks, CA: Sage.

Bradshaw, T. K. (1999). Communities not fazed: Why military base closures may not be catastrophic. *Journal of the American Planning Association, 65,* 193–206.

Brinton, C. (1938). *The anatomy of a revolution.* Englewood Cliffs, NJ: Prentice Hall.

Bruns, W. J., Jr. (1989). A review of Robert K. Yin's 'Case Study Research: Design and Methods.' *Journal of Management Accounting Research, 1,* 157–163.

Bryk, A. S., Bebring, P. B., Kerbow, D., Rollow, S., & Easton, J. Q. (1998). *Charting Chicago school reform: Democratic localism as a lever for change.* Boulder, CO: Westview.

Campbell, D. T. (1969). Reforms as experiments. *American Psychologist, 24,* 409–429.

Campbell, D. T. (1975). Degrees of freedom and the case study. *Comparative Political Studies, 8,* 178–193.

Campbell, D. T., & Stanley, J. (1966). *Experimental and quasi-experimental designs for research.* Chicago: Rand McNally.

Campbell, J. P., Daft, R. L., & Hulin, C. L. (1982). *What to study: Generating and developing research questions.* Beverly Hills, CA: Sage.

Carr, P. J. (2003). The new parochialism: The implications of the Beltway case for arguments concerning informal social control. *American Journal of Sociology, 108,* 1249–1291.

Carroll, J., & Johnson, E. (1992). Decision research: A field guide. *Journal of the Operational Research Society, 43,* 71–72.

Caulley, D. N., & Dowdy, I. (1987). Evaluation case histories as a parallel to legal case histories. *Evaluation and Program Planning, 10,* 359–372.

Chaskin, R. J. (2001). Building community capacity: A definitional framework and case studies from a comprehensive community initiative. *Urban Affairs Review, 36,* 291–323.

Cochran, W. G., & Cox, G. M. (1957). *Experimental designs* (2nd ed.). New York: John Wiley.

Cook, T. D., & Campbell, D. T. (1979). *Quasi-experimentation: Design and analysis issues for field settings.* Chicago: Rand McNally.

Cook, T. D., & Payne, M. R. (2002). Objecting to the objections to using random assignment in educational research. In F. Mosteller & R. Boruch (Eds.), *Evidence matters: Randomized trials in education research* (pp. 150–178). Washington, DC: Brookings Institution Press.

Cooper, H. M. (1984). *The integrative research review.* Beverly Hills, CA: Sage.

Cooper, H. M., & Hedges, L. V. (Eds.). (1994). *The handbook of research synthesis.* New York: Russell Sage Foundation.

Corbin, J., & Strauss, A. (2007). *Basics of qualitative research: Techniques and procedures for developing grounded theory* (3rd ed.). Thousand Oaks, CA: Sage.

COSMOS Corporation. (1983). *Case studies and organizational innovation: Strengthening the connection.* Bethesda, MD: Author.

COSMOS Corporation. (1998). *Evaluation of MEP-SBDC partnerships: Final report.* Report prepared for the National Institute of Standards and Technology, U.S. Department of Commerce, Gaithersburg, MD.

Crabtree, B. F., & Miller, W. L. (Eds.). (1999). *Doing qualitative research* (2nd ed.). Thousand Oaks, CA: Sage.

Crane, J. (Ed.). (1998). *Social programs that work.* New York: Russell Sage Foundation.

Creswell, J. W. (2007). *Qualitative inquiry & research design: Choosing among five approaches* (2nd ed.). Thousand Oaks, CA: Sage.

Crewe, K. (2001). The quality of participatory design: The effects of citizen input on the design of the Boston Southwest Corridor. *APA Journal, 67,* 437–455.

Cronbach, L. J., & Associates. (1980). *Toward reform of program evaluation: Aims, methods, and institutional arrangements.* San Francisco: Jossey-Bass.

Dabbs, J. M., Jr. (1982). Making things visible. In J. Van Maanen, J. M. Dabbs Jr., & R. R. Faulkner (Eds.), *Varieties of qualitative research* (pp. 31–63). Beverly Hills, CA: Sage.

Datta, L. (1997). Multimethod evaluations. In E. Chelimsky & W. R. Shadish (Eds.), *Evaluation for the 21st century* (pp. 344–359). Thousand Oaks, CA: Sage.

Denzin, N. K. (1978). The logic of naturalistic inquiry. In N. K. Denzin (Ed.), *Sociological methods: A sourcebook.* New York: McGraw-Hill.

Derthick, M. (1972). *New towns in-town: Why a federal program failed.* Washington, DC: The Urban Institute.

Dion, D. (1998). Evidence and inference in the comparative case study. *Comparative Politics, 30,* 127–145.

Drucker, P. F. (1986). The changed world economy. In P. F. Drucker (Ed.), *The frontiers of management* (pp. 21–49). New York: Dutton.

Eckstein, H. (1975). Case study and theory in political science. In F. I. Greenstein & N. W. Polsby (Eds.), *Strategies of inquiry* (pp. 79–137). Reading, MA: Addison-Wesley.

Eilbert, K. W., & Lafronza, V. (2005). Working together for community health—a model and case studies. *Evaluation and Program Planning, 28,* 185–199.

Eisenhardt, K. M. (1989). Building theories from case study research. *Academy of Management Review, 14,* 532–550.

Elmore, R. F., Abelmann, C. H., & Fuhrman, S. H. (1997). The new accountability in state education reform: From process to performance. In H. F. Ladd (Ed.), *Holding schools accountable* (pp. 65–98). Washington, DC: Brookings Institution.

Ericksen, J., & Dyer, L. (2004). Right from the start: Exploring the effects of early team events on subsequent project team development and performance. *Administrative Science Quarterly, 49,* 438–471.

Feagin, J. R., Orum, A. M., & Sjoberg, G. (Eds.). (1991). *A case for the case study.* Chapel Hill: University of North Carolina Press.

Fetterman, D. (1989). *Ethnography: Step by step.* Newbury Park, CA: Sage.

Fiedler, J. (1978). *Field research: A manual for logistics and management of scientific studies in natural settings.* San Francisco: Jossey-Bass.

Fielding, N. G., & Lee, R. M. (1998). *Computer analysis and qualitative research.* Thousand Oaks, CA: Sage.

Flippen, C. (2001). Neighborhood transition and social organization: The White to Hispanic case. *Social Problems, 48,* 299–321.

Fowler, F. J., Jr. (1988). *Survey research methods* (Rev. ed.). Newbury Park, CA: Sage.

Galster, G., Tatian, P., & Accordino, J. (2006). Targeting investments for neighborhood revitalization. *Journal of the American Planning Association, 72,* 457–474.

Gans, H. J. (1962). *The urban villagers: Group and class in the life of Italian-Americans.* New York: Free Press.

Garvin, D.A. (2003, September–October). Making the case: Professional education for the world of practice. *Harvard Magazine, 106*(1), 56–107.

George, A. L., & Bennett, A. (2004). *Case studies and theory development in the social sciences.* Cambridge: MIT Press.

Gerring, J. (2004). What is a case study and what is it good for? *American Political Science Review, 98,* 341–354.

Ghauri, P., & Grønhaug, K. (2002). *Research methods in business studies: A practical guide.* Harlow, England: Pearson Education.

Gibbert, M., & Ruigrok, W. (2007). What passes as a rigorous case study? *Strategic Management Journal.*

Gilgun, J. F. (1994). A case for case studies in social work research. *Social Work, 39,* 371–380.

Glaser, B., & Strauss, A. (1967). *The discovery of grounded theory: Strategies for qualitative research.* Chicago: Aldine.

Gomm, R., Hammersley, M., & Foster, P. (Eds.). (2000). *Case study method: Key issues, key texts.* Thousand Oaks, CA: Sage.

Gottschalk, L. (1968). *Understanding history: A primer of historical method.* New York: Knopf.

Graebner, M. E., & Eisenhardt, K. M. (2004). The seller's side of the story: Acquisition as courtship and governance as syndicated in entrepreneurial firms. *Administrative Science Quarterly, 49,* 366–403.

Gross, N., Bernstein, M., & Giacquinta, J. B. (1971). *Implementing organizational innovations: A sociological analysis of planned educational change.* New York: Basic Books.

Hamel, J. (Ed.). (1992). The case study method in sociology [Whole issue]. *Current Sociology, 40.*

Hammond, P. E. (1968). *Sociologists at work: Essays on the craft of social research.* Garden City, NY: Doubleday.

Hanna, K. S. (2000). The paradox of participation and the hidden role of information. *Journal of the American Planning Association, 66,* 398–410.

Hanna, K. S. (2005). Planning for sustainability. *Journal of the American Planning Association, 71,* 27–40.

Hedrick, T., Bickman, L., & Rog, D. J. (1993). *Applied research design*. Newbury Park, CA: Sage.

Herriott, R. E., & Firestone, W. A. (1983). Multisite qualitative policy research: Optimizing description and generalizability. *Educational Researcher, 12*, 14–19.

Hersen, M., & Barlow, D. H. (1976). *Single-case experimental designs: Strategies for studying behavior.* New York: Pergamon.

Hipp, J. R. (2007). Block, tract, and levels of aggregation: Neighborhood structure and crime and disorder as a case in point. *American Sociological Review, 72*, 659–680.

Hoaglin, D. C., Light, R. J., McPeek, B., Mosteller, F., & Stoto, M. A. (1982). *Data for decisions: Information strategies for policymakers.* Cambridge, MA: Abt Books.

Hooks, G. (1990). The rise of the Pentagon and U.S. state building: The defense program as industrial policy. *American Journal of Sociology, 96*, 358–404.

Jacobs, J. (1961). *The death and life of great American cities.* New York: Random House.

Jacobs, R. N. (1996). Civil society and crisis: Culture, discourse, and the Rodney King beating. *American Journal of Sociology, 101*, 1238–1272.

Jadad, A. (1998). *Randomised controlled trials.* London: BMJ Books.

Johnson, R. B., & Onwuegbuzie, A. J. (2004). Mixed methods research: A research paradigm whose time has come. *Educational Researcher, 33*, 14–26.

Joint Committee on Standards for Educational Evaluation. (1981). *Standards for evaluations of educational programs, projects, and materials.* New York: McGraw-Hill.

Jorgensen, D. (1989). *Participant observation: A methodology for human studies.* Newbury Park, CA: Sage.

Kaufman, H. (1981). *The administrative behavior of federal bureau chiefs.* Washington, DC: Brookings Institution.

Keating, W. D., & Krumholz, N. (Eds.). (1999). *Rebuilding urban neighborhoods: Achievements, opportunities, and limits.* Thousand Oaks, CA: Sage.

Kelling, G. L., & Coles, C. M. (1997). *Fixing broken windows: Restoring order and reducing crime in our communities.* New York: Simon & Schuster.

Kelly, A. E., & Yin, R. K. (2007). Strengthening structured abstracts for education research: The need for claim-based structured abstracts. *Educational Researcher, 36*, 133–138.

Kennedy, M. M. (1976). Generalizing from single case studies. *Evaluation Quarterly, 3*, 661–678.

Kidder, L., & Judd, C. M. (1986). *Research methods in social relations* (5th ed.). New York: Holt, Rinehart & Winston.

Kidder, T. (1981). *The soul of a new machine.* Boston: Little, Brown.

Kratochwill, T. R. (1978). *Single subject research.* New York: Academic Press.

Lavrakas, P. J. (1987). *Telephone survey methods.* Newbury Park, CA: Sage.

Lawrence-Lightfoot, S., & Davis, J. H. (1997). *The art and science of portraiture.* San Francisco: Jossey-Bass.

Liebow, E. (1967). *Tally's corner.* Boston: Little, Brown.

Lijphart, A. (1975). The comparable-cases strategy in comparative research. *Comparative Political Studies, 8*, 158–177.

Lincoln, Y. S., & Guba, E. G. (1985). But is it rigorous? Trustworthiness and authenticity in naturalistic evaluation. In D. D. Williams (Ed.), *Naturalistic evaluation* (pp. 73–84). San Francisco: Jossey-Bass.

Lipset, S. M., Trow, M., & Coleman, J. (1956). *Union democracy: The inside politics of the International Typographical Union.* New York: Free Press.

Lipsey, M. W. (1992). Meta-analysis in evaluation research: Moving from description to explanation. In H. T. Chen & P. Rossi (Eds.), *Using theory to improve program and policy evaluations* (pp. 229–241). New York: Greenwood.

Llewellyn, K. N. (1948). Case method. In E. Seligman & A. Johnson (Eds.), *Encyclopedia of the social sciences.* New York: Macmillan.

Lynd, R. S., & Lynd, H. M. (1929). *Middletown: A study in modern American culture.* New York: Harcourt Brace Jovanovich.

Magaziner, I. C., & Patinkin, M. (1989). *The silent war: Inside the global business battles shaping America's future.* New York: Random House.

Markus, M. L. (1983). Power, politics, and MIS implementation. *Communications of the ACM, 26,* 430–444.

Marshall, C., & Rossman, G. B. (1989). *Designing qualitative research.* Newbury Park, CA: Sage.

McAdams, D. R. (2000). *Fighting to save our urban schools . . . and winning! Lessons from Houston.* New York: Teachers College Press.

McClintock, C. (1985). Process sampling: A method for case study research on administrative behavior. *Educational Administration Quarterly, 21,* 205–222.

Merton, R. K., Fiske, M., & Kendall, P. L. (1990). *The focused interview: A manual of problems and procedures* (2nd ed.). New York: Free Press.

Miles, M. B., & Huberman, A. M. (1994). *Qualitative data analysis: An expanded sourcebook.* Thousand Oaks, CA: Sage.

Moore, B., Jr. (1966). *Social origins of dictatorship and democracy: Lord and peasant in the making of the modern world.* Boston: Beacon.

Morris, L. L., Fitz-Gibbon, C. T., & Freeman, M. E. (1987). *How to communicate evaluation findings.* Beverly Hills, CA: Sage.

Mosteller, F., & Wallace, D. L. (1984). *Applied Bayesian and classical inference: The case of "The Federalist" papers* (2nd ed.). New York: Springer Verlag.

Mulroy, E. A., & Lauber, H. (2004). A user-friendly approach to program evaluation and effective community interventions for families at risk of homelessness. *Social Work, 49,* 573–586.

Murphy, J. T. (1980). *Getting the facts: A fieldwork guide for evaluators and policy analysts.* Santa Monica, CA: Goodyear.

Nachmias, D., & Nachmias, C. (1992). *Research methods in the social sciences.* New York: St. Martin's.

Naumes, W., & Naumes, M. J. (1999). *The art & craft of case writing.* Thousand Oaks, CA: Sage.

Nesman, T. M., Batsche, C., & Hernandez, M. (2007). Theory-based evaluation of a comprehensive Latino education initiative: An interactive evaluation approach. *Evaluation and Program Planning, 30,* 267–281.

Neuman, S. B., & Celano, D. (2001). Access to print in low-income and middle-income communities: An ecological study of four neighborhoods. *Reading Research Quarterly, 36,* 8–26.

Neustadt, R. E., & Fineberg, H. (1983). *The epidemic that never was: Policy-making and the swine flu affair.* New York: Vintage.

Patton, M. Q. (2002). *Qualitative research and evaluation methods* (3rd ed.). Thousand Oaks, CA: Sage.

Perry, J. M., & Kraemer, K. L. (1986). Research methodology in the public administration review. *Public Administration Review, 46,* 215–226.

Peters, T. J., & Waterman, R. H., Jr. (1982). *In search of excellence.* New York: Harper & Row.

Peterson, K. A., & Bickman, L. (1992). Using program theory in quality assessments of children's mental health services. In H. T. Chen & P. Rossi (Eds.), *Using theory to improve program and policy evaluations* (pp. 165–176). New York: Greenwood.

Philliber, S. G., Schwab, M. R., & Samsloss, G. (1980). *Social research: Guides to a decision-making process.* Itasca, IL: Peacock.

Platt, J. (1992). "Case study" in American methodological thought. *Current Sociology, 40,* 17–48.

Pluye, P., Potvin, L., Denis, J.-L., Pelletier, J., & Mannoni, C. (2005). Program sustainability begins with the first events. *Evaluation and Program Planning, 28,* 123–137.

Pressman, J. L., & Wildavsky, A. (1973). *Implementation: How great expectations in Washington are dashed in Oakland.* Berkeley: University of California Press.

Ragin, C. C., & Becker, H. S. (Eds.). (1992). *What is a case? Exploring the foundations of social inquiry.* New York: Cambridge University Press.

Raizen, S. A., & Britton, E. D. (Eds.). (1997). *Bold ventures* (3 vols.). Dordrecht, The Netherlands: Kluwer Academic.

Randolph, J. J., & Eronen, P. J. (2007). Developing the Learner Door: A case study in youth participatory program planning. *Evaluation and Program Planning, 30,* 55–65.

Redman, E. (1973). *The dance of legislation.* New York: Simon & Schuster.

Richard, L., Lehoux, P., Breton, É., Denis, J.-L., Labrie, L., & Léonard, C. (2004). Implementing the ecological approach in tobacco control programs: Results of a case study. *Evaluation and Program Planning, 27,* 409–421.

Rog, D. J., & Huebner, R. B. (1992). Using research and theory in developing innovative programs for homeless individuals. In H. T. Chen & P. Rossi (Eds.), *Using theory to improve program and policy evaluations* (pp. 129–144). New York: Greenwood.

Rogers, E. M., & Larsen, J. K. (1984). *Silicon Valley fever: Growth of high-technology culture.* New York: Basic Books.

Rosenbaum, D. P. (Ed.). (1986). *Community crime prevention: Does it work?* Thousand Oaks, CA: Sage.

Rosenbaum, P. R. (2002). *Observational studies* (2nd ed.). New York: Springer.

Rosenthal, R. (1966). *Experimenter effects in behavioral research.* New York: Appleton-Century-Crofts.

Rubin, A., & Babbie, E. (1993). *Research methods for social work.* Pacific Grove, CA: Brooks/Cole.

Rubin, H. J., & Rubin, I. S. (1995). *Qualitative interviewing: The art of hearing data.* Thousand Oaks, CA: Sage.

Schatzman, L., & Strauss, A. (1973). *Field research.* Englewood Cliffs, NJ: Prentice Hall.

Schein, E. (2003). *DEC is dead, long live DEC: Lessons on innovation, technology, and the business gene.* San Francisco: Berrett-Koehler.

Schorr, L. B. (1997). *Common purpose: Strengthening families and neighborhoods to rebuild America.* New York: Anchor.

Schramm, W. (1971, December). *Notes on case studies of instructional media projects.* Working paper for the Academy for Educational Development, Washington, DC.

Selznick, P. (1980). *TVA and the grass roots: A study of politics and organization.* Berkeley: University of California Press. (Original work published 1949)

Shavelson, R., & Townes, L. (Eds.). (2002). *Scientific research in education.* Washington, DC: National Academy Press.

Sidowski, J. B. (Ed.). (1966). *Experimental methods and instrumentation in psychology.* New York: Holt, Rinehart & Winston.

Silverman, D. (2000). *Doing qualitative research: A practical handbook.* Thousand Oaks, CA: Sage.

Spilerman, S. (1971). The causes of racial disturbances: Tests of an explanation. *American Sociological Review, 36,* 427–442.

Stake, R. E. (1995). *The art of case study research.* Thousand Oaks, CA: Sage.

Stake, R. E. (2005). Qualitative case studies. In N. K. Denzin & Y. S. Lincoln (Eds.), *The Sage handbook of qualitative research* (3rd ed., pp. 443–466). Thousand Oaks, CA: Sage.

Stake, R. E. (2006). *Multiple case study analysis.* New York: Guilford.

Standerfer, N. R., & Rider, J. (1983). The politics of automating a planning office. *Planning, 49,* 18–21.

Stein, H. (1952). Case method and the analysis of public administration. In H. Stein (Ed.), *Public administration and policy development* (pp. xx–xxx). New York: Harcourt Brace Jovanovich.

Stoecker, R. (1991). Evaluating and rethinking the case study. *The Sociological Review, 39,* 88–112.

Sudman, S., & Bradburn, N. M. (1982). *Asking questions: A practical guide to questionnaire design.* San Francisco: Jossey-Bass.

Supovitz, J. A., & Taylor, B.S. (2005). Systemic education evaluation: Evaluating the impact of systemwide reform in education. *American Journal of Evaluation, 26,* 204–230.

Sutton, R. I., & Staw, B. M. (1995). What theory is *not. Administrative Science Quarterly, 40,* 371–384.

Szanton, P. (1981). *Not well advised.* New York: Russell Sage Foundation and The Ford Foundation.

Thacher, D. (2006). The normative case study. *American Journal of Sociology, 111,* 1631–1676.

Towl, A. R. (1969). *To study administrations by cases.* Boston: Harvard University Business School.

Trochim, W. (1989). Outcome pattern matching and program theory. *Evaluation and Program Planning, 12,* 355–366.

U.S. Government Accountability Office, Program Evaluation and Methodology Division. (1990). *Case study evaluations.* Washington, DC: Government Printing Office.

U.S. National Commission on Neighborhoods. (1979). *People, building neighborhoods.* Washington, DC: Government Printing Office.

U.S. Office of Technology Assessment. (1980–1981). *The implications of cost-effectiveness analysis of medical technology: Case studies of medical technologies.* Washington, DC: Government Printing Office.

Van Maanen, J. (1988). *Tales of the field: On writing ethnography.* Chicago: University of Chicago Press.

Veerman, J. W., & van Yperen, T. A. (2007). Degrees of freedom and degrees of certainty: A developmental model for the establishment of evidence-based youth care. *Evaluation and Program Planning, 30,* 212–221.

Voelpel, S., Leibold, M., Tekie, E., & von Krogh, G. (2005). Escaping the red queen effect in competitive strategy: Sense-testing business models. *European Management Journal, 23,* 37–49.

Warner, W. L., & Lunt, P. S. (1941). *The social life of a modern community.* New Haven, CT: Yale University Press.

Wax, R. (1971). *Doing field work.* Chicago: University of Chicago Press.

Webb, E., Campbell, D. T., Schwartz, R. D., Sechrest, L., & Grove, J. B. (1981). *Nonreactive measures in the social sciences* (2nd ed.). Boston: Houghton Mifflin.

Wholey, J. (1979). *Evaluation: Performance and promise.* Washington, DC: The Urban Institute.

Whyte, W. F. (1955). *Street corner society: The social structure of an Italian slum.* Chicago: University of Chicago Press. (Original work published 1943)

Wilford, J. N. (1992). *The mysterious history of Columbus.* New York: Vintage.

Windsor, D., & Greanias, G. (1983). The public policy and management program for case/course development. *Public Administration Review, 26,* 370–378.

Wolcott, H. F. (1990). *Writing up qualitative research.* Newbury Park, CA: Sage.

Yin, R. K. (1970). Face recognition by brain-injured patients: A dissociable ability? *Neuropsychologia, 8,* 395–402.

Yin, R. K. (1978). Face perception: A review of experiments with infants, normal adults, and brain-injured persons. In R. Held, H. W. Leibowitz, & H.-L. Teuber (Eds.), *Handbook of sensory physiology: Vol. 8. Perception* (pp. 593–608). New York: Springer-Verlag.

Yin, R. K. (1980). Creeping federalism: The federal impact on the structure and function of local government. In N. J. Glickman (Ed.), *The urban impacts of federal policies* (pp. 595–618). Baltimore: Johns Hopkins University Press.

Yin, R. K. (1981a). The case study as a serious research strategy. *Knowledge: Creation, Diffusion, Utilization, 3,* 97–114.

Yin, R. K. (1981b). The case study crisis: Some answers. *Administrative Science Quarterly, 26,* 58–65.

Yin, R. K. (1981c). Life histories of innovations: How new practices become routinized. *Public Administration Review, 41,* 21–28.

Yin, R. K. (1982a). *Conserving America's neighborhoods.* New York: Plenum.

Yin, R. K. (1982b). Studying the implementation of public programs. In W. Williams, R. F. Elmore, J. S. Hall, R. Jung, M. Kirst, S. A. MacManus, et al. (Eds.), *Studying implementation: Methodological and administrative issues* (pp. 36–72). Chatham, NJ: Chatham House.

Yin, R. K. (1986). Community crime prevention: A synthesis of eleven evaluations. In D. P. Rosenbaum (Ed.), *Community crime prevention: Does it work?* (pp. 294–308). Thousand Oaks, CA: Sage.

Yin, R. K. (1994a). Discovering the future of the case study method in evaluation research. *Evaluation Practice, 15,* 283–290.

Yin, R. K. (1994b). Evaluation: A singular craft. In C. Reichardt & S. Rallis (Eds.), *New directions in program evaluation* (pp. 71–84). San Francisco: Jossey-Bass.

Yin, R. K. (1997). Case study evaluations: A decade of progress? *New Directions for Evaluation, 76,* 69–78.

Yin, R. K. (1999). Enhancing the quality of case studies in health services research. *Health Services Research, 34,* 1209–1224.

Yin, R. K. (2000). Rival explanations as an alternative to "reforms as experiments." In L. Bickman (Ed.), *Validity & social experimentation: Donald Campbell's legacy* (pp. 239–266). Thousand Oaks, CA: Sage.

Yin, R. K. (2003). *Applications of case study research* (2nd ed.). Thousand Oaks, CA: Sage.

Yin, R. K. (Ed.). (2004). *The case study anthology.* Thousand Oaks, CA: Sage.

Yin, R. K. (Ed.). (2005). *Introducing the world of education: A case study reader.* Thousand Oaks, CA: Sage.

Yin, R. K. (2006a). Case study methods. In J. Green, G. Camilli, & P. Elmore (Eds.), *Handbook of complementary methods in education research* (3rd ed., pp. 111–122). Washington, DC: American Educational Research Association.

Yin, R. K. (2006b). Mixed methods research: Are the methods genuinely integrated or merely parallel? *Research in the Schools, 13,* 41–47.

Yin, R. K., & Davis, D. (2006). State-level education reform: Putting all the pieces together. In K. Wong & S. Rutledge (Eds.), *Systemwide efforts to improve student achievement* (pp. 1–33). Greenwich, CT: Information Age Publishing.

Yin, R. K., & Davis, D. (2007). Adding new dimensions to case study evaluations: The case of evaluating comprehensive reforms. In G. Julnes & D. J. Rog (Eds.), *Informing federal policies for evaluation methodology* (New Directions in Program Evaluation, No. 113, pp. 75–93). San Francisco: Jossey-Bass.

Yin, R. K., & Oldsman, E. (1995). *Logic model for evaluating changes in manufacturing firms.* Unpublished paper prepared for the National Institute of Standards and Technology, U.S. Department of Commerce, Gaithersburg, MD.

Yin, R. K., Schmidt, R. J., & Besag, F. (2006). Aggregating student achievement trends across states with different tests: Using standardized slopes as effect sizes. *Peabody Journal of Education, 81*(2), 47–61.

Zigler, E., & Muenchow, S. (1992). *Head Start: The inside story of America's most successful educational experiment.* New York: Basic Books.

Author Index

Subject Index

About the Author

Robert K. Yin was born and raised on the upper west side of Manhattan. He does not remember encountering case studies then, or at Harvard College where he received his B.A. (magna cum laude) in history, or even at M.I.T., where he received his Ph.D. by doing laboratory experiments in brain and cognitive sciences. Nor, to his knowledge, were case studies among the major works published by *The Commercial Press*, founded by his grandfather in 1897 (the publisher's main line of books consisted of textbooks, journals, and reference works—a familiar sounding niche). *The Commercial Press* has been China's largest publishing house and has survived to this day, despite two major regime changes in China (both were called revolutions).

Dr. Yin's exposure to case studies occurred during his first few years as an analyst at the New York City-Rand Institute, which conducted applied studies to improve the quality of then-declining urban living conditions, including life in city neighborhoods, citizen participation, and the provision of urban services. The rest, as they say, is history. Thus, for the past thirty years Dr. Yin has completed numerous qualitative (field-based) and quantitative (statistical) studies, also serving for many years as the President of COSMOS Corporation. He has produced another case study book (*Applications of Case Study Research*) and two readers containing lengthy excerpts from exemplary case studies (*The Case Study Anthology and Introducing the World of Education*). In addition, he has taught courses related to case study topics at the Department of Urban Studies and Planning (M.I.T.), the School for International Service (The American University), and multi-day seminars in the United States and abroad.

During this time, Dr. Yin has published widely on education and urban topics, also contributing to methodological advances. Among these have been the various editions of the present book, whose first edition was published in 1984 and which has now been translated into seven languages. The first translation was into Japanese, followed by multiple Portuguese and Chinese translations of multiple editions of the book. Korean, Italian, Romanian, and Swedish have been the most recent translations. Dr. Yin hopes that readers will find this Fourth Edition to be an improvement over previous editions as well as a book presented in legible English.